CRIME AND THE DRAMA

SIR JOHN MARTIN-HARVEY
as the falsely accused hero in *The Lyons Mail*

CRIME AND THE DRAMA

OR

DARK DEEDS DRAMATIZED

by

H. CHANCE NEWTON

WITH AN INTRODUCTION BY

SIR JOHN MARTIN-HARVEY

KENNIKAT PRESS
Port Washington, N. Y./London

CRIME AND THE DRAMA

First published in 1927
Reissued in 1970 by Kennikat Press
Library of Congress Catalog Card No: 77-102850
SBN 8046-0761-3

Manufactured by Taylor Publishing Company   Dallas, Texas

To ALBERT LAKER,

Editor of the *Referee*.

Loyal alike as Chief and Chum,
  Ever at hand to aid ;
Playing the Game in Life's wild " scrum,"
  Just as it should be played.
I gladly dedicate to you
  This Book of Crimes and Plays ;
For you have been my helper true,
  In countless kindly ways.

In this, and in that After Life,
God bless you—and your Loving Wife !

CONTENTS

CONTENTS

LIST OF ILLUSTRATIONS

INTRODUCTION

By SIR JOHN MARTIN-HARVEY

WHY my old friend " Carados " should choose me
to sponsor his book on *Crime and the Drama; or,
Dark Deeds Dramatized* [how well he realizes the
value of " apt alliteration's artful aid "], I do not
know. Except to my devoted and faithful Company
at rehearsals, I am quite an inoffensive person. My
old chief, Irving, even described me on an occasion
as " lamblike." True, there are within me hidden
depths of villainy and rascality to which I am able
to give vent in *Richard III, Dubosc,* and *Eugene
Aram,* and I should perhaps be flattered that I
have disclosed these lurid qualities so realistically
in my performances that " Carados " has quite
naturally chosen me as a " sponsor " for the " Dark
Deeds " which he has chronicled with such rich
appreciation and with such a loving hand in the
work which follows. Perhaps no such subtle com-
pliment is implied, and I merely have the gracious
task of saying a foreword in the same manner as
most chairmen of meetings which gather to hear a
distinguished public speaker, such as " Mr. So-and-so,
ladies and gentlemen, needs no introduction from
me." And was there ever a man who less needed
an introduction to the great public to which he will
speak than our old friend " Carados " ? An old
friend to the Drama, an old friend to the countless readers to whom he speaks through that famous
organ, the *Referee,* an old friend who has guided

and encouraged the first uncertain steps of many a young actor and actress and manager—myself among the number. One of the pleasantest recollections of my life immediately springs to my mind, though I knew nothing of the circumstance until a year or two ago when our friend " Carados " divulged the fact at a dinner given to mark the launching of *The Only Way* film. It seems that when I had the foolhardiness to take the great old Lyceum Theatre from my chief, Irving, for the production of *The Only Way*, he wrote in the generosity of his heart to the author of this book and asked him as a personal favour to do all he could for " the boy Jack "—for that was how I was known at the Lyceum. Right royally did " Carados " respond to my great chief's request, and no encouragement in those early and difficult days of management gave me more cheer than the hearty clap on the back which I received from my old friend through the columns of his popular journal.

CRIME AND THE DRAMA

OR

DARK DEEDS DRAMATIZED

***

CHAPTER I

BLOOD AND THUNDER'S BIRTHPLACE

"ON Horror's Head, Horrors accumulate," said Shakespeare in connection with a certain very bloodthirsty but marvellous domestic tragedy.

I have often thought that this line, taken apart from its awful happenings, may have been meant by its writer to indicate something of the state of the Stage Plays of his own period. Or, as one may say, a satirical touch regarding what I shall not hesitate to call the Elizabethan Blood and Thunder Drama.

This leads me to put a leading question.

What is the Blood and Thunder Drama which some critics and others regard so scoffingly, and, in some cases, so inaccurately? It is still the fashion, as it has been ever since I can remember, to speak of the Blood and Thunder Drama as having been the sole theatrical output of what the scoffers call "The Trans-Pontine Theatres." I venture to say that this view is as idiotic as it is incorrect.

Those of us who know anything at all about the sanguifulminous stage (and I have known it since

I was a child), both back and front of the curtain, know very well that the Blood and Thunder Drama did not originate in what is so often reportorially called " Transpontia."

The awful murder and other horrific merchandise of the stage really started, of course, in Elizabethan times, very soon after the real drama emerged from the Mystery and Miracle play state.

For example, surely Kit Marlowe, apart from his " Mighty Line " form of verse, is the first, or one of the first, and the worst, or one of the worst, purveyors of dramatic horrors for horror's sake. The unfortunate Kit, whose tragical end, by being stabbed in the eye in a Deptford disorderly house, has itself formed the story for more than one Blood and Murder play.

In regard to poor Christopher's very gory output, even those of us who value him are bound to confess that in *Doctor Faustus,* and certainly in the *Jew of Malta,* young Marlowe went the limits in horror-piling. In his glorious play, *Edward the Second,* to which his pupil Shakespeare's *Richard the Second* owed so much, the horrors themselves are of course unavoidable, for *Edward the Second* is one of the very real crime dramas which come into my category.

In this case the marvellous Kit was dealing with one of the foulest murders ever committed on King or commoner, and it must be said also, that although Marlowe does not mince matters in this connection, he does not, as in his other tragedies, carry out the well-known artisan aphorism and " Lay it on with a two tye brush."

So much for Marlowe !

I have hinted above that poor Othello's exclamation might also be held to indicate the drama of horrors of Shakespeare's period. That author himself is comparatively reticent in dealing with Blood and Murder themes. Whenever he does have a wholesale order to that effect, as in *Macbeth*, *Hamlet*, and *King Lear*, he carries those murders out in a perfectly natural and non-volcanic manner.

True, such a play as *Titus Andronicus* is surely the very limit of Horrors accumulating on Horror's Head. Its foul and reeking crimes seem to have been chosen and displayed solely with intent to horrify and disgust. We are by no means sure, however, that this unspeakable tragedy, which is in itself a transcript from real Crimes, was the work of Warwickshire William or not.

Anyhow, apart from the other tragedies issued wholesale, retail, and for exportation in the spacious days of Great Elizabeth, the dramatists of that time very soon began to dramatize contemporary crimes. One of the most famous examples, of course, is that very fine, but very unequal, tragedy entitled *Arden of Feversham*, which is often attributed to Wondrous William himself! Merely waiting to express the opinion that there are some few touches of his genius in that very Blood and Thunder play, I will pass on to say that it was based upon one of the most famous and most eagerly devoured murder cases in the whole history of such horrors.

The direful deed itself may perhaps be sufficiently explained if I quote here part of the tragedy's description from the title page of the original copy.

"The lamentable and true Tragedie of M. Arden of Feversham in Kent. Who was most wickedlye murdered, by the meanes of his disloyall and wanton wyfe, who for the love she bare to one Mosbie, hyred two desperat ruffins, Blackwill and Shakbag, to kill him. Wherein is shewed the great mallice and dissimulation of a wicked woman, the unsatiable desire of filthie lust and the shamefull end of all murderers."

Another "local" murder case dramatized very speedily, and also sometimes attributed to Shakespeare, is that strange little play, one of the few one-act pieces of the period, *A Yorkshire Tragedy*. Despite its one-act form this play contains enough sanguifulminosity to furnish forth ten acts! In spite of its crudity this tiny tragedy, so purely domestic in its nature, is very touching, and so true that it might be used for many a murder story in this very time of ours.

The tale is only too " topical " for any period. As is the fashion in certain highbrow plays of to-day, the *dramatis personæ* have no names. They are principally set forth as follows : Husband ; Wife ; a little Boy. This little lad, however, does not constitute the whole of the family. There are two other smaller children who are, as one may say, only " thinking " parts.

It is the old story. A young husband is led by bad companions into gaming, drink and drabbing. Too late he finds that he has exhausted all his patrimony, and even the food and other necessaries of his loving wife and dear little kiddies.

Shame, despair, and the " D.T.'s " do their fell work only too well, and eventually this half-hour playlet ends in the following terrible fashion. I quote from a very ancient and scarce copy of this little piece, the following few extracts :—

> . . . Now Glides the Devil from me,
> Departs at every joint, heaves up my Nails,
> O, catch him new Torments, that were ne'er invented,
> Bind him one thousand more, you blessed Angels,
> In that bottomless Pit, let him not rise,
> To make Men act unnatural Tragedies,
> To spread into a Father, and in fury,
> Make him his Children's Executioner,
> Murder his wife, his Servants, and who not ?
> For that Man's dark, where Heav'n is quite forgot.

Henry Irving
as Mephistopheles

Facing p. 12

Henry Irving
as Philip the Second, husband of
"Bloody" Queen Mary
(From a picture by Sargent)

WIFE. O my repentant Husband!

HUSBAND. My Dear Soul, whom I too much have wrong'd.
For death I die, and for this I have long'd.

WIFE. You should not, be assur'd, for these Faults die,
If the Law could forgive as soon as I.

(Children are here laid out!)

HUSBAND. I kiss the blood I spilt, and then I'll go,
My Soul is bloodied, well may my Lips be so,
Farewel, dear Wife, now thou and I must part,
I of thy wrongs repent me with my Heart.

*   *   *   *   *

(Here the officers enter to arrest the Husband, who holds forth thus :)

HUSBAND. That's but in vain, you see it must be so
Farewel ye bloodey ashes of my Boys,
My Punishments are their eternal Joys
Let every Father look well to his Deeds.
And then their heirs may prosper, while mine bleeds."

*(Exit HUSBAND, with OFFICERS ;
To be executed.)*

Another terrible tragedy, also founded upon a real crime, is a very excellent play called, *A Warning for Faire Women.* This crime really resembles that of the husband-murder in *Arden of Feversham,* but it is perhaps a little more complicated. One of the complications is due to the fact that the author has embodied as much of warning to Fortune Tellers and their victims as to Fair Women.

The reading of the hand of the heroine, Mrs. Sanders, is a sort of incentive to her joining in the crimes which follow. The flattering gipsy leads the beautiful young wife to suppose that she will soon be a widow, and that in succession to Sanders, she will espouse a very wealthy captain, who is " much enamoured of her."

The Satanic fortune-teller acts as a kind of pan-deress anon between the captain and the young wife, and indeed this go-between, Mrs. Drury by name, makes a pretty penny out of the transaction. (By the way, the word "Drury" has here a subtle unpleasant meaning which will be easily grasped by students of Old English phraseology and slang. Hence "Drury" Lane !)

After several Acts of amorous "negotiations" the Captain, Browne by name, feeling that he will and must "possess" Mrs. Sanders, easily becomes lured into a plot to compass the death of her young husband, who is also the Captain's host. Terrible scenes lead up to the murder of the husband. Then ensues a very dramatic pursuit of the guilty wife and her paramour and of the artful Mrs. Drury herself.

After a few more murders, and other crimes, to save themselves, all three are arrested, but the hapless Captain endeavours to the end to exculpate the wretched wife, and eventually flings himself on to the scaffold and hangs himself !

Mrs. Sanders and Mrs. Drury both pay the extreme penalty of the law, and in due course the three are hanged in chains as a "Warning to Faire Women."

It may be as well to give a part of the tag speeches of this reeking, but certainly religious, tragedy.

MRS. DRURY.　And yet we may obtaine forgivenes,
　　　　　If we will seeke it at our Saviour's hands.
　　　　　But if we wilfully shut up our hearts
　　　　　Against the holy spirit that knockes for entrance,
　　　　　It is not this world's punishment shal serve
　　　　　Nor death of body, but our soules shal live
　　　　　In endless torments of unquenchèd fire.

　　　　　*　　*　　*　　*　　*

MRS. SANDERS.　Here I confesse I am a grievous sinner,
　　　　　And have provok't the heavy wrath of God,
　　　　　Not onely by consenting to the death
　　　　　Of my late Husband, but by wicked lust,
　　　　　And wilful sinne, denying of the fault ;
　　　　　But now I do repent, and hate myselfe
　　　　　Thinking the punishment preparde for me
　　　　　Not halfe severe enough for my deserts.

　　　　　*　　*　　*　　*　　*

As in the case of *Arden of Feversham*, I give the title page of this terrible tragedy :—

"A WARNING FOR FAIRE WOMEN"

containing

The most Tragicall and Lamentable Murther of

MASTER GEORGE SANDERS OF LONDON,

Merchant, nigh Shooters Hill ; consented

unto by his owne wife.

Acted by M. Browne, Mistris Drewry and Trusty

Roger, agents therin ; with

thier seuerall ends. As it hath beene

lately diuerse times acted by the right Honorable

the Lord Chamberlaine his

Seruantes.

CHAPTER II

A Murder Drama Ordered by the Government

This play is no other than the famous *George Barnwell; or, The London Merchant.* It is one of the most famous and longest-lived of crime plays that can be discovered. As in the case of many another fine play, which appears to have escaped critical observation, I saw this dark deed drama many times, especially in my early youth. On several occasions it was called *George Barnwell, the London Apprentice,* or *The London Apprentice* only. The last-named title, however, in my young days, was found to clash with sundry versions of an equally famous crime drama written around the notorious Jack Sheppard.

When I first struck the Jack Sheppard series of dramas in my boyhood, it was towards the end of a long-existing prohibition by the Lord Chamberlain of the time, as to the performance of any Jack Sheppard play whatever! Anon I shall give chapter and verse of the way in which the different censors' ban on *Jack Sheppard* was evaded by every possible loophole.

I was myself concerned, with some of my own relations, in these evasions, for *Jack Sheppard* was still played under every other name it was possible to find, and one of its names was *The London Apprentice,* as often applied to the drama written around George Barnwell.

This George Barnwell drama, produced just about

two hundred years ago, was founded by George Lillo (a very diligent dramatist) upon a ballad based upon a real murder of a city merchant, by his apprentice and nephew, the said Barnwell. It was quite a novel sort of play; certainly it was the first, or one of the first, dramas, not only to take its subject from prosaic domestic and commercial life, but also to treat the subject in very ordinary prose instead of the usual blank verse, which was very often at that time very blank indeed! There was also a very banal street ballad concerning poor George!

The story of the Barnwell play is the same old story which (alas!) continues in our own time and is indeed often being enacted under our eyes at the present day. Here is a young and promising apprentice, good-looking, industrious, affectionate, loyal, in fact in every way a satisfactory character, until he meets with bad company. This bad company includes villains and impostors, who tempt him on to gaming, etc. The chief lurer, however, is a very beautiful syren of the shadiest character. She doesn't seem to have any front name, but is always spoken of, and speaks of herself, as Millwood.

The usual thing happens. Poor young George, having been tempted by the fair but frail Millwood to rob his employer's till from time to time to supply her greed of gold, is at last induced by her, on pain of her thrusting him forth for ever, to murder his benefactor so as to secure his wealth in bulk.

After a series of very wordy but mostly worthy scenes, this Barnwell tragedy becomes very intense. The poor prentice, now disguised in a mask, dodges the footsteps of his unsuspecting and deeply religious helper. George starts to shoot the good old man, but dropping his pistol, and thus attracting the attention of his victim, the wretched boy draws a dagger and stabs his benefactor through the heart !

Notwithstanding this fateful thrust, the pious old fellow is spared to give off several very sermonic speeches. George is speedily arrested by the Bow Street runners, and next cast into a dungeon at Newgate. Here he is visited and consoled by a fellow prentice named Trueman, one of the finest fattest parts for giving off " sentiments " that I have ever met in the range of the British Drama.

Happily the Messalina-like Millwood is also arrested in due course, and almost simultaneously she is executed with Barnwell on the gallows tree !

The wretched wanton, before treading the scaffold, expresses herself thus with regard to Us of the Inferior Sex.

MILLWOOD.   Men of all degrees and all professions have I known, but in their several capacities all were alike, wicked to the utmost of their power. In pride, contention, avarice, cruelty and revenge, the Reverend Priesthood were my unerring guides . . .
    (This was a topical gag against the Roman Catholics by this very Protestant playwright.)

Millwood continues thus :—

What are Men's Laws of which you make your boast ? But the fool's wisdom and the coward's valour—the instrument and screen of all your villainies, by which you punish in others that which you are yourselves. . . . Thus you go on deceiving and being deceived, plaguing and destroying one another, but Women are your Universal Prey.

This sordid but sincere drama not only had a big run for its time, and enjoyed many a revival, but also it was ordered by successive English governments to be played at least every Boxing night at old Drury, in front of the pantomime—and at other holidays . . . as an awful warning to the apprentices of London Town, numbers of whom were sent into the gallery to learn their moral lesson !

This lesson was enforced, or rubbed in, by poor George Barnwell in his farewell to his own true and pure sweetheart Maria, who long had loved him from afar, and especially by his rhymed tag which ran as follows ; spoken underneath the gallows' rope.

> " If any youth, like you, in future times
> Shall mourn my fate, tho' he abhor my crimes :
> Or tender maid, like you, my tale shall hear,
> And to my sorrows give a pitying tear ;
> To each such melting eye and throbbing heart
> Would gracious Heaven this benefit impart.
> Ne'er to know my guilt nor feel my pain,
> Then must you own, you ought not to complain ;
> Since you nor weep, nor shall I die, in vain.

Curtain.

BARNWELL BURLESQUED

I have seen *George Barnwell* played on many occasions, to flowing tears, and a sobbing accompaniment, especially from kind feminine friends in front. And many an excellent actor have I seen play the ill-fated George, and many a powerful actress as the meretricious Millwood.

The last time I saw *George Barnwell* at a regular West-End theatre was at the Gaiety when John Hollingshead revived it for a few matinées together with that old crusted grizzly skeleton melodrama, *The Castle Spectre*, of which more anon.

The Gaiety performance of *George Barnwell* was unintentionally given in burlesque fashion, although with the original solemn text, with the result that the fine old " moral lesson " was received with roars of laughter.

Even I (I now blush to confess) went back to the *Referee* and wrote my notice of that *George Barnwell* revival in rhymed travestic form, and with your kind permission I will append an excerpt or two from that, alas! very irreverent carolling criticism.

GEORGE BARNWELL

ACT 3

(Hurried music. Enter FORMOSA MILLWOOD*)*

BARNWELL.

    Behold me . . . I have done the deed . . . and now I'm filled with grief.

    Henceforth, the honest Barnwell, men will point at, saying ' Thief ! '

    Observe, 'tis here *(producing property pie)*. Now let us feed. Alas ! methinks that pie

    Will fill me with remorse (or indigestion) by and by.

FORMOSA.

    I had another favour, George, to ask you ere you go.

    You have an uncle (that's it ! start . . . to music tremolo).

    Go, get a fiver out of him . . . at once ! . . . delay's absurd.

    If he refuses, bash his hat *(chord)*. Go, vanish ! . . . not a word !

BARNWELL.

    Oh, cruel gyurl, would'st drive me mad, to finish act the third ?

Duet.

(Air : " *Tommy, Make Room for Your Uncle !* ")

FORMOSA.   George, go and ' bonnet ' your uncle,
                There's a little dear.

BARNWELL.   O, why should I ' bonnet ' my uncle ?
                'Tis very wrong, I fear.
                I know his Sunday ' chimney pot '
                Is worth a trifle too.

FORMOSA.   Now, don't annoy, faint hearted boy,
                But ' bonnet ' your uncle, do !

ACT 5.—*Central Criminal Court.*

MILLWOOD and BARNWELL in Dock.

JUSTICE JAWKINS.

Well, having heard the evidence, O pris'ners at the bar,
'Tis firmly my opinion that a naughty pair you are.
To go purloining people's pies . . . and bashing one's best
  hat ;
It strikes me that throughout the piece you two have had
  the ' fat.'
Millwood, I shall sentence you to quit the London stage
Until you learn to act (by then you'll be a tidy age).
You, Barnwell, take hard labour at the hands of actor men
At sundry minor-theatres . . . till eighteen-eighty, when
We'll transport you to the Gaiety. . . .

BARNWELL.

Ha . . . not that ! They'll chaff me then !

[N.B.—I changed the name Millwood to Formosa, because of
the then notorious Drury Lane drama siren of that " sobriquet."]

Just before finishing these *Barnwell* mems. I have
of course seen the burlesque performance of Lillo's
tragedy given in *When Crummles Played*, at the
Lyric, Hammersmith. But even that travesty
could not " kill " the real pathos of that drama.

CHAPTER III

BOWL AND DAGGER TRAGEDIES

Undoubtedly one of the most terrible examples of this kind of crime was the murder of Sir Thomas Overbury in the reign of our James the First. This awful crime, of which you will find the actual details in any History of England worthy of the name, grew out of the jealousy, or the Woman Scorned, kind of revenge which the Countess of Somerset wreaked upon the ill-fated Sir Thomas.

This lady, lovely to look upon, but most unlovely in disposition, had formerly been the wife of the Earl of Essex, but having been divorced by him, afterwards married the Earl of Somerset. There came a time when she cast herself, so to speak, at poor Sir Thomas Overbury, but he scorned to betray his friend, her husband, and in point of fact, being of virtuous habits, was speedily marked down by her Countess-ship for destruction, both morally and physically.

Like another Mrs. Potiphar, our Countess made and laid and matured her plans. Speedily she found means to denounce Overbury to her husband, charging him with immoral disloyalty to his friend.

This tragedy was speedily dramatized for the English stage, both of the period and a little later. I know of three such dramatizations, but I need only quote from one which is the most peculiar. The original edition of this play lies before me. It is by Richard Savage, the very minor poet, who was so fond of describing himself as " The Bastard " and alleging himself to be the illegitimate son of Earl Rivers. In my copy that poet is simply described as the son of the late Earl Rivers. Savage not only used his alleged base birth very much as a publicity stunt, but even wrote a poem, which, although scarce, exists to this day, under the title of *The Bastard.*

Richard's Sir Thomas Overbury play, like all his other works, is of the most bombastic kind. Here are a few quotations.

The Earl of Northampton, her ladyship's uncle, happens to state that Sir Thomas Overbury is about to pay a visit to herself and husband. Her ladyship explodes thus :—

> He ! Overbury !
> Then aid me, Indignation . . . Rage . . . and Vengeance.
> I am a Woman ! nay, a Woman wrong'd !
> And when our Sex, from Injuries take Fire,
> Our softness turns to Fury . . . and our Thoughts
> Breathe Vengeance and Destruction !

Her ladyship's next move is to tell her husband that Overbury has made designs against her honour. She adds :—

> He told me you were false . . . designing, jealous.
> Try'd every Art of Treachery to supplant you ;
> And when he found his Wiles were unsuccessful,
> Attempted Force, and threaten'd me with Slander.

Next this " Serpent and Woman " (as someone calls her) prepares her plans to poison poor Thomas, who still refuses to take notice of her ! She also plots to include her husband in her slaying vengeance, exclaiming thus :—

> Die, Overbury . . . Somerset . . . die all !
> Let the World burn to be my Funeral Pile,
> And Nature groan as I do !

Just another instance of the blood and thunder style of Savage. Here is what poor Overbury says after swallowing the awful potion :—

Ha ! What a shoot was there ! . . . My blood boils in me.
Flames wind about my breast . . . my Brain burns red
And my Eyes swim in a blue Sea of Sulphur !
Stand off . . . and let me breathe . . . what's that grim
    Form,
That stalks along . . . and creep to pale upon me !
I know the meagre Phantom now ! 'Tis Death !
He's gone ! . . . and now the heav'ns all open to me !
A Flight of Angels swoop upon my Head,
And clap their Wings about me !

Hark ! The Wind roars ! . . . The Seas begin to swell.
The Billows roll ! . . . now ! Now they drive upon me !
Oh, save me, or I'm lost . . . What ! Must I perish ?
Is there no Hold ? . . . not one kind, friendly Plank !
Helpless, indeed ! . . . thus in the Gulph I sink
Never to rise again. (*Dies.*)

So much for this strange dramatization of the Sir Thomas Overbury tragedy. Certain variants of this play I have seen in my youth, in Blood and Thunder drama circles.

It may surprise some to learn that the very first play in which the now Sir James Barrie, Bart., was concerned was a drama written around this very Richard Savage, who gained so much of his livelihood out of his alleged illegitimacy !

Now for another and more modern famous poison episode, the chief character of which was one of the most brilliant and deeply educated men it was possible to find in either our literary or criminal history.

WAINEWRIGHT THE POISONER

This historical criminal more skilled in toxicology even than Palmer, the Rugeley poisoner (of whom more anon), was a very shining light in literary circles, illuminative alike as essayist, poet, and linguist. A very handsome fellow was this Wainewright, and for a good while, before he was found out, he was the bosom friend of Coleridge, Wordsworth, Southey, Leigh Hunt, Walter Savage Landor, and even of the gentle " Elia," otherwise Charles Lamb.

It was Wainewright's secret habit to effect insurances on certain people's lives, or otherwise to extract money from them by " removing " them. So polished and so apparently innocent was this drug-administering demon, that it was impossible to suspect him until the terrible truth became plain for all men to see.

I could describe in full detail some at least of the many poison plots worked by this fiend of hell, who seemed so much an angel. It will assist my readers, however, if they will take my tip to read a certain short story by Charles Dickens. That story is called *Hunted Down*, and Dickens wrote it late in his career, receiving for it a thousand pounds down !

In this *Hunted Down* tale, C. D. has used Wainewright the poisoner in every possible detail. He calls him Julius Slinkton, but the description is in every way Wainewright's, even to his polished head of hair with the wide parting, which, whenever its owner bent it towards you, seems to say (as Dickens put it), " Keep off the grass ! "

This story was dramatized in due course, and indeed Wainewright the poisoner received stage honours on several occasions. I saw sundry stage plays based upon his darksome deeds. One of these dramas I recollect was called *Who Did It ?* and I shall never forget watching it in a very excited condition while I was a youth at the Britannia Theatre, Hoxton, J. B. Howe giving a very thrilling performance of the Poison Fiend.

THE PRICE OF THIS BILL IS ONE HALFPENNY!

New Britannia Theatre

SO CALLED BY ORDER OF THE LORD CHAMBERLAIN.

PRICES AS USUAL. Private Boxes £1 1s Seats in Private Boxes 2s and 1s 6d each Person. Boxes 1s each Orchestral Stalls 1s each Box Slips and Pit 6d. Lower Gallery 4d Upper Gallery 3d

Second Price to Pit and Gallery 3d at half-past 8 o'clock. Box Entrance open 5 o'clock, admission 1s to all parts, except Private Boxes No Person admitted to Boxes or Stalls unless SUITABLY ATTIRED Doors open at 6 o'clock, Performances to commence at half-past

On Monday, Evening, November 22, 1858, and all the Week,

BEGUILED ONE

OR THE

DUKE'S VICTIM

Part 1.--Rural Happiness!

Rustic Joys-The Foundling-Youth and Hope-Brilliant Prophets of the future-Nefarious Scheme-An honest Lawyer-Innocence in Danger-Atrocious Enterprise Successful!

Part 2.--Splendour & Trouble!

Friendship and Fidelity-The Betrothed Duke-The unhappy Victim-Villany Foiled The Forced Nuptials!

Part 3.--Captivity & Danger!

The Wife and No Wife-Temptation to Crime-Schemes to release the Captive-Desperate risk Horrible Suspense-CLIMAX OF INTEREST!

WONDROUS DENOUEMENT!

MR. G. W. ROSS

BRIGAND'S SECRET

Part 1.--The Vineyard of Molinari, by Sunset

The Hurdy Gurdy Girl menaced with death The Combat and Rescue!

Part 2.--Banks of the Tiber and terrace by the River!

Part 3rd.--- PAVILION IN THE CHATEAU!

A Grand Pas Seul de Basques,

By Madlle. CELESTE STEPHAN

And the Corps de Ballet.

The Brigand's Daughter accused! Sacrifice of the Band The Victims astounded The Lost Daughter Found Revenge of the Betrayed!

DEATH of the BRIGAND

And Restoration of the Lost Girl of Portici!

A typical playbill of crime dramas at the old "Brit" in Hoxton.

Irving's Version

Henry Irving was, I remember, always much interested in the case of Poisoner Wainewright, and more than once he talked to me very learnedly on that subject, almost, in fact, as learnedly as his son H. B. (really a great criminologist) would have done. Irving Père often seemed to yearn to have a play upon Wainewright's misdeeds, and hinted that someone sketched him a drama of the sort.

The nearest thing, however, to the actual facts in the way of a dramatization of this sort for Irving was *The Medicine Man*. This play's chief character was undoubtedly a kind of dramatic photograph of Poisoner Wainewright, but instead of being a literary light, he was a medical ditto.

Irving thought highly of this piece, but when he showed it to me, *I* didn't. He asked my opinion (as he often did), and I, having gone through the script, warned him that it was not a good play for the Lyceum, nor was the character a specially good one for him, although he was even then the greatest " villain " of our stage.

I warned Irving (among other things) that he had not been for some time so suitable as before to " coat and trousers " characters. He seemed very much obsessed with the part, however, and presently he produced the play. It failed signally.

The Criminal and the Canaries

And hereby hangs a tale. This awful poisoner in *The Medicine Man* had on the stage in several of his chief scenes a large cage of beautiful canaries on which he alternately bestowed his pettings and his poisons. That batch of birds had cost Sir Henry Irving a good deal of money.

When he was showing me the accounts of the unhappy "returns" of *The Medicine Man*, that cage was on his large dressing-room table. And as Sir Henry remarked, "I've lost £9000 on *The Medicine Man*," he glanced at the cage and exclaimed fervently, "*But thank God, I've got the canaries!*"

The following additional facts concerning Poisoner Wainewright, culled from the reports of the respective trials of that polished villain, for what might be called his toxicological inexactitudes, may be found interesting in connection with the plays written around him.

Thomas Griffiths Wainewright, to give him his full name, was born at Chiswick in 1794. He was brought up by his grandfather, Doctor Ralph Griffiths, founder of the *Monthly Review*, and before growing up to be an essayist, art critic, poisoner, and even forger, T. G. W. held a commission in the Guards. While thus engaged, he soon got into debt and started his various forgery feats. Finding himself in still further difficulties, he conceived and carried out a plan to poison his uncle, his sister-in-law, and a friend of his, who had been kind to him in Boulogne.

Thomas's wife very kindly arranged to be an accomplice in her sister's murder, and was herself fraudulently insured by her husband for £18,000. After having made his busy little start, with his nefarious arrangements, Thomas was arrested and transported to Van Diemen's land. And after several other crimes and crimelets had been proved against him, Wainewright the poisoner showed his consistency in that part of his profession, by poisoning himself. He chose opium for this purpose, and died therefrom in Hobart Town Hospital in 1852.

Wainewright, besides being the polished poisoner

and first-class forger in real life, was not only, as
I have shown, the dramatic original of Dickens's
Julius Slinkton, of the often dramatized Dickens
story, *Hunted Down*, but was also the original of
the villain Varney, of Bulwer Lytton's story of
Lucretia, which also was dramatized more than once.

THE MAYBRICK MYSTERY

It is not often that crime cases are dramatized
right away in these days as they were in olden times.
In the matter, however, of the celebrated Maybrick
poison tragedy, it was not very long before two or
three dramas on the subject appeared. The best
and most daring of these dramas was by that
brilliant playwright, Sydney Grundy. He very soon
came forth with a very powerful society play which,
when he asked me to see it on its trial performance
at the Greenwich Theatre, was called, *The Mouse
Trap*—a reference, of course, to Hamlet's retort
to King Claudius' question at the famous matinée
at Elsinore Castle.

I advised Grundy, however, to choose a better
title, at least one more understandable by the general
public, who might not be supposed to know their
Hamlet. Grundy did choose another title, but I do
not think his new name for it was any better, if so
good. He renamed it, in fact, *A Fool's Paradise*,
and in it he gave a very fine character to the late
Sir John Hare who played a kind of medical detective.
Call the play what he might, however, or disguise it
as he would, Grundy had dramatized the great
Maybrick Mystery in every detail !

It may be interesting to add that in this poison-
play the character drawn from the victim Maybrick
was acted by that afterwards great criminologist,
H. B. Irving.

3

CHAPTER IV

A CLERGYMAN CRIMINAL AND LEARNED MURDERER

The Reverend Doctor Dodd, whose forgeries while
in Holy Orders have been dramatized in divers
directions, was indeed an extraordinary person, even
for a clerical criminal.

After a distinguished career at Clare Hall, Cambridge, he became a very popular preacher and wrote
what was described as " a series of edifying books."
The prospective forger also became editor of *The
Christian Magazine*. Next he was made King's
Chaplain, and anon tutor to the Earl of Chesterfield's
nephew. Thus our parson began to earn a very
large income, but he soon drifted hopelessly into
debt, and also into even still more shady practices.

His reverence, however, was soon helped by many
friends to make a fresh start, whereupon he bought
the Charlotte Chapel in Pimlico. Even there poor
Dodd couldn't run straight, for he speedily made
" a simoniacal attempt " to buy the living of St.
George's, Hanover Square, and was speedily thrown
out of his chapel which he had bought.

This ecclesiastical " wrong 'un " then went to
Geneva with his aforesaid pupil, who was now Lord
Chesterfield. This nobleman eventually gave Dodd
a living at Wing, in Bucks. Dodd soon sold this,
however, and also forged a deed for £4000, a deed
purporting to be signed by Lord Chesterfield himself!

During the rumpus that succeeded this very
irreverent forgery, Dodd managed to borrow and to
refund a part of the money which he had gained

therefrom. He was, however, tried and sentenced to death. Despite the earnest efforts of Dr. Johnson and others to get him pardoned, this wretched poet, preacher, and wholesale felon was hanged at Newgate in 1775.

I confess that when I first became acquainted with the Dark Deeds of this Divine, in my later 'teens, it gave me considerable pain. I felt this because, as soon as I began to learn to read, my first knowledge of the Bard of Avon, in a literary rather than a dramatic sense, was derived from this unhappy clergyman's still famous compilation, *The Beauties of Shakespeare.*

I think I may also confess that I still feel something of pity for this criminal clergyman, because I have here at my elbow a most remarkable and very scarce book by the Reverend Doctor Dodd, setting forth, mostly in poetry, his terrible penitence (real or assumed) as written by him in Newgate jail while waiting his execution.

Also I always feel sorry for the fact that the Doctor's Dark Deeds gave a chance for that wholesale religion-mocking satirical playwright, Samuel Foote, to write around him a characteristically " profane " play.

Happily Foote, on his deathbed, was converted to Christianity by that stodgy but sincere dramatist, Richard Cumberland.

So much for Doctor Dodd and the dramas concerning him.

The celebrated case of Eugene Aram, Scholar and Murderer, now claims our attention, and although so much has been written concerning that mysterious homicide in books of trials and criminology, yet a good deal of interesting matter can be put forward treating of that unhappy wretch, especially in regard to his stage history.

Strangely enough the late H. B. Irving, one of the greatest of our criminologists, although concerned with the Dramatic World for so many years, in his remarkable study of Eugene Aram, omits all mention not only of the many dramas concerned with that learned miscreant, but even is silent touching his great father's famous recitation of Hood's "Eugene Aram" poem in the theatres. Stranger still, H. B. also ignores the Aram drama, which that illustrious actor-manager played in at the Lyceum Theatre.

Of course it was that wonderful comic-tragic poet, Thomas Hood, who first put Aram in the public limelight something like a century after that murderer's trial and committal. Hood's poem has always been a favourite with reciters who love to be what one might call "Mummers of the Morbid." I will confess that even I, although of a much more festive temperament, have been guilty of giving this gloomy, ghastly recitation on certain of our public stages. But that by the way.

Both the lamented H. B. and the happily still surviving Lord Birkenhead, each of whom has given a most exhaustive account of the brutal murder committed by Schoolmaster Aram, and his savage accomplice, Houseman, give conclusive proof that Aram was an absolute criminal in heart and mind. He was horrible alike in his treatment of his long-suffering wife, and cunning in every possible way. The fact that Lord Birkenhead does not mention any stage play concerning Eugene Aram is perhaps not altogether surprising, but one is rather astonished at H. B. Irving's silence in this matter.

Strange, indeed, for I have myself seen several of these dramas, to say nothing of those which I have read. One of the earliest, also one of the first seen by me, was entitled, *Eugene Aram; or, St.*

DYING SCENE OF BEVERLEY IN "THE GAMESTER"
(Written by the Rev. Edward Moore for David Garrick)

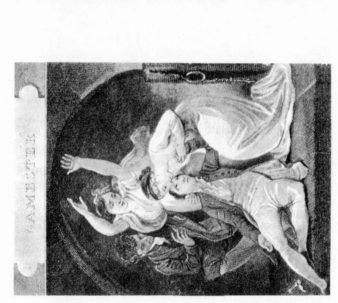

LOVE SCENE FROM "GEORGE BARNWELL"
(The "Vamping" Siren and the Guileless 'Prentice)

Facing p. 32

Robert's Cave, a three-act play by the prolific dramatist, W. T. Moncrieff. W. T. M., in addition to having been a very sensational playmonger, has the honour of sharing with actor-manager Edward Stirling (husband of the famous Mrs. Stirling), the renown of having been among the first " pirates " of Dickens's stories for stage purposes.

If a digression may be permitted here, I feel that it is only right that I should give good old Moncrieff credit for being the chief dramatizer of that not too salubrious story, *Tom and Jerry; or, Life in London.*

The sub-title of Moncrieff's *Eugene Aram* is of course connected with the fact that, owing to Eugene's co-criminal Houseman " peaching," the body of the murdered Daniel Clarke was found in that cave.

Without entering into the abundant horrible details of this absolutely brutal murder, I may say at once that the undoubtedly gifted Aram, a learned self-deceiver and utterly dangerous man, was hanged in chains near Knaresborough. Also that one of his daughters, described as " a very wild girl," ran home gleefully to tell her mother that she had seen her father hanging up on the hill ! Mrs. Aram, who was then keeping a pie and sausage shop in Knaresborough, is alleged to have picked up her husband's bones as they fell from the gibbet !

About the time of Moncrieff's drama, which was originally played at the Surrey (a " prompt " book of which lies near me), Edward Bulwer Lytton came forward with his well-known romance whitewashing Eugene Aram and making him like poor old King Lear, " more sinned against than sinning."

Many will remember that Lytton's slavering of this cultured criminal was very soon burlesqued by Thackeray in his famous travesty, *George de Barnwell.*

Eugene was not the only villain " sainted " by Lytton, whom Thackeray called " Mr. Bullwig,"

for that lordly romancer also bestowed quite a lot
of spring-cleaning on Paul Clifford and other
criminals mentioned herein.

SOME "SAINTED" ARAM DRAMAS

Unhappily for what the late Charles Hawtrey used
to describe in one of his characters as "simple beautiful manly straightforward unadulterated truth,"
most of the writers of plays around Eugene Aram,
not only stole Lytton's chief episodes, but also
slavishly followed his whitewashing and sickly
sentimental views of that murderer.

One of these Bulwerian blends was written by a
French *émigré*, a Royalist, who, when he became a
play-writer for the London stage, engaged me as
a lad to copy his playscripts, and to do certain other
work in connection with several theatres at which
he was engaged. His name was Adolf Faucquez.
His Eugene Aram drama produced at the Standard,
Shoreditch (now the Shoreditch Olympia), over forty
years ago, was very dramatic, as indeed all his plays
were. I very soon "spotted" that Adolf's writing
of this Aram play had been inspired by what was
perhaps the most astounding stage distortion
ever known of the Eugene Aram murder facts,
namely, W. G. Wills's drama named after that
murder, and produced at the Lyceum in the mid
seventies.

In this sloppily sentimental, treacly tragedy,
utterly unworthy of its gifted writer, Irving, who
had done so much for the Eugene Aram recitation,
played the learned homicide whom Wills had made
quite an injured innocent "hero." To match this
haloed saint, this facile Irish dramatist and poet
invented a new romantic heroine for Eugene to
espouse ! That romantic miss was played first by

Miss Isabel Bateman, and afterwards even by the great Ellen Terry, if you please !

Houseman was, I remember, acted with tremendous force by E. F. Edgar, whom Irving had brought over from the Surrey Theatre.

I often used to " chaff " Henry Irving about this idealized Aram of his of Wills's, but his general excuse was that just then, " sentimentality held its sway upon the stage."

Wills did away with all the murder and trial scenes and concerned himself mainly with Eugene's emotional sufferings and terrible " temptations " ! Poor Wills, however, whose history in his plays was always chaotic, was not the only dramatic whitewasher of Eugene.

A good many years later, W. G. Wills's brother, the Rev. Freeman Wills, and another clergyman, the Rev. Frederick Langbridge to wit, concocted a Eugene Aram drama on similar very sentimental lines for no less a popular star than the since knighted Martin Harvey ! This play was called (as several farces had been before it), *After All*.

The Rev. Freeman Wills was a very " advanced " cleric of the muscular Christian type, and I used to know him during his ministrations at a very large and very useful church in Sun Street, Finsbury. My knowledge of his clerical collaborator, the Rev. Frederick Langbridge, who became Canon of Limerick, is still more peculiar.

When as a youngster I began to vary my stage work with writing for the papers, the then "lay" Langbridge was a fellow comic poet with me. We both worked on that very droll but, alas, long defunct humorous periodical called *Fun*.

Both my reverend friends, in romanticizing Eugene for Martin Harvey, unfortunately forgot to make the drama at all dramatic. Not to put too fine a point upon it, the play failed to repeat the signal success which those two ecclesiastical playwrights had achieved for the present Sir John with their masterly dramatization, *The Only Way*, based of course upon Dickens's *Tale of Two Cities*.

Without proceeding to harrow the feelings of my readers by any special intimate description of some of the horrors of the Eugene Aram plays which I have seen or perused, I may perhaps be allowed to add that even a romantic opera called *Eugene Aram* was produced some twenty-five years ago !

BULLWIG'S OWN UNFINISHED PLAY

One especial addition must be mentioned. That is that the great and gushing Bulwer Lytton himself actually started an Eugene Aram tragedy for stage use.

A striking example of the Lyttonian method in this scarce tragedy runs as follows :—

Would . . . would my life might boast one year of wealth
Though death should bound it !

BOTELER.   Thou mayest have thy wish.

ARAM (*rapt and abstractedly*).   Who spoke ?   Methought I heard
my genius say . . .
My evil Genius.   Thou mayest have thy wish.

BOTELER.   Thou heard'st aright.   Monson, this eve will pass
By Nid's swift wave ; he bears his gold with him.
The spot is lone . . . untenanted . . . remote ;
And if thou hast but courage . . . one bold deed.
And one short moment . . . thou art poor no more !

And later we have these gems of dialogue :—

ARAM.   Go on.   I pray thee pause not.

BOTELER.   There remain
Few words to body forth my full design.
Know that . . . at my advice . . . this eve the gull'd

And credulous fool of Fortune quits his home!
Say but one word, and thou shalt share with me
The gold he bears about him.

ARAM. At what price?

BOTELER. A little courage.

ARAM. And my soul! . . . No more.
I see your project. . . .

BOTELER. And embrace it.

ARAM.   Lo!
How many deathful, dread and ghastly snares
Encompass him whom the stark hunger gnaws.
And the grim demon Penury shuts from out
The golden Eden of his bright desires.
To-day, I thought to slay myself, and die,
No single hope once won! And now I hear
Dark words of blood, and quail not, nor recoil . . .
'Tis but a death in either case; or mine
Or that poor dotard's. . . . And the guilt . . . the guilt.
Why, *what* is guilt? A word! We are the tools,
From birth to death, of destiny; and shaped,
For sin or virtue, by the iron force
Of the unseen, but unresisted hands
Of Fate, the august compeller of the world.

*   *   *   *

And now perhaps enough has been said to cause
the reader to feel no especial wonder that, to quote
the tag from Hood's poem—

That very night, while gentle sleep
    The urchins' eyelids kiss'd,
Two stern-faced men set out from Lynn,
    Through the cold and heavy mist,
And Eugene Aram walk'd between
    With gyves upon his wrist.

CHAPTER V

HERE'S ANOTHER . . . LOT OF GUYS

'Tis time to remember the Fifth of November
Gunpowder Treason and Plot.
For there still is reason why gunpowder treason
Should never be forgot.

The chief of these reasons—putting aside, of course, all theological or credal views concerning the conspiracy by Guy Fawkes and Company—is that it is necessary for our purpose to inform the Gentle Reader that this great Political Crime was not only dramatized, but dramatized at least a score of times in my own personal experience.

The first of the Guy Fawkes plays which I met was written by one George Macfarren long before I was born. To be exact, a hundred and four years ago, when it was produced at the old Coburg Theatre, which became the Victoria when the Queen of that name ascended the Throne. It is now known to all and sundry as the Old Vic.

This extraordinary Guy Fawkes play (of which I have some old prompt books) was one of the earliest Blood and Thunder dramas I have ever met. I have seen it many times at two theatres especially. One is the aforesaid Vic, and the other is the famous Britannia Theatre, Hoxton. I have also seen it played elsewhere, but these are the two chief dramatic temples at which it flourished, and it was always revived at both houses on Guy Fawkes night. On these occasions I have seen marrow-freezing performances of Guy, by eminent Blood and Thunder tragedians, such as Joseph Reynolds, John Bradshaw, and Cecil Pitt, younger brother of the famous author of *Sweeney Todd, the Demon Barber of Fleet Street.*

Macfarren's Guy Fawkes, with its Lord Mounteagle (discoverer of the plot), its heroes, Catesby and Tresham, and its very extraordinary low comedy character known as Sir Tristram Colly Wobble, was in itself a fearsome thing for us youngsters, even familiar as we became with it through the making of our own guys. But above all, the tremendous "attraction" announced on the playbills for these Guy Fawkes nights revivals was that the performance finished always with—

BY SPECIAL REQUEST!

A GRAND DISPLAY OF FIREWORKS !!!

Several of my relations not only acted in these revivals of *Guy Fawkes,* but also on more than one occasion got more or less badly injured through the aforesaid pyrotechnic display.

It has always been a matter of deep regret to me that I was not born in time to see the original Guy Fawkes of Macfarren's drama. That was the terrific, terrible O. Smith, the "creator" of perhaps more villains and monsters than any other player to be named. Always excepting perhaps the great sailor actor, T. P. Cooke, whose early stage life was devoted to demons of the deadliest die!

Not only have I seen the above-named *Guy Fawkes* at the Vic, but also other famous impersonators at the Standard, Shoreditch, the Grecian and the City of London Theatre, Norton Folgate. I can call to mind many another Guy Fawkes play dealing in more or less detail with the Conspiracy, the Trial, and the Execution or hanging, drawing and quartering, of the grim Guy himself.

These plays include specimens respectively entitled *Guido Faux; or, The Gunpowder Plot*, by Sydney Hodges, at the old Olympic; *Guy Fawkes the Traitor*, by Charles Whitlock, around the provincial theatres; *Guy Fawkes; or, The Fifth of November*, a very old Haymarket piece; and a very strange drama called *Ordsall Hall*, by Charles Herman, a famous tourer of *Uncle Tom's Cabin*.

This last specimen, a very melodramatic, meaty one, was honestly announced (as the others were not) as based upon the famous romance *Guy Fawkes*, by Harrison Ainsworth, Esq. It is not generally known, I think, that no less a critic of culture than the gifted John Oxenford, so long of *The Times* newspaper, wrote a Guy Fawkes drama for the Lyceum, nearly ninety years ago.

There have been several burlesques of these Guy Fawkes marrow-freezers, the authors being respectively Tom Taylor, Albert Smith, Fred Leslïe the actor (with his collaborator Herbert Clarke), Sir F. C. Burnand, Henry J. Byron (of course), and naturally, at the Gaiety. Also last, but not least, John T. Douglass, who from the time I first knew him as a boy somewhat older than myself, ran or helped to run the famous National Standard Theatre, Shoreditch, and who, alas! met his death in an air-raid outside that very theatre, through a German bomb.

Harking back a moment to famous impersonators of poor old Guy, it is fitting that I should give some account of one of the most powerful Blood and Thunder players of the part.

This was the long-resident " heavy " man of the old Vic, the hereinbefore-mentioned John Bradshaw, whom the Vic audiences always called " Jack," when they roundly hissed him, as they always did for his many deeds of horror per night.

When I was a youngster at the Vic, when Joseph Arnold Cave was running it, naturally I saw the desperado " Jack " in quite a number of sangui-fulminous rôles. I grew to know him well, and I soon discovered that it was he, and no other, who was the hero, or original, of Henry S. Leigh's Carol of Cockayne, entitled, *The Villain of the Vic,* which was long a very popular recitation.

I append a few stanzas therefrom by way of illustration.

In Lambeth, at the " Dragon " tap,
    Upon a day it came to pass,
I met as affable a chap
    As ever took a friendly glass.
We drank . . . a very little while,
    Dissolved one shilling and a kick ;
And then he told me with a smile,
    He play'd the villains at the " Vic."

" Methinks," I said, " I see thee now
    On Queen Victoria's classic boards ;
There sits a frown upon thy brow,
    That cork . . . and only cork . . . affords.
Thine ev'ry act proclaims thee ripe,
    At nothing but thy foes to stick ;
I hail thee as a goodly type
    To play the villains at the ' Vic.' "

I envied him with all my heart. . . .
    I feel it would have been my pride
To act a very wicked part
    In dramas on the Surrey side.
Had I to seek a fresh career,
    If Fate would let me have my pick,
I'd say, " Well, Destiny, look here,
    I'll play the villains at the ' Vic.' "

Serene my days would be and bright,
    My deeds exceptionally good ;
But I would cork my brow at night,
    And be as naughty as I could.

And on my grave, when I am dead,
I'd plant no *jacet* with its *hic*,
But just this little phrase instead . . .
" *He play'd the villains at the ' Vic.'* "

Bradshaw's thirty odd years at this popular New
Cut playhouse naturally made him a great favourite.
Well do I remember the strange proof of this
popularity on Manager Cave's last night at the
Vic, when, as I have stated elsewhere, its opening drama, *Trial by Battle*, was hooted from its
boards.

On that eventful night Bradshaw, like the whole
strength of the company, was affectionately greeted,
and as one may say, " Farewell'd." So much so
that in the front row of the gallery a playgoer, in
great enthusiasm and his shirt sleeves, drew from
under the seat a huge stone bottle containing beer,
or " Pongelo," as he called it. Raising this liquor-
laden utensil aloft he singled out Bradshaw and
shouted, " Hi, Jack! Us and my pals 'ere is going
to drink to your blinkin' good 'ealth ! "

Demanding silence, he then passed the bottle
along each side of him to several of his fellow-lovers
of dramatic art, and when they had quaffed their
fill, these toasters arose in their seats and hurled
at Bradshaw the benediction, " Gawd bless yer,
Jack ! "

That heavy villain who had probably committed
more murders on the stage than even Henry Irving
in his career, responded in broken tones, husky with
emotion. [N.B.—John's voice was always husky at
other times, but no matter.]

Now comes a pathetic Guy Fawkes touch, concerning the Old Vic. Some time had passed since
the evening of the Bradshaw Beery Benediction,
and I found that good old Jack was wandering about
" out of a shop."

This enforced " resting " (as modern pro.s call it) had lasted some time when one day this Veteran Villain was standing by the corner of the New Cut talking to a friend who was also of what the Americans love to describe as the " blue-chinned " profession. Suddenly a little group of ragged urchins chanced to pass by and then halted.   One of the boys looked up into Bradshaw's face and, turning to his pals, yelled, " Blimey! if it ain't old Guy Fawkes! " Anon they hooray-ed him and ran away !

Then the poor old " villain " remarked pathetic- ally to his companion, " There, laddie, you see a proof that though one is still disengaged, one's artistic efforts are not en-tirely forgot-ten ! "

Good old Jack ! If ever there was a portentous gunpowdery plotting Guy Fawkes, he was that very Guy !

The last Guy Fawkes play which has come my way is quite a polished literary drama entitled, *The Fifth of November*. It is a brilliant piece of work by Howard Peacey, and was recently published in the Benn Series of " Contemporary British Dramatists."

Whether the devourers of the usual Guy Fawkes legends and dramas will agree with this Peacey play is perhaps open to question.   To speak by the card, it seems constructed with a view to whitewashing " Guy, Guy, Guy ! " and to use for its principal hero Catesby, who becomes really a very finely drawn character.

By way, however, of restoring balance of opinion in this matter, it is perhaps fit that I should quote at least part of that famous song, which was very popular in my young days in the theatres and music halls, especially with that famous comic singer, Sam Cowell, the grandfather of the brilliant comedy actress, Miss Sydney Fairbrother.

GUY FAWKES

I sing a doleful tragedy . . . Guy Fawkes, the prince of sinisters,
Who once blew up the House of Lords, the King and all his
 ministers,
That is, he *would* have blown them up . . . and folks will
 ne'er forget him ;
His will was good to do the deed . . . that is, if they'd have
 let him.
    Bow wow wow.
    Tol lol de riddle lol, de rol lol de ray.

He straightway came from Lambeth side, and wish'd the
 State was undone ;
And crossing over Vauxhall Bridge, that way cum'd into
 London ;
That is, he *would* have come that way, to perpetrate his guilt,
 sirs,
But a little thing prevented him, . . . the bridge it wasn't
 built, sirs.
    Bow wow wow, etc.

Then, searching through the dreary vaults, with portable
 gas-light, sirs,
About to touch the powder [train, at witching hour of
 night, sirs ;
That is, I mean, he *would* have used the gas, but was prevented . . .
'Cause gas, you see, in James's time, it hadn't been invented.
    Bow wow wow, etc.

And when they caught him in the fact, so very near the
 crown's end,
They straightway sent to Bow Street, for that brave old
 runner Townsend.
That is, they *would* have sent for him ; for fear he is no
 starter at,
But Townsend wasn't living then . . . he wasn't born till
 arter that.
    Bow wow wow, etc.

So, then, they put poor Guy to death, for ages to remember ;
And boys now kill him once a year, in dreary dark November ;
That is, I mean his effigy (for truth is strong and steady).
Poor Guy they cannot kill again, because he's dead already.
    Bow wow wow, etc.

CHAPTER VI

A CRIME THAT CAUSED THE OLD VIC'S FIRST DRAMA

This was an extraordinary melodramatic spectacle written by W. Barrymore, who was not only a popular playwright of over a century ago, but was also an ancestor of the famous Barrymore family, who afterwards went to America. Their present chief representatives are the famous Ethel Barrymore and the fine tragedian and film actor, John Barrymore, who like the rest of the family was really born Blythe and is related to the famous Drew family.

This strange drama arose out of an awful crime case which had excited public interest just before the Vic opened, not only because of the mysterious murder concerned with it, but also because the man accused of that dire deed aroused consternation by demanding the exercise of a right which had lain in abeyance for several hundred years.

That is to say, he insisted upon being allowed to undergo the famous "Ordeal by Touch," wherein, as some will remember, the innocence or guilt of the accused depended on whether or not the blood of the victim gushed forth at his touch. Or, preferably, the most obvious form of such a test, namely, "Ordeal by Battle." In this case, of course, the accused man's innocence or guilt depended on whether he vanquished his opponent or not.

The newspapers of the period, all of which then,

4

of course, were compelled to bear a sixpenny stamp
whether the price was a penny or otherwise, teemed
with sensational reports of this strange and antique
form of trial. The aforesaid Barrymore, whose
many plays in my possession prove him to be very
smart indeed, seized upon that tragic topic and soon
turned out the above-named *Trial by Battle.* He
was one of the many hack playwrights of then and
since, and even now, whose business boast it is,
that they can turn you out any sort of drama while
you wait !

Trial by Battle, therefore, was produced in the
year 1818 with such tremendous success apparently
that I feel compelled to quote some startling incidents from the play, which has long been out of
print. Happily I possess an original prompt
copy.

Trial by Battle opens in a smuggler's cave where
a band of defiers of the Revenue are debating as to
whether they shall accept a large purse of gold from
a local Baron who bears the more or less honoured
name of Falconbridge. This bold bad baron is
anxious to secure the smugglers' services in order
to carry off a local beauty, one Geralda, to add to
the number of his many other feminine victims.
One elderly smuggler is for defying the baron and
his bribe. His arguments are very cogent ; for
example, he says :—

> As a smuggler I can follow my trade without a blush, for
> having been cheated by the laws, with pleasure will I cheat
> the laws. But, an assassin ! . . . my heart revolts at the
> idea."

A little later, on being still further pressed to
accept with his comrades a heavy sum to be divided
equally among the band, for any who may secure
the possession of this " female," the gentle-hearted

smuggler becomes still more insistent in the cause of
Lovely Woman.   As thus :—

> As yet this band is ignorant of the crime of murder . . .
> to gain possession, then, of this female, loss of lives must
> ensue and some of ye may fall victims.   Therefore I abjure
> the deed, nor will I longer belong to a band who, for the sake
> of gold, would sacrifice a helpless female at the altar of Lust
> and Infamy !   (*Chord.*)

Not unnaturally the band become somewhat
annoyed at this saintly smuggler's denunciation.
Wherefore say Omnes :—

> Stab him to the heart !   (*Crash of Music.*)

From this we run briefly on through several
scenes to the end of Act I, which culminates in the
bold bad baron carrying off the fascinating " female "
by the aid of many of the band, with the exception
of the aforesaid saintly smuggler, and his young son
who endorses his father's virtuous sentiments.

The pursuit of the lordly abductor and his fiendly
friends by the father of the heroine, results in the
baron stabbing that parent, and also in slaying
another kindly helper of that gyurl !   From this
point " Vengeance arises from her hollow cell " (as
poor Othello puts it), and after what the author in
his stage directions keeps calling " *ad libitum* business," things begin to look black for the bold bad
baron.   For lo !   the usual faithful low comedian
begins now to loom large upon the scene and to
help all the virtuous in their righteous cause !

Short scene follows short scene in rapid succession,
even the music, or melos, being described in these
episodes as a " wild hurry."   The nefarious nobleman
and sundry confederates arrange, by dint of daggers,
and at pistol point, to push their way through to
escape and freedom !

Eventually our villain finds means to have one of the young heroes, Henrie, arrested for one of the murders which he has himself committed! It is then that the falsely accused person demands the right of Trial by Battle.

Scene the last, and shortest of these short specimens, hardly possessing, as one may say, " an ounce of dialogue to a pound of action," is called the Tournament, and I do not think I can do better than quote it in full, or nearly so.

At this point the Judges are discovered surrounded by different knights, and after a Grand March there is a crash of chords, and the Baron enters, with one of the smugglers named Rufus, whom he has chosen to be his champion in the coming combat.

At this point also Henrie enters.

JUDGE. We, the judges, command in the King's name, that no person of whatsoever estate, degree or condition, that he, being present, so hardy, to give, take or sign, by wanton speech or language, either to the prover or to the defendant, whereby the one of them may take advantage of the other upon pain and forfeiture of lands, tenements, goods, chattels, and prisonment of their bodies. Such is the law, and may Heaven defend the Right!

Flourish. HENRIE and RUFUS retire. *Heralds sound.*

Enter HENRIE. Enter RUFUS.

HENRIE throws down gauntlet. RUFUS picks it up.

GRAND COMBAT.

RUFUS is Defeated.

BARON. Hold! though my champion falls, my honour shall ne'er be tainted with the crime of murder . . . either therefore pronounce me innocent, or in honourable combat let me wipe off disgrace. Falconbridge was nobly born, and honoured will he live or nobly fall.

JUDGE. Baron! Still do I pronounce thee assassin, and with my champion will I prove the charge.

THE HERO IN "TRIAL BY BATTLE"
(From a "Penny Plain and Tuppence Coloured"
Tinselled Engraving)

THE BOLD BAD VILLAIN IN "TRIAL BY BATTLE"
(Another popular "Tinsel")

Facing p. 48

BARON.   Then so be it . . . this my fence.

FLOURISH.   Takes up Gauntlet.

Combat between HENRIE and BARON.

BARON killed . . . Shout for OMNES!

The Curtain Falls.

I omitted to mention that the heroine Geralda, in *Trial by Battle,* never speaks a single word and yet she is not dumb!   Even if the author had permitted her to say, as so many Blood and Thunder heroines do at the end of such plays, " Thank Heaven, I am spared ! " one could hardly have called her a chatterbox !

CHAPTER VII

CURIOUS CONTINENTAL CRIME DRAMAS

The chief specimens of such plays as these quoted in these series are described as Continental because they have all been borrowed by the British for the British boards.

One of the most famous of these pieces, based upon real crimes, is, of course, the renowned melodrama, *The Lyons Mail*, in which Sir Henry Irving made such a pronounced and memorable success in the dual rôle of the falsely-accused hero and the revolting real murderer.

Long before Irving produced the play which follows in almost every detail the celebrated case of this French highway robbery and the murders concerned therewith, I had myself seen and shuddered at several other dramas founded upon the same historic tragedy.

One of these vivid concoctions was *The Courier of Lyons*, founded upon the popular French play of much the same name. It was by Edward Stirling, the wholesale dramatizer (in the piratical sense) of Dickens and other famous novelists.

I might almost confess to be *particeps criminis* with the late Stirling in these matters, especially in his later life, for even in my youth I was engaged by Stirling, then stage manager at Drury Lane, to copy his playscripts.

Stirling's adaptation of *The Courier of Lyons* had been inspired by the fact that Charles Reade, before

he became more famous as a novelist, had prepared
a version of this crime drama for Charles Kean to
enact the dual rôle of Lesurques and Dubosc at
the Princess's. That was before I was born, and I
did not catch this Kean in this or any other play
in my time.

I did, however, see many popular performers in
this difficult double character, both in Stirling's
version and in Reade's, to say nothing of many a
hotch-potch version around the minor Surreyside
and East End theatres.

In later years I struck this good old crime drama
at the Gaiety Theatre of all places in the world . . .
and there I saw the famous tragedian, Hermann
Vezin, give a wonderfully effective and stirring impersonation of Lesurques and Dubosc, the hero and
villain respectively. Vezin's was undoubtedly the
finest performance of these two parts until Irving
outrivalled him, as it were, at the Lyceum some
years later.

One of these latest strong impersonators of this
double character is Bransby Williams.

As in so many dramas based upon real crimes,
starting with the hugely successful *Jonathan
Bradford; or, The Murder at the Roadside Inn*, the
English dramatizers also falsified their respective
adaptations of the *Lyons Mail* melodramas by making
the innocent victim escape scot free !

Alas ! it was the innocent Lesurques who was
guillotined ! The real murderer (or chief of the
murderers), Dubosc, was not caught till long after.

In the original French play written by Moreau,
Siraudin and Delacour, the real end of the tragedy
was shown. A very interesting " human document "
concerning the innocent hero's awful and unjust fate
lies before me as I write. This document, dated
March 15th, 1850, is addressed by the family of

14 — THE COURIER OF LYONS. [ACT I.

Marduet ✕✕ *Click* ✕✕

Duboso. Well, there was one advantage in being imprisoned, I was free from such absurd and intolerable intrusions. Ah, footsteps! (*sits*) (*clock strikes three*)

Enter CHOPPARD *and* FOUINARD / R. U. E.

Duboso. It strikes three—Ah! here is some one.
Chop. (R., *pushing* Fouinard) Go on!
Fou. (R. C.) But suppose it shouldn't be——
Duboso. Garçon!

Enter WAITER *from* L.

Some brandy.
Chop. (R.) Eh!
Fou. (R. C.) Oh!
Waiter (L.) A small glass?'
Duboso. (L. C.) A bottle and a large glass.

Exit WAITER, *who returns with bottle and tumbler, which he places on table and goes off.*

Chop. (L. C., *to* FOUINARD) Do you see? (DUBOSO *pours out a glass and drinks*)
Fou. Oh! la, la, la! (*singing to himself joyfully*)
Chop. It must be he.
Duboso. (*regarding them*) All right I think. (*pours out second glass and drinks it rapidly, they gazing upon him with admiration*)
Chop. Citizen, in the manner in which you have rinsed down those two tumblers of brandy, I believe I can perceive —
Duboso. That I shall soon finish the bottle. (*drinks*)
Fou. I am sure it is he.
Chop. It is Duboso. (*they bow with reverence, he extends his hands, which they shake with respect and fervour*)
Duboso. You know me—how is that?
Chop. All the army know their general; but the general knows not all his soldiers.
Duboso. You reason well, thank you!—it is flattering, but long, and we have no time to lose.
Chop. Come, let us have something to drink.
Duboso. (C.) Yes, I am thirsty. ~~Garçon, some brandy!~~ *Come & drinks*

~~Enter WAITER, after decanter and glasses and exit.~~
(*they sit*) Which of you is a lender of horses?
Chop. I, Pierre Choppard, the jockey, generally known and appreciated as the amiable.
Duboso. And this imbecile is, Fouinard, whom they call the philosopher.
Fou. (*flattered*) He knows me—the great thief knows me—Oh, Citizen! (*bows*)
Duboso. We want a third.
Chop. We want Courriol, who is never to his time.
Duboso. I cannot wait for him—I have business—here! (DUBOSO *makes sign to* FOUINARD *to come near to him, he pours out a glass and they touch glasses and drink; to* CHOPPARD) You have four horses?

Transcript of the original Prompt-book of

CHOP. Yes.

DUBOSC. They will be ready!——

CHOP. In an hour.

DUBOSC. At the barrier of Charenton!

CHOP. Good.

FOU. (*timidly*) And—the object—for which we shall employ these quadrupeds?

DUBOSC. Fifty-five thousand livres in gold; thirty for me, forty-five, you three.

FOU. Oh! oh! (*singing and dancing*)

DUBOSC. You shall know more when we are on horseback and upon our road. You will let Courriol know? (*going*)

Enter COURRIOL, L. D.

COUR. Here I am! here I am!

CHOP. Ah, Monsieur Courriól! always behind time!

COUR. (L.) It was not my fault. (*perceives* DUBOSC) Ah! (*in amaze*)

DUBOSC. Explain all to him, I am going to the bar. Adieu, my chickens, adieu!

Exit, R. U. E.

FOU. What is the matter?

COUR. Who is this man?

FOU. The famous Dubosc—the Man and the Brandy!

COUR. Dubosc! is it Dubosc? If I had not left Lesurques on horseback this very minute, I could swear—what a resemblance!

CHOP. Come, come, we have but one hour, come!

FOU. Seventy-five thousand livres—oh! (*sings and dances in delight*)

CROPPARD *pushes* FOUINARD, *and they exeunt,* R. U. E.

SCENE II.—*The front of Jerome Lesurques' Cabaret at Lieursaint, with sign. The high road from Paris to Lyons.* R. U. E. *to* L. U. E.; *time, five o'clock in the afternoon: in the chamber (the floor of which is raised), open to the audience, candles, buffet, bottles and glasses, tables and stools: chamber door at back; three steps to descend from house to stage, and air holes of the cellar in front.* L.

Courier of Lyons (or *The Lyons Mail*).

Lesurques to the authors of the drama, and to the theatrical managers concerned who produced *Le Courier de Lyon* at the Théâtre de la Gaieté, Paris, on the following day !

These descendants of the unhappy victim had attended a Répétition Générale two nights before the production, and this is part of their collective letter :—

> We cannot but feel the liveliest gratitude for the interest you have throughout attached to our unfortunate ancestor, the unhappy victim of the most lamentable of Judicial mistakes, and we beg to offer you the assurance of it.
>
> We do not hesitate one moment, then, in authorizing you to give the real name of the principal personage.
>
> Accept, gentlemen, etc.
>
> For the descendants and heirs of Joseph Lesurques—
>
> D'ANJOU, his Grandson.

In addition to the letter which I have quoted from the descendants of the innocent ill-fated Lesurques, it should be interesting to note the accompanying inscription which is on his tombstone in the famous cemetery of Père Lachaise.

> A la mémoire de Joseph Lesurques, victime de la plus déplorable des erreurs humains, 31 Octobre, 1796. Sa veuve et ses enfants, martyrs tous deux sur la terre, tous deux sont réunis au ciel.

This letter of 1850 was written fifty-five years after Lesurques was guillotined for the foul murder committed by Dubosc !

Among my many copies of adaptations of *Le Courier de Lyon* is a wonderful prompt book, seventy-seven years old, the one first used on the London stage.   I have also the prompt copy of the Charles Kean version produced four years later.

The principal version of *The Courier of Lyons*

murder and its innocent victim, namely, *The Lyons Mail*, has (while I write) been acquired by my old friend, Sir John Martin-Harvey, who has taken up, and with striking success already, the trying "dual rôle" of the guilty murderer and the innocent hero, so long played by his great manager and mentor, the late Sir Henry Irving.

I am glad that Sir John has taken over this terrific melodrama, for undoubtedly it gives him the greatest chance he has ever had of showing dramatic contrast in one performance.

It is interesting to note, for future reference of students of the Drama, that when Sir John began to be a member of Irving's company, and was known to that great chief and to all of us connected with him as " the Boy Jack," that afterwards knighted youngster acted a peculiar little part in *The Lyons Mail* at the Lyceum, the part of the frightened tavern boy, Joliquet. This was played with Charles Kean by Ellen Terry's sister Kate, then ten years old.

When not quite out of his 'teens, " the boy Jack " began to court, and afterwards successfully won, the esteemed Lyceum girl actress, Nina de Silva, who is now Lady Martin-Harvey.

CHAPTER VIII

MORE POISON PLAYS

Of course there are numerous, and indeed almost numberless, poison crimes which have been dramatized, especially of the historical kind, such as that concerned with the previously-described poor Sir Thomas Overbury. The toxicological tragedies caused by the infamous family of the Borgias alone would fill not only pages, but volumes.

From my earliest youth until the present time I have seen and read a large number of Borgia crime plays, quite distinct from the famous opera, built or composed around the libidinous Lucretia of that fearsome family.

My fresh batch of poison plays includes *The Borgia King*, an old Adelphi drama written by A. R. Slous, born Selous, and father of the famous explorer and war correspondent of that name. Slous was also the author of the first T. P. Cooke naval prize drama, *True to the Core*, which was based on Kingsley's nautical romance, *Westward Ho!*

Another far more terrible play of this kind was ranting Nat Lee's blank verse (very blank verse) tragedy entitled, *Cæsar Borgia, Son of Pope Alexander VI*. This was originally produced at the old Duke's Theatre, close upon two hundred and fifty years ago, and were I to quote (as I may yet have occasion to do) some of Nat Lee's speeches, you will not wonder why the poor fellow was called " Mad Nat." Another *Cæsar Borgia* play was a four-act tragedy of comparatively recent date, for t was written by my friend Justin Huntley McCarthy and tried out about fourteen years ago. Like most of the younger McCarthy's works, it is full of sterling artistry, although it lacks that " full i' the mouth " quality which I found in these nightmare plays and in sundry other *Borgia* blood and thunder pieces which I have encountered.

Two of these Lucretia Borgia Chamber of Horrors plays were respectively written by Frederick Belton and J. Weston, the former being produced at Sadler's Wells and the latter at the Victoria, in the Waterloo Road, and the Effingham, in the White-chapel Road.

Of course the greatest Lucretia Borgia tragedy is that of grand old Victor Hugo's originally produced nearly a hundred years ago in France, and often translated, or adapted, for the British boards. It was Hugo's Borgia poison-drama which formed the libretto of Donizetti's famous opera.

Henry J. Byron wrote a splendid burlesque on this terrible theme. It was called *Lucrezia Borgia, M.D.*

Another loathsome lot was the Cenci family, whose crimes toxicological and otherwise have furnished forth dramatic fare in plenty. Not always, however, with the family name attached. I take it that this omission is largely owing to the family name having been associated with a certain nameless crime which the marvellous but misguided Shelley seemed to think a fit subject for a play—*The Cenci* to wit. He took care, however, to warn all and sundry that he did not really intend it for public presentation. Until a few years ago, *The Cenci*, which I mention here chiefly because it is one of the most horrible of all real crime dramas, was for a long while very rightly forbidden by our Censorship.

Why that ban was ever lifted, and why certain otherwise sensible tragediennes and others should think fit to present it publicly is, as Lord Dundreary used to say in the play, " One of those things which no fellah can weally understand."

Anyhow, the Cenci family, like the Borgias, certainly provided by their poisoning, their poniarding, etc., much dramatic fibre for crime dramas British and foreign.

I may wind up my present survey of poison plays by alluding briefly to the fact that you will find much interesting dramatization of such crimes in such dramas of unadulterated horror as Webster's tragedy, *The Duchess of Malfi*, one of the earliest stage horrors I had to do with in my youth, behind the scenes and in front thereof. Also there is much such material in an extremely nightmarish tragedy which deserves a paragraph all to itself !

A Poison Bowl and Gibbet Drama

This play is entitled *Hoffman ; or, Revenge for a Father*, and it is the work of Henry Chettle, a very wayward " terrible trial " of a fellow who had, however, sufficient playwriting ability to cause him to become a sort of " ghost " to no less a dramatist than W. Shakespeare ! Those who are at all acquainted with Chettle's work (and I fancy they are but few, for his plays are very scarce) may trace his hand in several Shakespeare plays as well as in the works of other Elizabethan dramatists.

This tale of Hoffman is so terrible and so varied, in its vampirish villainy, that I may be compelled to refer to it in fuller detail in further remarks on blood-and-thunderism. For the present I will only say that Hoffman, a sort of Hamlet, without that fascinating Prince's poetic philosophy, like him seeks vengeance for a murdered father. In order to provide gibbets for that parent's murderers, to be hanged up beside the gibbet of his father, whose skeleton is discovered rattling in chains at curtain-rise, Hoffman prepares here and there more than one poisoned chalice !

His favourite habit, however, with the murderers of his father, whom they hanged—poor fellow !— merely for being a pirate, is to make a steel circlet or crownlet red-hot in a fiery furnace, and coming behind each wretched murderer, to press it down upon that victim's skull and thus make him ready for gibbeting !

But no more of this Hoffman, however, at present ! Except to say that its nerve-knocking story is considered by some commentators to be based upon a series of historical crimes of the period !

CHAPTER IX

HIGH TOBY AND CRIB-CRACKER CRIME DRAMAS

I have a suspicion that, whether we confess it to ourselves or others, my otherwise gentle readers, like myself, have a special fondness for dabbling in crime stories both printed and play-acted. Also that we are especially moved by the lives and adventures of the Knights of the Road, or "High Toby Merchants," as they were wont to be called. And even the more romantic housebreakers, or crib-crackers, from Jack Sheppard downwards, we study with especial interest.

Moreover, that species of murderers and desperadoes known as Burkers, who gleefully slew unoffending citizens for the sake of selling their corpses to surgeons for anatomical vivisection, have also thrilled us, have they not ? Far into the night have we panted with secret excitement as the Bow Street Runners gained nearer and nearer on their prey, or were spoofed from time to time by such great criminal heroes as the aforesaid Jack or his terrible traitorous companion, Jonathan Wild. And with what smothered joy have we read of such still more romantic criers of "Stand and deliver !" and "Your money or your life !" as Claude Duval, Paul Clifford, Tom King, Dick Turpin, Nick Nevison, the Golden Farmer, Jerry Abershaw, George Barrington, Old Mop, Sixteen String Jack, Springheel Jack, Scarlet Dick, and so on and so forth.

THE TERRIBLE BURKE AND HARE

Although I say it with bated breath and whispering humbleness, I really can claim to be able to speak with some authority on dramatizations of Dark Deeds because undoubtedly, from my earliest youth, I have been really saturated in such play fare, both behind the scenes and in front thereof.

Take the case of the above-mentioned Burkers. These bloodthirsty gentry took their name from a couple of men-slayers and body-snatchers, named Burke and Hare. They were brought to book after a trial which is well worth your perusing in the Newgate Calendar. B. and H. were succeeded in the dissection - body - providing business, mostly carried out on the banks of the Fleet River, by two even worse desperadoes respectively named Bishop and Williams, whose trial and description of execution I commend to my criminological readers.

Now although Messrs. Burke and Hare, and Messrs. Bishop and Williams finished on the scaffold, many years before I was born, it so happened that among the earliest crime dramas I saw, at the old Brit and elsewhere, were dramatizations of their Darksome Deeds. Well do I remember a thrilling melodrama called *Hawke the Burker*, based upon a penny " blood " of the same name, which I too kin, in my early boyhood. But by far the most striking, and to me most painfully striking, example of the Burking drama, was a play of which there is also no mention in any dramatic chronicles.

This latter marrow-freezing melodrama, constructed upon the *Hawke the Burker* lines, was entitled, *The Murder of the Italian Boy*. A little later I found it called, *Carlo Ferrari, the Hurdy Gurdy Boy*.

In my boyhood at the blood-and-thunder theatres with my play-acting and music-hall relations, this

5

Burker play shared with *Sweeney Todd, the Barber Fiend of Fleet Street,* and *Maria Martin; or, the Murder in the Red Barn* (of which classics more anon) the honour of freezing my young blood and making me temporarily hide myself, either in the wings or under the seat, according to the part of the theatre in which I was then situated.

With regard to *The Murder of the Italian Boy,* in which drama Burkers Bishop and Williams were dramatized by name, the slaying was effected by means of those revolting ruffians braining the young boy, forcing out his beautiful teeth, for special sale, and hurling his poor corpse down a well. From this they intended to extract the body later, in order to sell it to the surgeons as the Burking custom then was.

Now with regard to this melodrama, I can say with special emphasis that thereby hangs a tale, and it is a tale in which I was myself very strangely concerned. After my first time of seeing *The Murder of the Italian Boy* at the old Brit at Hoxton, I hurried home to a little truly rural cottage in which I then dwelt with my grandmother. It lay off a then very countrified thoroughfare called Birdcage Walk, running out of the Hackney Road. In the garden of this cottage was a well, and on my reaching home that night, I remembered that it had been said that the well in the pretty little back garden of this cottage had been the scene of a murder of a boy by two villains, chiefly, as I had heard, on account of his beautiful teeth. It flashed suddenly into my mind that the episode I had just seen in the Brit drama was this very crime, and I soon found out that it was!

I have described in some measure, in my earlier reminiscences of the Brit in the *Referee,* something of the appalling terror which I felt as a youngster all the night following that awful Britannia experience, and how I kept peeping out of my bedroom window, in horror, to look at the Fatal Well!

Not long ago a *Referee*-reading friend, knowing of this nightmare episode of mine, sent me proof not only that this was the very well where Bishop and Williams slew the poor little hurdy-gurdy lad, but also that it was the very spot of the arrest of those murderers about fifty years before I was born!

CHAPTER X

ALL THE JACK SHEPPARDS

Here again I can claim something of a monopoly in regard to a certain class of crime drama, especially in the case of dramatizations of the housebreaking, prison-breaking, and other daring exploits of John Sheppard, otherwise known as Jack. I began to be concerned with plays written around that young rebel from my early boyhood. That acquaintance of mine began, strangely enough (as I hinted earlier), towards the end of a period during which all plays concerning Jack Sheppard had been banned by the Lord Chamberlain. This prohibition had lasted from soon after the production of the best Sheppard drama I have ever met, namely, Old Buckstone's, which was first done at the Adelphi with Mrs. Keeley as Jack a great many years before I was born.

Buckstone's drama, like his one hundred and ninety-nine other plays, was full of clever touches and of splendid opportunities for acting, not only in the character of Jack, but also in the rôles of Jonathan Wild and Blueskin, enacted respectively by the terrible O. Smith and the huge Paul Bedford.

"Bucky" had adapted this play from the then tremendously popular romance of the same name by Harrison Ainsworth. I say "romance" advisedly, for, as in the case of his Dick Turpin, Ainsworth had whitewashed the young scoundrel Jack almost out of all recognition.

MRS. KEELEY
(one of our greatest comic and pathetic actresses who
lived till the age of 94)
as the original Jack Sheppard

Facing p. 64

And yet Ainsworth had at hand (as *I* soon had) no less an authority than Daniel Defoe, who, stern realist as he always was, gave the full, true, and particular account of Jack Sheppard right up to his last dying speech and confession ! I may add that it was Daniel who also compassed, and apparently actually carried out, the arrest not only of Jack Sheppard, but of his infamous tutor and fence, Jonathan Wild, whose last dying speech Defoe also gives. In fact, D. D., the greatest (as he was the first) journalist, "interviewed" both Jack and Jonathan in their respective condemned cells in Newgate Prison.

In treating this young king of housebreakers, who was executed at the age of twenty-one, Buckstone. and most of the dramatizers who succeeded him, opened the play with Jack carving his name on a ceiling beam in the shop of his employer, Mr. Wood, a house which then stood in Wych Street, now part of Aldwych.

Then it is that Jack gives off the famous song stave :—

> When Claude Duval was in Newgate thrown,
> He carved his name on the Dungeon stone ;
> With a fal lal la, fal lal la,
> With a chisel so fine, tra la la !

Subsequently the young villain breaks forth into another ditty, which has since become famous. Its opening lines run thus :—

> In the box of a stone jug I was born.
> Fake away . . . fake away !
> Of a hempen widow the kid forlorn.
> Fake away !
> My noble father, as I've heard say,
> Was a flash merchant of capers gay.
> Nix my dolly, pals, . . . fake away !
> Nix my dolly, pals, . . . fake away !

I daresay many people know the meaning of the thieves' slang in the above verse, but I may just mention that " the box of a stone jug " means the cell of a prison, and a " hempen widow " is the widow of a man who has been hanged !

The dramas of Jack Sheppard, especially of the best kind, contain several strong dramatic situations. There is, of course, in the first place, a great storm in the Thames, an historical event which in this case is utilized for the rescue of a babe from the swirling torrents, under Old London Bridge.

This babe, because of that incident, is named Thames Darrell, and becomes the real romantic hero of the play and the rightful heir to certain estates and portable property all coveted by the play's second villain, the horrible Sir Roland Trenchard.

Jack is shown in these whitewashed plays to defend and aid the hero Thames, and to help him in his love affairs. Jack's own love affairs, alas ! do not end too happily, for as some will remember it was one of the poor lad's " blowens," named Edgworth Bess, who helps his pretended pal Jonathan Wild to give that boy burglar " up to Justice," as they always say on the stage.

The wholesale villainy in *Jack Sheppard* is carried on still further by another " fence," of a Fagin kind, named Abraham Mendez, one of the many very vile stage Jews. One of the big scenes affects two of these villains, namely, Jonathan and the aforesaid Sir Roland Trenchard. Jonathan having got Roland into a secret spot and having " done him in " for various valuables and sundry priceless " papers," persuades Trenchard to descend a very deep well in order to secure sundry " Jew-els," etc. He then contrives to bash with a bludgeon and to cut with a terrible knife Sir Roland's hands as they cling to the well top, and so consigns his fellow-brute,

down . . . down . . . down, to the bottom of the
well, from whence he will never emerge again !

It is here that Jonathan, while dispatching his
criminal confederate far below, croaks the famous
exclamation (to a crash of music), " You have a long
journey before you, Sir Roland."

I have said that I came into the Jack Sheppard
domain towards the end of its long period of prohibition, but, " believe me or believe me not " (as Dan
Leno used to say), my relations and others continued
to play *Jack Sheppard* in all sorts of theatres ! This
drama was at that time, and for some years later,
played not only in the East End, but in the West.
In order to evade the law, however, *Jack Sheppard*
bobbed up in all sorts of versions and under all
sorts of names !

The disguised Sheppard dramas with which I have
either been concerned in some way or another, or
have seen as playgoer, or read with increasing
interest, include the following : *The Idle Apprentice ;
The London Apprentice ; The Boy Burglar ; The
Young Housebreaker ; The Storm in the Thames ;
Thames Darrell ; Jack Ketch ;* and *The Stone Jug.*
In all these, of course, Jack Sheppard had another
name. In the last-mentioned drama he was called
Bob Chance.

Later Jack Sheppard plays which I came across
comprised four very important versions. One was
Old London, adapted from a French version of *Jack
Sheppard*, called *Les Chevaliers du Brouillard.* The
English adapter, announced, I remember, as F.
Boyle, was afterwards said to be no other than the
great *Times* dramatic critic, John Oxenford, a very
prolific playwright in his time, and one of whom I
could tell (and may yet tell) some strange stories !

The Jack Sheppard of this version was called Dick
Wastrel, and was played by no less an actress than

Henrietta Hodson, who at that time and for some years later was running the Queen's Theatre, Long Acre, on the site of which Odhams' the printers now stands. It was not long after this that Henrietta became the wife of Henry Labouchere, the famous journalist, founder and editor of *Truth*. H. L. was a brilliant but most eccentric personage, even for a Member of Parliament.

Another of these versions was also called *Old London*, and was by the late Arthur Shirley and William Muskerry Tilson. It was first done in the provinces and afterwards came to that popular melodrama house, the Marylebone, just over thirty years ago. This was adapted from Ainsworth's novel. So was the third of this batch, the title of which dramatization, however, done at the Standard in the early nineties, was *Old London Bridge in the Days of Jack Sheppard and Jonathan Wild*, which title may be said "to get it all in." The fourth and perhaps most peculiar dramatization of J. S. was called—as of yore—*Jack Sheppard*. It was by the celebrated journalist and novelist, Joseph Hatton, and was produced at the Pavilion, Mile End, in the spring of 1898. This version, I think, was the first to use the original title, since the famous version by Buckstone.

The housebreaking hero in this was played, strangely enough, by my late beloved friend, that fine comedian, Weedon Grossmith.

I say "strangely enough" because, brilliant actor though he was, Wee Gee's sole qualifications for playing Jack Sheppard was, as I used to tell him, his extensive and peculiar knowledge of the lives and adventures of highwaymen and others, and his possession of certain of their business utensils and weapons, in his marvellous collection of such treasures.

There were two other immensely popular dramatizations: one by the prolific Moncrieff for the Vic ; the other was by that equally ingenious dramatist, J. T. Haines, for the Surrey. There have been, of course, many burlesques in which Jack has figured. Of these perhaps it is enough to say at present that the two most famous Jack Sheppard burlesquers were the late Nellie Farren and the still surviving Jennie " Jo " Lee.

Those who are interested, like the mystical Hervey, in *Meditations among the Tombs*, will doubtless be glad to note that the great little Jack Sheppard, the wholesale prison-breaker, is buried in the long crypt of St. Martin-in-the-Fields, not far from the sepulchre of Mistress Nell Gwynne, whose funeral service at that church was preached by Archbishop Tillotson.

The dearly loved Rector of St. Martin-in-the-Fields (who, alas ! has partly retired on account of ill-health ; namely, the Reverend "Dick" Sheppard) has often smilingly alluded to the fact that his church contains the sepulchre of his famous, or infamous, sur-namesake.

CHAPTER XI

JONATHAN WILD AND CLAUD DUVAL

By this label I refer to certain plays which were written around the earlier mentioned "fence" and so-called thief-taker, Jonathan Wild. Of course Jonathan figures very largely in all the Jack Sheppard plays which I have indicated. But there came a time when Jonathan had several dramas named after him, even as he had narratives all to himself! Undoubtedly of all the undramatic or especially literary "lives" of this unspeakably contemptible villain, the very finest is that gloriously satirical one written by the great novelist (if not exactly great dramatist), Henry Fielding, and entitled, *The Life of Mr. Jonathan Wild the Great*.

It is not generally known that Jonathan Wild was really a Brum. Like many another criminal he soon found that a weekly wage earned by honesty was not sufficient for his various needs. After serving a little while, like Jack Sheppard, in the carpentering line, Jonathan Wild descended upon London and became a gentleman's servant, and then his extravagant notions seemed to grow. Also like most of his burglar and highwayman class, Jonathan spent a good deal of his nefarious earnings on the fair sex or "blowens," as they were then called. With one of these sirens, a rather attractive and very artful damsel, named Mary Milliner, Jonathan began to form a kind of syndicate. It was Mary who put him up to a very lucrative dodge. This was to get hold of the " bustle " (or booty) of various footpads and other felons, and either to sell the same at a higher price or to make arrangements to restore them to their rightful owners—for a suitable reward, of course, and on the understanding that no questions would be asked.

The ingenious Mary and the by now equally ingenious Jonathan, posing as Mr. and Mrs. J. W., soon formed another useful " joint," as their class calls it. By means of this new idea Mary would go out and entrap other thieves (such as Jack Sheppard) and by means of her blandishments would possess herself of their secrets and their illgotten gains.

And when these criminal victims would not agree to the terms proposed by Mr. and Mrs. Wild, Mary, by means of information received from her so-called husband, would cause the non-complying criminals to be speedily nabbed by the local Bow Street runners !

This department of the Wild collaboration proved very valuable to them both, for by Jonathan's apparent unselfish assistance of the law, Jonathan, the " fence," was admitted by the authorities to interview in Newgate and elsewhere the felons whom he had assisted to " bag." Thus Jonathan was able to learn where such and such plunder had been deposited, and while promising to do his best to help the poor victim in the dungeon, he was able to lay his hands on all the portable property they had hidden. Whereupon, of course, Wild took care not only *not* to keep his promise to the felon who had confided in him, but even to make it considerably hotter for the poor dupe !

It was thus that Wild served Sheppard, and as in Defoe's searching analysis, so happily also in the plays built around Jonathan, this unspeakably contemptible side of his character was mercilessly depicted.

In all the dramas I have seen concerning this " fence " fiend, even up to the latest which was given at the Elephant and Castle Theatre not many years ago, Jonathan has been so painted in his true colours that he has been not only soundly and roundly hissed by audiences *en masse*, but some of them, especially in the pit and gallery, have called him such names that they are not printable in these respectable chronicles !

By way of finale concerning Wild, I may mention that his end at the gibbet was terribly and unromantically unlike the winding up of most crib-crackers and Knights of the Road.

In their cases, for the most part, ladies of fashion, and even of peerless beauty, were known to flutter around the scaffold and to offer to marry this or that highwayman " hero " to save him from the rope ! As will be seen in due course, this was especially the case of the so-called " gallant " Claude Duval.

When Jonathan Wild, however, came to the gibbet, no fair damsel, not even his charming co-crookess, Mary Milliner herself, thus offered to save him by substituting the matrimonial noose for that of Tyburn Tree. No ! Jonathan Wild, like his fellow but far less horrible criminal, Macbeth, had to put up with curses both loud and deep. In fact, but for the intervention of the authorities themselves the wretched Jonathan Wild would have been disembowelled at the gallows.

And now for an alien artist on the High Toby !

By this description I refer to that apparently artistic and attractive Adonis of a highwayman, Claude Duval. Claude was a native of Normandy and came over to England, as so many other aliens have done, as a spy. We had spies enough at that time in all truth, for the time was that of Charles II, who, whatever may be said of some of the other Stuarts, was traitor enough to his English subjects to encourage all sorts of spies, especially of the foreign persuasion. And more especially so when they were in any way concerned with this or that one of his light o' loves.

Young Claude became the most romantic of all the professional footpads that even padded foot in the British Isles. We have seen, and we have heard, on our stages, the young' London Cockney Jack Sheppard singing reverently of " Claude Duval when in Newgate thrown." There is no doubt that Jack, even though more of a crib-cracker than property pincher on the highway, regarded Claude as the god of his idolatry. We have seen the famous picture, in some form or other, showing Claude Duval dancing the Coranto on Hounslow Heath with a beautiful aristocratic lady whom he has enticed out of her coach, while engaged in his depredations. Moreover, we have met his Apollo-like form in many a drama and in several comic operas and burlesques. Nay, we have even known him to be " cried up " by poets and novelists galore.

As regards poets, the great Samuel Butler, author of *Hudibras*, wrote what he called a pindaric ode entitled, *To the Happy Memory of the Most Renowned Duval*. This was written in 1671, two years after the fascinating footpad had been executed at Tyburn at the age of twenty-seven !

There is no doubt that Duval's end was hastened by his excessive vanity, a quality so largely possessed by all criminals, and in this case accelerated by the vast numbers of fashionable and other women whom Claude was said to have—" enslaved " !

In proof of this enslavement one may quote a few lines from Butler's Ode :—

> Thither came ladies from all parts,
> To offer up close prisoners their hearts,
> Which he received as tribute due,
> And made them yield up love and honour too.

And it was evidently some of these very women who came to the scaffold and offered to release him by marriage.

Another writer on Duval, dropping into prose, refers to Claude's capturing of the fair sex as follows :—

> The adventures of his gallantry are, however, of such a nature that decorum forbids their recital ; and certainly it is no great compliment to the delicacy or taste of him who first recorded them. It is sufficient to mention that his gallantries emptied his coffers, and excited him to renewed depredations to feed his licentious desires, until he became confirmed in every species of vice !

In the case of Duval's fearful end at so young an age, I am afraid one must use the quotation of W. E. Henley, " the booze and the blowens cop the lot," for after Claude had been " given away " by several of his lady loves, he was captured in a cellar beneath a tavern, up in Chandos Street in the Strand. The fascinatingly handsome youth might have eluded his pursuers once again, but for the fact that he was as drunk as an owl !

In the Claude Duval dramas I have seen, and have been otherwise concerned with, I call to mind many an attractive impersonation of that " hero," notably in that strange but gripping melodrama, *White-friars*. In this play Claude was originally played by the famous Bravo Hicks, who, by the way, was not called Bravo by the plaudits he gained, as people seem to think, but because of the fact that he always

played bandits, pirates, smugglers, wreckers, or
" bravoes."

One of the finest Claude Duvals I saw was also
one of the handsomest that ever trod the stage.
This was the late Frank Celli, father of Miss Faith
Celli. He played Claude Duval in the comic opera
of the same name written by the late " Pot "
Stephens and set to music by the late " Teddy "
Solomon.

I could tell of many another Duval drama, but
these I have mentioned may suffice, especially as my
conscience is pricking me for keeping waiting a
highwayman who was by no means fascinating and
by no means heroic. I mean the one to whom Sam
Weller referred in song as " The Bold Tur-*pin*,"
who, according to Sam, " put a bullet into somebody's knob, and perwailed upon him to stop."

CHAPTER XII

DRAMAS OF THE SO-CALLED TURPIN

I say the "so-called" Turpin because, as some know (but many don't), that desperado's real name was Jack Palmer. I think I may claim to have read everything, or certainly almost everything, that has ever been written about Dick Turpin both as regards plays and novels, trials, and so forth. But although it suited some romancers, such as our old untrustworthy friend Harrison Ainsworth and others of his class, to whitewash and to treacle-gush over Jack Palmer, *alias* Dick Turpin, I have long come to the conclusion that that highwayman was one of the most brutal, unromantic, bloodthirsty pigs who ever dared to take to the High Toby and call himself a Knight of the Road! So there!

And I say this with all due respect to my old friend, Matheson Lang, and to Citizen Tom Mix (U.S.A.), who have regaled us (more or less) with such gloriously gilded impersonations of this scoundrel on the film!

Poor old Ainsworth, it will be remembered, puts his "Turpin" hero in his very blood-and-thundery romance called *Rookwood*. By the way, I may remind some who may have forgotten it that this strange and fitful tale starts thrillingly enough to suit even a modern American crook mystery melodrama. It shows how the real sentimental hero, who gives the book its name, descends into a family vault and, uncovering the coffin of his mother, cuts off one of her hands to wear next his heart to remind him (forsooth) to seek revenge for the villain who compassed that mother's death!

Turpin turns up later in this "romance" as a sort of semi-spectral rider, urging on his wild career beside the similarly urgeful hero. Indeed, it is the "Bold Turpin" who helps that sometime unfortunate young person and always behaves (according to Ainsworth) in most generous and self-sacrificing nature. Quite in the same spirit, you see, in which, as we are so often told by these romancers, these same Knights of the Road made it a habit to rob only the rich—only to give to the poor! As the gentleman says in the comic song, "Yes, I *don't* think!"

Anyhow, Ainsworth was obviously so fond of his sentimentalized highwayman in this story that he remarks very pathetically towards the end, "Dick Turpin, alas! (Why disguise it?) was hanged at York."

Of course the unreliable but always deeply interesting Harrison Ainsworth makes a great feature of Turpin's supposed Ride to York on his famous mare, Bonnie Black Bess. H. A. also makes use of the ballad concerning that very noble steed. I am afraid that Ainsworth must really have known that Dick Turpin did *not* perform the Ride to York feat at all!

This feat, or something very like it, was achieved by Highwayman Nevison, and oftentimes have I sat and listened to that keen criminologist and quaint comedian, Weedon Grossmith, enthusiastically holding forth on Nick Nevison and similar High Toby "heroes."

I suppose it is sad to relate that Nevison, like Jack Dick Palmer Turpin, was also hanged at York. He was then forty-five, while, if I remember rightly, Turpin was only thirty-seven.

6

Most of the vile deeds of Turpin, either by himself
or in connection with Tom King and Co., are fully
set forth in certain chronicles of crime, including, of
course, the Newgate Calendar.

Therefore I will proceed to treat of some of the
many dramatizations of Dick's Dark Deeds, dramas
which I have seen or been concerned with, from
childhood's days until almost the present time.
Several of these Turpin plays were, of course, taken
for many years in succession from the above-named
romance, *Rookwood*. Indeed, one of the latest and
one of the most successful of these *Rookwood* dramatizations was acted for many years up till recently
by my happily still surviving comrade, the Anglo-
Australian actor, Frank Gerald. His version, which
he played in four acts at the theatres and one act
in the music halls, was called, like so many other
Turpin plays, *The King's Highway*. For the Ride
to York business friend Frank rode gaily a very noble
steed, whose portrait and that of its rider as Turpin,
upon its back, is in my proud possession.

Another tremendously successful Turpin on the
Halls was another old friend of mine, namely R. A.
Roberts. His performance, it may be remembered,
was quite a *tour de force*, for he played not only
Turpin but all the other dramatic personæ. He
could also, I feel sure, have played Black Bess, if
he could have found a sufficiently realistic make-up.

Harking back to my earliest Turpin dramas, I
saw most of these at the famous melodrama houses
such as the Standard, City of London, Norton
Folgate, the Pavilion and Effingham in the Mile
End Road, the Oriental (now the Queen's Palace),
Poplar, and such-like. But especially, of course, at
good old Astley's, where I was engaged for awhile.

Two of the versions I saw at Astley's from time
to time were written or nailed up, respectively, by

two very smart and clever playwrights, H. H. Milner and W. E. Suter. Both these versions would be now nearly a hundred years of age, and they were getting fairly venerable when I first met them.

Milner's version was an unabashed crib from *Rookwood* with this daring variant, that whereas Ainsworth was compelled to "hang" Turpin, Adaptor Milner causes him to stand astride the body of poor Black Bess, who has been shot by the Bow Street runners, and covering those officials with a brace of pistols, is enabled to arrange a very happy tableau for himself and his fellow-crooks !

Suter's version was more of a knockabout kind and more avowedly for circus use. It had a very effective comic episode for the turnpike-gate minder and, as well I know, in my experiences with my character-acting uncle in this very play, the man in charge of the turnpike gate had a very risky job, beside having to give a very special and dangerous cue for Bess to jump over him and the toll gate.

Of course the great pathetic situation in every one of these whitewashed Turpin plays was, firstly, where Dick accidentally shoots and kills his pal, Tom King, outside the " Spaniards " at Hampstead Heath, while aiming at a Bow Street runner. And the second big episode was where Turpin laments the death of the gallant steed who (in the play) carries him on his two-hundred-mile ride.

I confess that when I was a youngster I, like all the other youngsters present, shed many a tear over these two situations. And indeed I have not been utterly unmoved even of recent years when this scene has cropped up.

Although I am not of sufficient venerableness to have seen the great original Dick Turpin, yet I have seen many of the best during the last half-century. Among these I may mention the famous Henry

Powell, a very fine equestrian actor, Fred Marchant, Fred Thomas, William Travers, the great little J. B. Howe (whom I saw in sundry versions, including two of his own) ; and my aforesaid uncle, W. W. Lacy, who was a fine equestrian as well as a splendid acrobat. Also certain members of the Footitt family, and those wonderful circus fellows, The Ginnetts. The famous Fred Ginnett, like the above-mentioned Frank Gerald, played Turpin a good deal in the Variety Theatres. Indeed, I fancy one of the latter-day versions which he used was by the late humorist, Wal Pink.

Like every other hero real or false, Dick Turpin has figured in many a burlesque. After I had had a long course of the above-named dramas at such blood and thunder and equestrian houses which I have named (especially some startling personal experiences with the Sangers), I revelled in some of these extravaganzas, although of course it was always difficult to make them as funny as the original melodramas were.

One of the smartest of the Turpin play parodies was *Dick Turpin the Second*, which was produced at the Gaiety about thirty-seven years ago. You can guess that this was a smart skit, for it was written by that chartered humorist, one of the cleverest we have ever had, poor little Willie Goldberg, the renowned " Shifter " of the so-called *Pink 'Un*. Good little kind-hearted " Shifter " had won his Oxford degree and other things in his day, but he died very young, like several of his too Bohemian but equally kind colleagues.

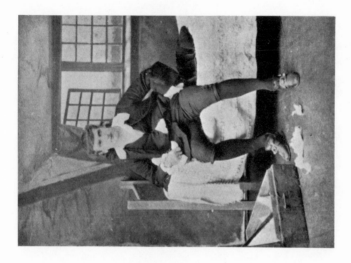

WILSON BARRETT
as Chatterton, the Boy Poet

E. S. WILLARD
as "The Spider" or Burglar-Chief in *The Silver King*

CHAPTER XIII

ANOTHER ROMANTICIZED ROBBER

This High Toby merchant is no other than Paul Clifford. Paul's crimes can be studied in detail in the trials of the period, but if my readers would prefer to view Paul in an idealized and highly innocent light, I advise them to turn to sundry whitewashing novelists. Perhaps the most important romancer who treated Clifford, and who indeed made him something of an Angel of Light instead of a Devil of Darkness, was that famous " cleanser " of criminals, Lord Lytton, otherwise Bulwer Lytton.

Even when glorifying that sordid but scholarly scoundrel, Eugene Aram, Lytton spoke quite tenderly of what he called " The milder guilt of Paul Clifford."

It may be granted that Clifford did not have too encouraging a start in life, and that like many other criminals (especially those described by Defoe), he owed much of his pegging-back in life to a mother whose morals were anything but moral!

There was probably some basis for the assertion of Lytton and other romancers of Paul's career that his illegitimate father subsequently became a learned judge. This dramatic point very naturally and very properly was seized upon by novelists and dramatists alike to work up a very terrible episode.

I allude, of course, to that tremendous situation wherein Judge Brandon, at the moment of sentencing

Paul Clifford to the gallows, learns that he has sentenced his own son !

This was too strong a dramatic notion to be missed, and I have seen it used in all sorts of forms of Paul Clifford dramas. In some cases the hanging judge has smothered or concealed this terrible fact and has gloated over getting rid of his inconvenient son. In others he has shown a relenting mood and has endeavoured to secure the reprieve of his victim.

In almost every dramatization, however, the hapless Paul has been shown to fall in love with the beautiful Lucy Brandon, who is sometimes depicted as the daughter or sometimes the niece of the famous judge.

Several very powerful Paul Clifford plays have I met during my varied career. If you will promise not to let it go any farther, I will confess that one of these Paul Clifford dramas was written by *myself* !

The hero, Paul, was played by the handsome George Leyton, for whom I wrote a very High Toby-like carol entitled, *Hurrah for the Road!* which you will find (if you want it) at Francis Day and Hunter's. It was composed by that excellent all-round musician, Denham Harrison, who also contributed some very dramatic music for the several situations of this play.

In this perpetration of mine, the very wicked Judge Brandon (and I made him very wicked) was played by an actor of very wide renown, namely, the Australian tragedian, J. Hastings Batson, who had been a very celebrated Hamlet " down under." After playing in my *Paul Clifford,* he obtained an engagement with the late Sir George Alexander.

One of the more famous Paul Clifford plays was written by the prolific blood-and-thunder playwright, Fitzball. One of the other early ones (a far better

version) was by no other than old Ben Webster,
the famous actor, and was played at the Vic just
after its name was changed from the Coburg.
Another renowned man who wrote a Paul Clifford
play was my late esteemed friend, that noble poet and
true genius, Robert Buchanan. His play was called
Lucy Brandon and was played at the Imperial a
little over forty years ago. I am sorry to say it
failed lamentably.

Another version was done at Astley's under the
name of *Fate's Decree,* and was by a very clever
dramatist and very smart sporting man named
H. W. Williamson. I forget the name of J. B.
Howe's version at the Brit, but I know he wrote a
very successful one for that house, and so did that
theatre's resident dramatist, Colin Hazelwood.

In later days I saw another *Paul Clifford* at
the Old Vic. This was by H. M. Pitt, a member
of the far-flung theatrical family of the same name.
Its title was perhaps the most effective of any. It
was called *Paul Clifford ; or, the Highwayman of
Life.*

Of course Paul, like Turpin and other exclaimers
of "Stand and deliver!" or "Your money or your
life!" also suffered from the hands and pens of the
burlesque writer.

CHAPTER XIV

Dog and Dumb Play Specimens

I have in my time met a great many crime dramas, both of French and English origin, in which the leading character was either a dog, or a dumb boy or ditto girl.

Of the first, or canine kind, doubtless the most popular specimen is *The Forest of Bondy ; or, The Dog of Montargis*, which is founded upon a real crime which took place in the more foresty part of France about the middle of the eighteenth century.

Those who have not seen this thrilling drama, so frequently played in my early days, can have no idea of the deep interest aroused by its swift and brief action. As to the story, it is enough to say that two brutal murderers of a gallant French officer are eventually hunted down by that victim's faithful hound, under the direction of a faithful friend.

I can assure you that I have seen vast audiences hang spellbound over the final episode in *The Forest of Bondy*, which culminates in the wonderful animal leaping at the throat, first of one villain, and then at the other. Each miscreant yells forth the long celebrated, and one time often quoted shriek of terror, " Take off the dog ! "

Having had to do with a great many stage productions myself, I can and I would tell you exactly how we used to make sure of our dog star seizing the villain exactly at the right spot and without, of course, real danger to his epiglottis. But having

resolved never to give away a stage illusion under
any circumstances, I must ask you to excuse me in
this, or any similar case, from telling you "how it
is done."

And now for some account of dramas concerning
the Dog and the Dane.

The Dane in this case is not really the dog, but
our solemn old friend Hamlet the Prince of Denmark,
and I have two reasons for bringing him in here.
One is that the crime committed by Hamlet's uncle
upon that Prince's father, by slaying him in the
orchard as he slept, was a real crime, the full details
of which may be found in Saxo-Grammaticus, and
other antiquarian historians consulted by Shakespeare
and his preceding authors of *Hamlet* plays.

My second reason is that, strange as it may seem,
I have many times in my stage experience, before
and behind the scenes, seen and been concerned with
several condensed versions of *Hamlet* in which
we used a real dog star to work the *dénouement*.

These "Dog Hamlets" (as they were called) were
mostly played by clowns and pantomimists of note
at their benefit time. Then Mr. Merriman would
don Hamlet's inky cloak, and would go through the
real text of the tragedy in a condensed form and
would play it for "all it was worth" plus its famous
performing dog! This faithful sleuth-hound was
first brought in while the Ghost was giving his son
a description of this "murder most foul."

The talented animal was next introduced in the
play scene to keep its "eye" on the guilty Claudius,
especially where that murderous monarch is caught
out by Hamlet's "Mousetrap" matinée.

The lynx-eyed dog finally was brought into the
corner to watch during the fencing bout of Hamlet
and Laertes, and when that murderous trick was
disclosed, the dying Dane called his dog forward

and that canine star at once leapt at the throat of the gory sovereign and pinned him to the earth until he perished miserably !

The English stage can boast of a great many strong plays in which the hero or the heroine (and sometimes both) enact a dumb part character throughout. In a few cases the dumbness is cured towards the tag. Of course I am only speaking of such plays based upon real trial and crimes, for, sooth to say, dumb dramas abound among blood-and-thunder specimens.

Right away from our first melodrama, *A Tale of Mystery*, based by Holcroft the Shoemaker dramatist upon a *cause célèbre* of the middle eighteenth century, a play in which the villain has something like four hundred music cues, and the dumb show hero almost as many, most of our leading actors and actresses have played these great dumb - show characters.

For example, the hereinbefore-mentioned T. P. Cooke revelled in such silent heroes and even dumb fiends. The great Madame Celeste, in all her plays, enacted either an entirely dumb heroine or hero or one partly so.

The most widely popular of any dumb-show real crime drama in all my varied experience of such thrillful concoctions was undoubtedly one which is usually played under the title of *The Dumb Man of Manchester*.

This play, originally adapted from the French for the great Ducrow of Astley's, was taken from a play which was founded upon a French crime, namely, the murder of a benevolent employer, a factory owner, by an avaricious, villainous nephew.

The crime was fastened on to an innocent person, of course, and in the unfolding of the piece and the bringing home the terrible deed to the real culprit, the guiltless dumb hero, Tom by name, was made to enact many a stirring and deeply pathetic episode.

All of course was worked, as in all these plays, with a most ingeniously arranged set of music cues. In the finale of this play, poor Tom has a hand-to-hand combat with the villain and is nearly murdered in the process. Generally in the play, Tom climbs up and down a rope in order to focus his attempts upon the villain. The combined effect of this struggle undoubtedly forms what has been described as the greatest fight on any stage.

The most successful performers of *The Dumb Man of Manchester* (into which were afterwards worked the threads of a local crime, and played under various names, such as *The Factory Assassin*, etc.) have included, in addition to Ducrow (the original), Henry Irving, Dick Kitchen (father of Fred), Fred Evans (father of Will), and all sorts of wonderful pantomimists, chiefly clowns, among them the Three Paynes, Charles Lauri, senior and junior, the Rowellas, the Crouestes, the Hulines, the Deulins, the Martinettis, and my own aforesaid uncle, W. W. Lacy. I confess that this uncle of mine also dared often, in my presence, to play the Dog Hamlet !

I have played in *Hamlet* a good deal myself (sometimes going on for five parts a night therein !), but (thank Thespis) I never sank to playing a canine " Moody Dane " !

A MODERN MARROW-FREEZER, AND OUR MONARCH

This blood-curdling specimen which I am about to describe is a play of to-day, so to speak, and was entitled, *The Monk's Room.* It was the work of a most estimable gentleman named John Lart. He was a man full of culture and of cash, and the latter commodity enabled him to take several theatres in which to produce this Blood and Thunder Drama. For instance, he started at the Shaftesbury, got down to the Olympic, and then across to the Opéra Comique.

The Monk's Room, which came out somewhat like *Hamlet* in Plus Fours, was mostly costumed in coat and trousers, etc. It was a terrible story of a haunted chamber, in which a monk had been cruelly murdered centuries earlier. Before dying he had left a permanent curse upon that house, and all who should ever be concerned therewith.

And very terribly did that curse work, from generation to generation, until it reached our own time, when the play proper commenced. I can call to mind the sundry murders, the murderers going and coming by sliding panels, and the harrowing ghosts with blood-stained breasts, and so forth, that hovered around us from time to time !

Now this drama, enacted by a most powerful cast, including the late Hermann Vezin, and other famous players, when it reached the Opéra Comique had a tremendous effect one night upon the late King Edward, who, alas ! poor Sovereign, did not know what he was in for.

His Majesty (as a matter of fact he had not quite come to the throne) instructed our old friend, " Librarian " George Ashton, to book him a box at the old Globe Theatre, which then stood in Newcastle Street, Strand, all of which has been wiped out to assist in forming Aldwych.

It was the heir-apparent's intention to see at the Globe that then tremendous success, *The Private Secretary,* and especially to exercise the Royal risibility upon little Penley, as the persecuted parson in that play.

As many will remember, the Globe Theatre and the Opéra Comique were side by side, that is, as regarded their respective stage doors and ditto Royal entrances. By an evil fate Ashton and his Royal master were taken through the Opéra Comique stage entrance instead of the Globe's. For a good while the Royal visitor sat in his box waiting to laugh at Penley, but there was no sign of that popular little droll. Instead of laughing at laughable episodes, the heir to the throne was being regaled (or otherwise) by the successive spectres and other things I have mentioned. At last, quite marrow-frozen, he sent for the manager of the theatre.

On that manager arriving the Prince asked him what had become of Little Penley. The manager, who happened to be John Lart himself, humbly explained that the play which His Royal Highness was then witnessing was his (John's) very own drama of phantoms and many murders, *The Monk's Room*.

The much perplexed manager offered to send into the Globe and arrange for His Royal Highness to go there. But, as all remember, the Prince, and subsequently our beloved King, was in every way a true playgoer, and therefore he cheerfully asserted that he would see *The Monk's Room* through. And he did to its bitter, and bloodthirsty, end!

Ashton confessed to me later that his Royal employer rubbed it into him after he went away, and said that if he did not fix up the Globe for the next night so that he could enjoy little Penley, he (Ashton) would hear of it!

A Drama by Disraeli.

It is not generally known that the late Lord Beaconsfield, born Disraeli, and christened Benjamin by his father Isaac, who was a " Meshumad," wrote a marrow-freezing real crime drama on his own account.

This " Dizzy " drama was called *Alarcos*, and it was based by Benjamin upon one of Lockhart's Spanish ballads, which in turn was based upon a real crime of the period.

In this tragedy, which Disraeli audaciously announced as "A return to the Shakespeare method" (which it wasn't), the Count Alarcos was a most terrible personage who, having gone in for eternally triangular habits, murdered his long-suffering wife in full view of the audience. He also caused the death of many other personages concerned.

Among the other innocent sufferers who thus expired was a very faithful Moor who had befriended the unhappy Countess and eventually was attacked for so doing by a batch of bandits "specially engaged" by the criminal Count.

This blend of blank verse (*very* blank verse) horrors was a great failure at Astley's Theatre when I was a youngster there with the producer thereof, in the very same week that its author, the great Benjamin, was made Prime Minister for the first time.

Well do I remember that awful first night ! Also how narrowly the new Prime Minister escaped being " booed " by the irate audience.

CHAPTER XV

" A Terrible Tragedy of Tongs "

Doubtless there are a good many living now who, like myself, remember more or less vividly the awful tragedy indicated above. It took place in Northumberland Street, Strand, which now forms part of Northumberland Avenue, and the period was the early sixties.

I call to mind that the pictorial papers of that time, such as the *Illustrated London News* (still flourishing) and the *Illustrated Times* (long dead), were full of awful pictures of this shocking affair. It was really a fight to a finish between two scoundrels of whom it was difficult to say which was the darker desperado.

These two villains were respectively surnamed Murray and Roberts. Roberts, who was a money-lender, met and lured Murray into his chambers in Northumberland Street, and proceeded to blackmail his guest with regard to a very shady transaction which Murray, as a solicitor, had engineered.

Murray resenting Roberts's financial attempts, a terrible quarrel ensued. This led to what is generally called in the Blood and Thunder Drama, " a fearful combat to the death."

Roberts, roused to frenzy, produced a pistol from his pocket and shot a bullet into Murray's temple without, however, slaying him on the spot.

Murray, pretending to be dead, wriggled along the floor and, getting hold of the fire tongs, bashed

Roberts almost to pieces. As Roberts had locked the door in order to have this duel, when the cries for help arose it was a long while before anybody could come to their assistance. In the meantime, both the terribly injured miscreants rallied sufficiently to endeavour to choke each other and to hurl all sorts of furniture, jars, etc., at each other's heads.

When assistance eventually arrived, both combatants were in a frightful state of batteredness and bleeding, and they were taken away for medical treatment.

Roberts, the original assailant, died very soon afterwards in the Charing Cross Hospital, but not before he had made some remarkable lying statements, as they were proved to be. Roberts, on his death-bed, swore that Murray first shot himself, and then attacked him (Roberts) with the terrible tongs.

Murray lingered on awhile, and in the meantime all London (to say nothing of the provinces) was aroused to the most feverish point of excitement concerning what was undoubtedly one of the most startling tragedies ever known.

This awful case was eventually increased in interest and dramatic power, by the fact that a woman named Annie Maria Moodey, who was made to give evidence at the inquest, described herself as Murray's mistress. She added that Roberts had made illicit advances to her and that this was the real reason why Roberts first attacked Murray!

Undoubtedly, however, although this tragedy, like so many others, was not utterly unconnected with the old proverb, "Cherchez la femme," yet it was evident from what transpired later that the main reason of the fight was a matter of each man seeking, or having sought, to blackmail the other.

Of course it was not long before Messieurs the

Playwrights seized upon this awful conflict for use in this or that play, especially in the Blood and Thunder Theatres. I remember several such dramas, but at the first the use of the crime itself was not acknowledged on the playbills.

In due course, however, such acknowledgments were made, and especially with regard to two melodramas. The first of these, which came out twenty odd years after the fearful fight, was the work of Hugh Marston and Leonard Rae. It had its first London production at the Standard, Shoreditch (now the Shoreditch Olympia), at the Easter of 1882, and well do I remember that first night. Strangely enough this melodrama was entitled, *Humanity; or, a Passage in the Life of Grace Darling*.

You will perhaps wonder how the heroic Grace managed to get into this play. She was utilized, however, for assisting in the rescue of several shipwrecked voyagers, some of whom had been in the toils of the two principal villains. Without going further into the many more or less shudderful episodes of this four-act melodramatic mixture, I may as well say that these two villains were based upon Murray and Roberts. Also that the last act of the play was devoted entirely to these two desperadoes disintegrating each other in exact imitation of Murray and Roberts in Northumberland Street. And the playbills gave a description of the original fight. At the end of this episode the falsely accused and other innocent persons rushed in to find the battered bodies of the assailants, and the curtain fell to general joy!

One of these Murray and Roberts characters was, I remember, acted by that versatile and powerful player, the late Edward Sass, who was the brother-in-law of the late great manager, George Edwardes. Sass, when off the stage, was one of the finest

7

humorists I have ever met. In fact, I have never encountered so truly humorous a player of awful villains in my life.

I might mention that "heavy villain" Sass was also a great devotee of that very innocent pastime floriculture. In this regard the late Edward was a determined and ceaseless rival in the gentle art of rose-growing against his next-door neighbour, who was that quaint low comedian and variety artist, the late Fred Emney.

What proved to be a still more popular dramatization of the Murray-Roberts fight was in the form of a sketch produced by the late semi-Jewish actor-manager, John Lawson. And this was how John managed it.

Some years after the above-named Standard play was produced, I was "approached" (as old actors say) by Lawson, then a young low comedian, who had been a trapeze artist. He wanted from me the provincial rights of a burlesque called *Lancelot the Lovely*, which I had written with Richard Butler (then Editor of the *Referee*) under our collaborative stage name of "Richard Henry." These provincial rights had already been secured by the droll comedian Arthur Roberts, for whom the burlesque was written, so John Lawson bought instead the touring rights of *Humanity; or, a Passage in the Life of Grace Darling*. In this piece he played a comic Jew, and he travelled this melodrama for a good many years.

Presently there arose in the music halls a demand for sketches, and John came soon to me telling me he had a brain wave. This brain wave took the form of John cutting out the first three acts of that play, and making the fourth (or Roberts and Murray fight) into an eighteen minutes' sketch.

In this terrible thriller as it proved to be (and so

successful that I nicknamed it in the *Referee*, the *Money Spinner*), John introduced the Jew as the hero, and kept only one of the villains, so that he should fight him himself!

With even more audacity, Lawson introduced a song called *Only a Jew*, which he sang (or rather intoned) in such a manner that I am afraid he aroused more laughter than tears, which he intended to extract. Anyhow, the Murray-Roberts fight was carried out with the utmost intensity and realism. Fire-irons and furniture, mirrors, pictures and bric-à-brac were alike flung by the combatants at each other, until at last the villain was battered to death, and when John arose exhausted, perspiringly to take his curtain call, the stage was one mass of wreckage!

So real, however, was the half-Levite Lawson in his " art," that he bought a fresh set of china and glass, mirrors and what not to smash at every performance!

Plucky John made quite a fortune out of this bloodthirsty bit of drama, but, alas! he lost most of it with other sketches, even far wilder, but not so convincing, and also with sundry other speculations which were (as I often vainly told him) outside of his play-acting and play-producing province.

But John was one of the dearest fellows and friends, and he passed away far too soon. God rest him!

CHAPTER XVI

SOME MORE CENSORED CRIME DRAMAS

Jack Sheppard was by no means the only play which gave the censors of the period grounds for great uneasiness, and which in point of fact was banned, with no uncertain ban.

I have an old prompt book of a play called *The Gamblers* which was brought out at the Surrey Theatre just over a hundred years ago, but which I have seen revived in sundry forms. The theatre had just been taken over by a Mr. Williams, who was the proprietor of a celebrated boiled beef shop a few doors from Newgate Prison. *The Gamblers* was written around the terrible murder case wherein one Thurtell slew a Mr. Weare just before the play came out. All England was agog concerning this terrible deed, the chief perpetrator of which was the shocking gambler.

The play itself was a poor thing, even for those days of nailed-up melodrama, but its chief attraction lay in the fact that the very gig in which the murderer escaped *pro tem.*, the identical sofa on which he slept on the night of the murder, and the real table at which he had supped with his victim just before the terrible deed, were all shown upon the Surrey stage.

The " props " of the play also included the very jug out of which the unsuspecting victim had drunk punch with his waiting destroyer !

Daniel Bandmann · George Conquest
(Both famous impersonators of gory criminals)

William Creswick · John Ryder
(Both eminent tragedians who often revelled in Real Crime Dramas

Facing p. 96

All these grimly realistic "props," being vouched for as to their correctness, drew vast audiences to that old Surrey Theatre in the Blackfriars Road. But only for a few nights, as it fell out. By that time the Lord Chamberlain and Licenser of Plays for 1824 swooped down upon the Surrey and threatened to shut it up unless the play and its "props" were withdrawn forthwith.

And so the poor boiled beef merchant–theatrical manager had to do as he was bid, and the gruesome gig, etc., were seen no more—not on any stage, anyhow.

Of course when I struck *The Gamblers* in after-years, there was no attempt to restore these awful relics. It was always advertised, however, by way of an extra "draw," that this play dealt with the murder of Mr. Weare, and with his murderer who happily in due course (to use a favourite reportorial expression) "had paid the last penalty of the Law." I should add that "Justice" was still further satisfied by the fact that Probert, who assisted Thurtell to murder Weare and anon turned "King's evidence," was afterwards hanged for a minor crime, namely, sheep-stealing !

Other crime dramas of real life which came under the Licensers' lash in due course included several of the Dick Turpin dramas and one or two concerning Claude Duval and Paul Clifford. And here is a case of a very peculiar play, which in one of its more extreme forms was banned from the "boards."

This drama, or, rather, the special version of it concerned, dealt in the then too prevalent, felon-worshipping fashion with the great George Barrington, otherwise known as the "Gentleman Pickpocket." Its episodes were of the usual dashing criminal kind, in which the chief blackguard concerned was of course the chief hero.

Despite the dramatic whitewashing of this contemptible scoundrel, the " Gentleman Pickpocket," as history shows, was sent to Botany Bay with a gang of similar felons. It was in connection with this transportation that the polished " cly-faker " above mentioned turned poet for the nonce, and wrote that effusion which contains the often-quoted couplet :—

> True patriots we, for be it understood,
> We left our country for our country's good.

Within comparatively recent years several real crime melodramas have been dropped upon by the authorities. Among those which I can call to mind were two wretched blood - and - thunder affairs written just over thirty years ago around that wholesale murderer, Deeming. One was called *Deeming ; or, Doomed at Last*, the other was entitled *Deeming, Man and Monster*.

Another similar homicidal mixture, a very strange one I remember, was entitled, *The Mysterious Drama ; or, The Camden Town Murder*. It was produced in 1908 and, like the Deeming and similar dramas, was played principally at certain "portable theatres" and booths around the suburbs and in the provinces.

These plays, together with dramatic versions of such awful crimes as the Yarmouth Bootlace Murder, the Peasenhall Mystery, and certain other murder mixtures, based on even later crimes, were all brought out in defiance of the Licenser.

In most cases the authors of these plays did not seek for a licence, for they knew they would not get it ! Happily, in due course, however, I saw these horrible offensive mixtures driven from the boards by what are mostly called, in such plays, "the minions of Justice."

But notwithstanding the censorial fiat in these matters, you may still find several of these awful concoctions bobbing up (as *Jack Sheppard* did of old) under other names, and so evading the Law!

I might add here, that among other modern melodramas which flourished very briefly before achieving censorial banishment were strange concoctions concerning Charles Peace, Wainwright's murder of Harriet Lane in Whitechapel, the Coram Street murder, the Dr. Crippen horror, and even horrible dramatic depictions of certain of the unspeakable murders committed by Jack the Ripper.

CHAPTER XVII

THE RED BARN MURDER AND ITS DRAMAS

Now it is high time, methinks, that I treated one of the greatest murder trials in the annals of crime, and the dramas and plays written around it.

I allude to the famous case of Maria Martin, who, as everybody knows, was murdered in the Red Barn near Norwich by her lover, William Corder, in 1828. I think you will find that the details of this awful deed and of the trial and subsequent hanging of the brutal murderer are quite sufficiently depicted in the under-given scenes of the chief drama of that murder. These scenes I have taken bodily from the original prompt book, written out and scarred about as such old-time scripts used to be before the time of typewriting and printed play copies.

This script which I have used was lent to me (as I have mislaid my own written one) by a well-known "portable" theatre manager who is still touring *Maria Martin* in and around the minor districts of the industrial parts of the provinces.

I began to see and to know the *Maria Martin* melodramas when I was a very little youngster indeed. I suppose that perhaps the very earliest stage anecdote I heard was poured into my juvenile ears by one of my relations who often played the murderer Corder and other parts in the play. I allude to that old wheeze which says that on the day that murderer Corder was "turned off" (as Dickens's *Barnaby Rudge* hangman put it), a man in the gallery at the Norwich Theatre during a performance of *Macbeth* was suddenly startled to hear the question, " Is execution yet performed on Cawdor ? "

Whereupon that astounded galleryite shouted, " Yes, of course ; I saw him gibbeted this morning ! "

It seems strange that so many journalists and actors are so ignorant of this famous murder melodrama which has appeared in so many gory guises. Only the other day a theatrical reminiscence writer actually spoke of *Maria Martin, the Murderess* ! A few weeks before that, even in one of the Green Room Club " Rags " at a West End Theatre, the performance of *Maria Martin*, given as a joke, was utterly spoilt by the obvious fact that no one concerned with the cast, even the experienced actor who played William Corder, had any knowledge of that play, or how it should be acted !

The only way to play *Maria Martin* and to get laughs out of it at the present day, is not to speak and to make up in burlesque fashion, but to utter its peculiar jargon dialogue in a perfectly serious manner ! *Then* your laughs will come sure enough !

Maria's Own True Character

But mark you, although Maria was the murdered, and not the murderess, it is not true that she was quite an angel of virtue. If you read the trial for yourself in the Newgate Calendar you will find that she had already had two children by Corder. Also that it was the imminence of a third which caused Corder to slay her. More especially as he, being of good yeoman family, had a chance of " marrying money " in the neighbourhood.

And now I think it will be enough for showing

other real facts of the case, by proceeding to the selection from the original script, starting at the point where Corder entices Maria to the Red Barn, pretending that he will take her to London and marry her if she will come there disguised as a boy, which she does, as you will see.

MARIA MARTIN

SCENE V

Interior of the Red Barn. The interior empty. Spade and pick in R corner. Some dirty straw lying about. Door in flat L C. Red Mediums and Red Limelight from each side of the stage to give the red interior. Weird music agitate forte to open scene. Clock strikes 9 . . . at finish of music, or let music be very piano.

Enter BENGY D F.

BENGY. The natives round here shun this old Red Barn, because they've an idea it's haunted. No fear of a soul coming near after nightfall. It's just nine o'clock. I'll have a look round and see if my stores are safe. This old Red Barn is just the spot to hide my poachings and pickings. I'll stow these fowls of Martin's away. That thundering idiot came the double on me, but I followed him and saw where Martin's daughter hung these (*shows fowls*), and when she left the kitchen I nipped in and secured them again. It'll give 'em a bit of a startler to find 'em gone. What's that ? . . . (*Goes to door in flat and peeps out.*) Well, as sure as I'm a living Romany, if it ain't William Corder coming towards this barn. What's his game at this time of night ? (*Peeps out again, then creeps off* L.U.E.) *Weird music again.*

Enter CORDER *at door in flat with cloak on. He looks round barn.*

CORDER. Not arrived yet. All the better. It will give me time to think of some way out of the terrible fix I'm in. My love for Celia Malcolm is so intense, that I would go through fire and water to make her mine. Yet there is a yawning gulf that divides us . . . Maria Martin. She is the stumbling block that bars my way to marrying Celia. Shall I allow this woman to stand in my way of happiness and riches ? No. I must find a means of silencing her tongue for ever. *Alive* she's a menace to my marriage with Celia.

. . . *Dead*, I should have nothing to *fear*. Will she never come ? Perhaps her parents have persuaded her to forgo her journey. (*Goes to door in flat and listens.*) No sign of her in the distance, nor can I hear a sound of a person crossing the fields. Oh ! Has the devil foresworn me when I most need his aid ?

(BENGY *gives a fiendish laugh of* Ha ! Ha ! Ha ! *from* L.U.E.)

CORDER.   God in Heaven ! What was that ? The fiend is with me . . . she is approaching. The victim is walking to her doom.

(*He goes off* R.U.E. *Music like a shriek and a fierce howl of wind. Enter* MARIA, *in boy's suit. She is trembling with fear. Looks round barn in fear.*)

MARIA.   Why did William appoint so horrible a spot for our meeting place ? By daylight the Red Barn is a spot to be avoided, but at nine o'clock at night . . . Oh, it's too horrible to contemplate. I could not have entered had I known William was not here waiting for me. Oh, how my heart beats and my legs tremble beneath me. Oh, why is he not here ?

(*Enter* CORDER *at* R.U.E.)

CORDER.   He is here. Who calls ? (*Music crash.*)

MARIA.   I have been waiting anxiously for you.

CORDER.   You are pleased to see me ?

MARIA.   Can you ask . . . I am delighted. I feel quite safe now that you are here. Nothing can part us now.

CORDER.   Nothing but death ! (BENGY *repeats*, Nothing but death.)

MARIA (*looks about in terror*).   Did you hear that, William ? (*She clings to him.*)

CORDER.   It was but an echo of my own words.

MARIA.   Let us leave this terrible place. Where is your trap ? I shall feel happier when seated in it and on our journey to London.

CORDER.   I am not going to London ; neither are you.

MARIA.   Then for what purpose did you bring me here ?

CORDER.   I will tell you. I have something to say to you that I have no wish to reach other ears, so I judged the Red Barn the most fitting place for that purpose.

MARIA. Oh, William, your words and your actions fill my heart with fears. I will not remain another minute.

CORDER. Stop where you are. You came here at my bidding, and you cannot leave until we come to some settlement. You brought it upon yourself by your own stupid folly.

MARIA. I did it in the heat of passion and jealousy. But did I not ask your pardon and you freely forgave me?

CORDER. Do you imagine for one moment that a man of my temperament ever forgives the loss of the only woman I ever loved? I feel that I could kill you where you stand for bringing that about.

MARIA. How can you use such cruel words to me, the woman you once loved?

CORDER. That is all passed now; your conduct in denouncing me to Celia Malcolm has killed every atom of love I ever had for you.

MARIA. O God in Heaven, why ever did I come to such a place to hear cruel words from the lips of the man I love? Why did I not obey the " Gypsy's Warning." How her words stand out before me in flaming letters. " Go to your chamber, and lock yourself within it. . . . For your very soul's sake, take no journey to-night, for there is death at the end of it." I laughed at her words of ill omen. My God, why did I not take her warning?

CORDER. What is to be . . . will be. 'Tis your fate to die here to-night! (*Crash of Chords.*)

MARIA (*goes to him and pleads*). No, no, William, for your very soul's sake, spare me, and I will go from here this very night and never trouble you with my presence again.

CORDER. No! While you live you are a bar to my happiness with Celia Malcolm. Dead . . . the road will be clear for me.

MARIA. William, think of the old days. . . . Think of the ties that bind us. Let me go free, and I swear never to give one word against you as long as I live.

CORDER. It cannot be. You hold my sworn pledge to make you my wife. You also know that I caused the death of your child by poison. Once free you would denounce me. Death is the only way of silencing your tongue for ever!

MARIA. Then if I am to die you will bear the marks of my vengeance to your grave. (*She draws fancy dagger from her hair and stabs him in the face.*)

CORDER. (*Puts hand to face and, in terrific rage, he seizes her in his arms.*) That blow has sealed your doom !

(*She screams out* Help ! Help ! Help ! *Breaks from him and rushes to door in flat, he catches her, swings her body over his knee, she screams again for help and rushes up to back of Barn, seizes spade, she makes a blow striking him on shoulder, which causes him to stagger to ground. She drops spade and runs to door, he after her, and catching her throws her to the ground. She starts up and seizes him, he throws her off, and picking up the dagger she dropped . . . he catches her and forcing her on to her knees, he drives dagger into her breast twice. She falls down on the ground . . . dead ! He drops dagger and stoops over her and feels her heart.*)

CORDER. Dead . . . Dead . . . and I am Free. . . . Free ! To remove all traces of my crime, I'll fire the Barn.

(BENGY *has entered from* L.U.E. *Crosses to door in Flat.* CORDER *sees him.*)

A witness to my crime . . . then it shall be two deaths instead of one.

(*He seizes Bengy. Struggle. Throws him off. Corder picks up spade and makes a blow at Bengy, who gets spade by handle. Throwing Corder into L corner, stands with spade raised over head to strike.*)

BENGY. Mayhap you'd like to murder *me* like you did *that poor girl !*

* * * * * *

(*Quick Act drop. Hurried Music.*)

SCENE VII.

Condemned Cell. Prison cot C at back. Small grated window high up on scene over cot. Cell door on L side in return. Green Mediums and Green Limelight Mediums. Weird tremolo music to open.

William discovered lying on bed cot asleep. After pause he starts to his feet and looks about cell as if expecting to see something.

CORDER. I must have fallen asleep, and in that sleep I passed through a most terrible dream . . . It was the day of my trial. I saw the crowded court with its sea of faces with

their eyes fixed upon me.   The jury had just returned into
court to give their Verdict of Guilty . . . Guilty ! I heard
the deep voice of the Judge pronounce my sentence of
Death. . . . To be hanged by the neck until you are dead,
and may Heaven have mercy upon your soul.   Then all
was as black as night, but in the distance I saw a small light,
oh so small, but it gradually grew larger, larger, until I saw
a vision of myself standing in the Red Barn, with dagger
raised over my victim, . . . she on her knees begging for
mercy . . . but mercy is not for her. . . . In my rage at
losing Celia Malcolm through this one interference . . . I
drove the dagger into her heart, and she, with a loud,
piercing scream of agony fell at my feet. . . . Dead. . . .
Dead ! Oh, the horror of it all, when I beheld the woman
I had once loved . . . the woman I had cruelly wronged,
lying at my feet with face upturned . . . a look of horror
in her eyes.   Then in my dream I heard a voice in the distance cry out " Murderer . . . Murderer."   In my terror
I flung myself on the ground, and must have lain there for
hours. I awoke. On looking round my eyes fell on the
body of my victim. . . . It all came back to me . . . the
knowledge that I was a murderer. I started to my feet,
seizing an old spade I found in the barn, commenced to dig
the victim's grave, and when deep enough I placed the poor,
dead body of my victim in its last resting place and covered
it with earth.   But in spite of all my work with the spade
the hand of the dead woman wormed its way up through the
earth with finger pointing to me as her murderer . . . turn
which way I would I could not escape that pointing hand.
(*Music tremolo.*)

(*During this slowly lights go down to a Black Out and vision
of* MARIA *shows through back wall which is painted as transparency as cloth.* CORDER *on seeing vision of* MARIA *screams
and buries face in hands.   He gradually looks round to back of
stage when transparency lights it back, and shows the execution
of* CORDER. *Showing* CORDER *standing on the drop with
black cap over face. Hands bound to his sides, his feet tied
together at ankles. The hangman stands at his side and
Clergyman in surplice with Prayer Book in hand. The vision
of* MARIA *and the Execution of* CORDER.
Weird Music all through this Scene until end.*

    *   *   *   *   *   *

CURTAIN.

CHAPTER XVIII

Some Travesties and a French "Red Barn"

The *Maria Martins* which I have indicated were,
I blush to say, not the only stage exhibitions of
that terrible crime. There were even burlesques of
this awful case, and I blush still more to say that I
was one of the comic culprits!

In a comparatively early number of the *Referee*
I wrote what proved to be (if I may say so) a
universally popular recitation on this theme. It
was called *The Penny Showman; or, The Murder of
Maria Martin.* It is published by the playbook
firm, Samuel French Ltd. I am sure that that
firm will not object to my quoting a few verses
from this terrible travesty, which runs in rhyme and
as follows :—

THE PENNY SHOWMAN

I'm a showman by purfession, gents, so please to gather round
And see my grand theatrical performance, which is sound.
For the charge is but a penny, and the drammar in my
    show
Is about Mariar Marting, which was murdered long ago.

Come along, my little kiddies, nothing can my show surpass.
Wipe your heyes an' blow yer noses . . . do not breathe upon
    the glass !
Fix yer hoptics wery careful, and behold the startling play . . .
All about Mariar Marting, which was beautiful and gay !

Scene the Fust : A little cottage, where Mariar may be seen,
Wery deligently stitching at her Watsaname's machine ;
On the left her pore old mother's sittin' graceful on a tub,
A-peeling of pertators and attending to the grub.

* * * * * , *

On the right is William Corder . . . *he's* Mariar's nice young
   man.
He appears a-ruminatin' and rewolving of his plan.
And don't Mariar love him, cos he's so smart and spry ;
But if you look you'll see a willin's twinkle in his eye !

Scene the Second is a garding, where the sweethearts come
   to spoon,
While up above the chimbley pots, a-winking, there's the
   moon.
The willin arsts her to be his, for better and for wuss,
And he sayes, " Will you be myern ? " and Mariar whispers,
   " Yus."

Scene the Third, I think, my little dears, will fill yer 'arts
   with dread.
It represents a lonely Barn . . . and people calls it " Red,"
And nasty Mr. Corder, and Mariar too, is there. . . .
If you'll look you'll see a sort of willin's rustle in his hair !

On the right is William Corder, with Mariar havin' words,
Though only jest before they seemed as happy as two birds. . . .
And he lands her with a chopper, which is hung behind the
   dore ;
On the left you see the wretched wictim welt'rin' in her gore !

The next scene, boys, is Noogate, the interior inside,
Where Corder's caged, for slaughterin' of his intended bride.
He dreads the hexecutioner, who shortly will be seen,
Agoin' to chop his head off with the horrid GELATINE !

The hassassin, William Corder, is endeavourin' to snooze,
But, alars, that wretched murderer is sufferin' from the blues !
And 'twill make your hair stand up on end . . . your blood
   run cold, almost . . .
For in the middle of the cell's Mariar Marting's ghost !

(And so on.)

I doubt if what my dear old friend Haddon Chambers called in one of his plays, " the long arm of coincidence," has ever been illustrated more strikingly than in the following strange happening.

Almost about the same time that the real murder of the real Maria Martin took place in England, an identical murder was committed in France. As in the case of Maria Martin, the sordid lover who committed this terrible deed did it because he saw a chance of marrying a woman with money, and found his former sweetheart inconvenient and necessary to " be removed."

Also like William Corder this double-dyed villain lured his victim to meet him in order to convey her to the nearest town, where he proposed to marry her, but inveigled her into what was called the " Grange Rouge," and there did away with her. In this case, however, he disposed of her corpse in an adjacent well !

This *cause célèbre* aroused as much excitement in France as poor Maria Martin's did in England, and when the victim's body had been recovered and the bloodhounds of the Law swooped down upon the murderer, there was much rejoicing among the French population.

As in the case of William Corder and Maria Martin, melodramas based upon this awful crime soon appeared upon the local boards and elsewhere.

One special version has come into my possession since as a youngster I used to see it played. It is called *The Red Farm ; or, the Well of Sainte-Marie*, and is adapted from a French play by MM. D'Ennery and Lemoine.

The English adapter of this was none other than the famous old blood-and-thunder merchant, W. T. Moncrieff, and it was first played at Old Sadler's Wells Theatre nearly ninety years ago.

8

In this very vivid melodrama the authors have retained what happened in the real murder case as regards the discovery of the murder and the murderer. This was through a dream of the mother's exactly as happened in the case of Maria Martin. Unlike the Maria Martin play, however, this French crime drama does not end with the execution of the murderer, for the dramatizers so arranged that when the fatal well was searched, the murdered victim wasn't really quite murdered and soon afterwards recovered !

She had been thus rescued by a former, and of course guiltless lover, but in order that Justice might be done, these dramatizers took care that the would-be murderer stabbed himself to the heart and fell dead at the feet of his intended victim. Then the curtain fell with general joy and the pealing of wedding bells.

One of the most thrillful and shudderful performances of *Maria Martin* I have ever seen is the one which (even as I write) is cramming the Elephant and Castle Theatre every night, drawing playgoers from all parts of London, the suburbs, and even the provinces !

CHAPTER XIX

TICHBORNE TRIAL DRAMAS

Strange as it may seem in connection with several crimes mentioned previously in the semi-dramatic chronicles, that plays written around them do not seem to have been known to many writers and compilers concerned, it seems stranger still that such lack of knowledge should be apparent with regard to one of the most famous crimes and certainly the longest trial known in the annals of the English law courts.

I refer here to the great Tichborne Trial which began in 1872 and ended in 1874, occupying nearer three years than two, in emulating the great Mr. Pope's "Needless Alexandrine" and "dragging its slow length along."

A great number of people are still alive who, like myself, can recall all manner of incidents of this protracted trial, even though then they may have been, as I certainly was, only a youngster.

Moreover, among the countless descendants of those who lived at the time, there were to be found (as I have often found) large numbers who remember and who sometimes even continue the stormy dissensions and cataclysmic cleavages which occurred in families over that universally celebrated case.

Well indeed do some of us remember the volcanic debates and discussions which occurred in our respective places of business day by day, as to whether the claimant to the Tichborne Estate and title, namely, one described as Arthur Orton, butcher, of Wapping, was really entitled to those possessions. It will also be remembered at all events (the merest details are necessary now) that a real heir to the Tichborne barony went to Australia in his youth and was supposed to have been drowned in the wreck of a ship called the *Bella*. Also it will be recalled that there soon grew a rumour to the effect that that young heir had not been drowned, but was very much alive.

In due course one presenting himself as that still surviving heir, turned up, and by some means or other was able so to satisfy a great number of people that his claim was genuine that he was heavily backed !

This Claimant, asserted by the other side to be the butcher, Arthur Orton of Wapping, was mocked at and derided on the other hand, and all belief in him was utterly scouted by thousands of people. The trial itself was probably the most dramatic that has ever been known in any nation, and quite as dramatic as its own details were the family alarums and excursions which I have indicated above.

I was myself mixed up not only with my own relations, but with a large number of friends and acquaintances who joined in these pro- or anti-Tichborne combats. I even knew, and many can bear me out, testators alter their wills and cut out this or that intended legatee, on account of his or her fervid belief or disbelief in the Tichborne Claimant.

It matters little, of course, as to whether I, at my then youthful age, believed in Arthur Orton or not. As a matter of fact, however, if I may dare to say so, even at this distance of time, I never did believe in him, or if I did at the start, I very soon ceased to do so. This may be due to the fact that I had

SIR JOHN MARTIN-HARVEY
as the Real Murderer in *The Lyons Mail*

Facing p. 112

occasion to meet Arthur Orton a good deal, both during the trial as well as many times after, in the theatres and music halls with many of which I was at that time connected.

For, look you, this "Butcher of Wapping" (as the Claimant was subsequently proved to be, when he received a reward of fourteen years' penal servitude) was induced during the trial to give performances or, rather, to address audiences on his own behalf at such popular places as the Old Britannia, Hoxton, the Grecian Theatre, in the City Road, McDonald's Music Hall, near the Brit, and several other resorts of the so-called minor sort.

By these means the Claimant was able to increase and multiply the funds necessary for fighting in this great case. The fact that Orton, on being released after doing ten years of his fourteen " inside," again came into the theatres and music halls to " make a bit " does not, of course, matter as to whether he was the real heir or not. Certainly he always claimed himself to be to the day of his death. I think I am right also in saying, too, that when he died his coffin plate bore a Tichborne inscription !

Be all this as it may or mayn't, strangely enough while I am in the midst of writing these memories of that great trial, the newspapers are reporting the death of Arthur Orton's widow, who seems to have had quite a real belief in her husband's claim.

Also the death of the Wapping Butcher's widow has caused a report to be printed to the effect that Arthur Orton's mother had an illegitimate son by a previous Baron Tichborne, and that she was induced by the Tichborne family lawyer to accept a sum of money to keep silent on the affair and even to arrange

to marry the man who was afterwards the father
of the Tichborne Claimant.

The peculiar thing about this Orton report is that
it was not the alleged Tichborne natural son who
put in a claim to these possessions, but the legitimate
son born so much later.

Without taking up time and space by discussing
this report of a base-born Tichborne, or why it was
that the " legitimate " Orton should rise as claimant,
I will merely add that this said sensational and quite
stage-play-like report was very rife in the early
stages of this long-spun-out case.

Inasmuch as Tichborne chroniclers have not
mentioned or have forgotten that there were several
plays built round it, I may here in some measure
rectify that strange omission.

One of these plays came out at the Surrey Theatre
early in 1872, very soon after the trial started.   It
was entitled, *The Claimant; or, The Lost One Found*,
and was by H. P. Grattan, born Plunkett, an Irish
novelist and playwright of considerable ability
considering that he had to do his playwriting mostly
on hack-work lines, at any rate during all the time
I knew him at the West End and suburban theatres.
He had a wife who was a clever actress, and their
combined talents have descended in a great measure
to their grandson, Harry Grattan, the prolific revue
author and skilful producer.

This " Claimant " drama, I remember, caused
much sensation at the Surrey during the necessarily
limited run at that theatre, which was compelled to
change its programme often.

There was another Tichborne play called *The
Lost Heir*, a provincial production played in the same
year as Grattan's. This, however, did not reach
London, and as I was not much in the provinces at
that period I did not see it.

One of the most striking Tichborne dramas which I saw in one of the East End theatres was entitled, *The Wreck of the " Bella,"* the ship above mentioned. This play was very vivid and was a good deal concerned with a character which had been based upon the remarkable and mysterious Jean Luie, who was bos'n, or something of that sort, of that ill-fated vessel on which the real heir was supposed to have been drowned.

I confess that I have not been able to trace even the place or the date of the production of *The Wreck of the " Bella "* in any of the chronicles of plays produced in the British Isles. This, however, is not surprising, for even those chronicles, and especially carefully compiled stage encyclopædias, have omitted several Tichborne plays, and also a good many of the strange crime dramas of which I have given sound evidence.

The Tichborne trial cropped up in other entertainments than those in the theatre proper. While the dramas on the subject were (as the professional phrase goes) " pulling down the house," similar " pulling " was being exerted in the pantomime and burlesque places and in the music halls.

In these departments many a topical gag was cracked by low comedians, " dames," or theatrical and variety folk. These gags and wheezes took various shapes, and some consisted of back-chatters referring to each other as " a fat claimant " or mostly a " wopping butcher."

Verselets referring to the trial and to those chiefly concerned on both sides, were dropped into the lyrics in all manner of pantomimes and burlesques, and some songs were entirely devoted to this *cause célèbre.*

One of the most popular songs I remember in this matter was one called, " Would you be surprised to Hear ? " which was a catchphrase continually uttered throughout the hundreds of days of the trial by Serjeant Ballantyne, by way of starting his cross-examinations.

Naturally the poets of the period had their lines and rhymes playing on " Tichborne," Richborn, *which*born, and so on. I will confess that even I, being then a young worker in songs and skit-providing, used this famous trial a good deal in my lyrics, punful and otherwise. But do not be alarmed, gentle reader, I do not propose to give you any examples of my own Tichbornian travesties.

CHAPTER XX

My Own Tale of a Tichborne Type

One especial feature of the Tichborne trial, and one which was so strangely used by the Ortonites as a proof that Arthur Orton must have been the " rightful heir," was the fact that Lady Tichborne, the old mother of the missing Sir Roger, had on what was virtually her death-bed, declared that the Wapping Claimant was really her long-lost son !

We all know, and most of us believe, that a mother cannot very well be deceived in such a case as this. As the trial proceeded, however, it seemed pretty plain to all but the most extreme of Arthur Orton's advocates that in this case at least the maternal instinct was in error.

And now with your kind permission I will relate a true story of my own family, which has some resemblance in this respect to this historical case.

In earlier chapters I have made some mention of an actor uncle of mine, and it is that uncle to whom this true tale refers.

Some few years before the Tichborne trial, when this theatrical uncle was playing at the Standard Theatre, Shoreditch, a message was brought to the dressing-room that a gentleman wished to see him at once on a matter of life and death. The caller was ushered in forthwith and he proceeded to tell my uncle that he must come as speedily as possible to the bedside of his mother, who was ill and not expected to recover.

My relation, amazed beyond measure at this message, informed the caller, who was the stricken lady's family lawyer, that his (my uncle's) mother had died a good many years before. The lawyer would have none of this and insisted, stating that the refusal to come to the old lady might result in her death. "It is useless," he added, "for you to deny the relationship, for the family and I have traced you for many years right down to to-night, from the time when you ran away from home and went upon the stage."

My uncle still persisted in his statement, adding that for him to obey the injunction would be to act fraudulently towards the dear lady, whoever she might be.

Some little time later, the lawyer called again at my uncle's house bringing with him the lady's second son, who in the case of the death of the missing heir would of course inherit the property concerned. This property was a very large one growing out of one of the biggest advertising businesses in the City of London, and there were certain estates concerned therewith.

Now the strange thing is that when the lawyer, pointing to my uncle, said, "Mr. ——, who is that gentleman there ? " the younger son (the very image of my uncle) at once in my presence said, "That is my elder brother, and I demand that he shall come to see his mother before she dies."

Still my uncle persisted in his refusal, and a short time afterwards the dear lady, having recovered somewhat, was brought by her younger son to see my uncle, and there again, in my presence, both the son and the mother declared solemnly that he was the missing heir !

However, nothing was gained by their visit, but in spite of this they called again and again, and the lady was terribly upset that her supposed heir would not consent to come home and enjoy his inheritance.

I quote this case thus briefly because it gives once more a proof that even a mother can be deceived in recognizing what she believes to be her own off-spring.

In this strange case it was proved subsequently that on the very day when this lady's son fled from home, my uncle also left his parents to go upon the stage, and on that day those who were tracking the elder son of the above-named family suddenly happened on my uncle (on account of the extra-ordinary likeness to the missing son) and followed him year after year, while the real heir utterly escaped their vigilance.

Finally the lady and her second son called on my uncle, and after thanking him for having shown his supposed mother such great kindness in connection with his refusals, they told him that they had just received evidence proving the death of the elder son. Whereupon, of course, the second son, my uncle's "double," succeeded in due course and my uncle was left in peace to go on playing clown, harlequin and what-not, at not too swollen a salary !

CHAPTER XXI

SOME BLASPHEMY CRIME DRAMAS

Naturally the first and most important of these are the melodramas based upon the curse laid upon poor old Vanderdecken for his impious and apparently true imprecation whereby he vowed to keep his vessel, the *Flying Dutchman*, on the course round the Cape of Good Hope, even if he should have to navigate that former good ship until the Day of Judgment.

All my life from my very earliest stage recollections I have been concerned in front and back of the stage with plays about the hapless Van. One of the earliest was the version produced at the City of London Theatre, Norton Folgate, eighty years ago, and caught up by me there and at other playhouses later.

This and similar versions I have shuddered at more or less on many occasions at the Old Vic, the Surrey, the Britannia, Hoxton, etc. In later years I came across quite another drama based on this theme, the one based upon Captain Marryat's great story, *The Phantom Ship*. The hero of this, it will be remembered, is Vanderdecken's son Philip, who is haunted throughout his navigating, and also through his married career, by the Evil Spirit in the shape of the unspeakable monster, Shriften, the one-eyed pilot.

It was in this version that the late George Conquest, who had been helped in writing the play by Henry

Pettitt, gave a never-to-be-forgotten impersonation of Shriften. The hero Philip starts by vowing to his still mourning mother that he will go out on to the high seas and rescue his doomed father, even at the cost of his own life, both temporal and eternal.

Marryat's wonderful story has never been adapted much or since ; it is mostly the elder Vanderdecken's life and adventures which have formed the basis of the melodramas on that subject.

A very peculiar version of the Vanderdecken legend and based somewhat upon Wagner's marvellous opera, *The Flying Dutchman,* was produced at the Lyceum between forty and fifty years ago by Henry Irving, who played the Dutchman. This drama, which was by W. G. Wills, although full of that poetically gifted author's romantic fervour, lacked what so many of his plays did, true dramatic inspiration or sense of the theatre.

And so it happened that Irving, though a master of such uncanny character acting, was really a financial failure in the part.

A Boisterously Bloodthirsty Blend

This extraordinary play was a work concocted by the late eccentric actor-manager, John Lawson, with (please pardon my blushes) some assistance from myself. In it Lawson insisted upon showing that the unhappy Vanderdecken père was really a most virtuous-minded man, and that his terrible blasphemous event, together with any other villainies he might commit, was solely due to the evil influence of Sweeney Todd, the Demon Barber of Fleet Street !

In spite of my remonstrances, Lawson insisted upon showing as a proof of this evil influence that whenever the evil-spirited Todd entered into the body of Vanderdecken, an infernal blue light burned within that breast, which became conveniently transparent for that purpose !

Perhaps in these " Dracula " days this might seem a comparatively tame proceeding, but I can assure you that the twice-nightly audiences where we went with it deemed it both startlingly thrilling and ever-memorable.

So much for poor old Vanderdecken and the crime plays written around him.

CHAPTER XXII

A REAL CRIME DRAMA OF DOUBLE LIFE

In this case we return awhile to those famous authors, Robert Louis Stevenson and W. E. Henley, and once we find ourselves considering a lurid melodrama which deals with a criminal who caused alarums and excursions during his brief career.

This play is called *Deacon Brodie* and is named after the weird Edinburgh desperado who flourished towards the end of the eighteenth century. The word "Deacon" in this case has no ecclesiastical meaning. It is a word applied at that time to the master of a Guild or Trade Union. Brodie was a joiner and cabinet - maker of considerable skill, fashioning the most beautiful specimens of work by day, but, alas! very diligently applying himself to housebreaking and similar money-raising exploits by night.

In scrutinizing the life and adventures and subsequent trial of Deacon Brodie, one is forced to the conclusion that he had little of that chivalry to women or to the poor which has been attributed rightly or wrongly to so many celebrities engaged in crib-cracking or the High Toby.

In fact Brodie seems to have been disloyal alike both to his pals and his paramours. One of these latter figures very much in the real trial, and also in the play based upon these facts. Her name was

Jean Watt, and she had a child or two by Brodie, but in spite of his persistent ill-treatment of her, and his inconceivable amount of lying to her, poor Jean stuck to the scoundrel to the last.

The villainies of the " Deacon " and his nefarious colleagues, together with some rather artistic efforts at capture by the Bow Street runners of the period, will be found set forth in crude but correct fashion in the *Scottish Annals of Crime*, and with equal exactitude, but with greater literary finish, in Lord Birkenhead's recent volume concerning sundry criminal trials.

Strangely enough, like the late H. B. Irving, Lord Birkenhead, as in the case of Eugene Aram, etc., omitted all mention of any play written around Deacon Brodie. One would have thought that so important a work as the Brodie play of Henley and Stevenson would have had an attraction at least for these two famous criminological experts. Happily however, both as regards seeing this melodrama of R. L. S. and his renowned colleague, and also as regards the possession of the play, I may be able to give some special details thereof.

The play, *Deacon Brodie; or, the Double Life*, was produced, I remember, at a special matinée at the Prince's Theatre, now the Prince of Wales's, just over forty-two years ago !

It was presently put into an evening bill at the Comedy Theatre, but, unfortunately, although it is really Stevenson and Henley's best contribution to the dramatic stage, the play did not achieve a very long run. If anything it did rather better in America, where it was enacted by a part of the original London company.

The " Deacon " was played by a very brilliant young actor, E. J. Henley, who was a brother of Stevenson's collaborator.

Actor Henley, who gave a very brilliant performance of this double-life character, had won some notoriety earlier, not only as an actor, but as having mimicked Henry Irving so audaciously as to cause that eminent chieftain to feel insulted.

I remember the circumstance well at the old Gaiety, and there was quite a little rumpus about it, not only behind the scenes but also in the public prints.

The other principal characters in this dramatic version of the double-dyed " Deacon's " doings were played by a set of brilliant performers, including Minnie Bell, who gave a beautiful performance of Brodie's neglected unmarried wife, Jean Watt. Also the late Charles Cartwright, who afterwards became one of our most striking villains, and Edmund Grace, a remarkable new actor, who made quite a hit as a sordid thief, with the catchword, " Muck's my Motter ! "

The juvenile lover was acted by the late Brandon Thomas, who afterwards became, and is still, famous as the author of the " still running " farcical comedy, *Charley's Aunt.*

Everybody knows about R. L. S., for so much has been written about him.   Perhaps too much, to judge from recently published " Revelations " by Knowalls, mostly rubbish, or, as the gentleman crook said in the Brodie play, " muck."

I might add, however, that there is one especial book of Stevenson's and that is the Prayer Book written by himself and full of real Christian fervour. It may be additionally interesting to mention that the late really great little comedian, James Welch, was so obsessed by this book of prayer by R. L. S. that he bought hundreds of beautifully bound copies to give away, and I have one autographed by Jimmy, here at my elbow.

9

Now as to Henley not so much is known, because his work had by no means so much public appeal as Stevenson's, but Henley was really a wonderful fellow, as I know from personal contact.

He had been a street labourer or navvy in his early days, and met with a terrible accident that caused him to lie in the Edinburgh hospital for a long time, during which he studied every book he could lay his hands on, especially the works of the masters of Fiction and Poesy.

It was during this enforced physical idleness that Stevenson saw Henley and they became firm friends, and indeed Robert afterwards did a great deal to push William forward.

It must be confessed that in due course William did a great deal to help, and certainly to boost Stevenson. They became, as I have shown, collaborators, especially in dramatic work ; one of their other plays being *Admiral Guinea*, which will be treated more fully when I come to deal with the real crime dramas of pirates and smugglers.

After a time, unfortunately, Henley and Stevenson quarrelled, and it must be admitted that Henley was a very hot-headed fellow; in this respect indeed, and in appearance, he used to remind me a good deal of that other volcanic genius, Charles Reade.

W. E. Henley eventually tumbled into very warm Caledonian hot water owing to his extremely outspokenly audacious book on Robert Burns, but it is not to be denied that alike in literary and in vigorous poems, poor old Henley, who died comparatively young, possessed the real fire of genius. In the poetical line I need only remind my readers that he was the author of that wonderful poem, *Invicta*, which contains the lines :—

> I am the Master of my Fate,
> I am the Captain of my Soul.

And now, just by way of criminal tag, I may mention that it was Henley who did the wonderful thieves' slang translation of one of François Villon's remarkable ballads, written by that fifteenth-century felon-poet and cut-throat, to his co-criminals. Henley calls his version :—

VILLON'S STRAIGHT TIP TO ALL CROSS COVES

So here are a couple of verses and the envoi :—

> Suppose you screeve ? or go cheap-jack ?
> Or fake the broads ? or fig a nag ?
> Or thimble-rig ? or knap a yack ?
> Or pitch a snide ? or smash a rag ?
> Suppose you duff ? or nose and lag ?
> Or get the straight, and land your pot ?
> How do you melt the multy swag ?
> Booze and the blowens cop the lot.
>
> Suppose you try a different task,
> And on the square you flash your flag ?
> At penny-a-lining make your whack.
> Or with the mummers mug and gag.
> For nix, for nix the dibbs you bag !
> At any graft, no matter what,
> Your merry goblins soon stravag ;
> Booze and the blowens cop the lot.
>
> THE MORAL.
>
> It's up the spout and Charley Wag,
> With wipes and tickers and what not,
> Until the squeezer nips your scrag.
> Booze and the blowens cop the lot.

Isn't this " Booze and the Blowens " a splendid rendering of Ballad-Monger Villon's recurrent line :

Tout aux tavernes et aux filles.

Villain Villon has often been used in stage-plays, notably by Beerbohm Tree and George Alexander. Just now that French felon is the " hero " of *The Vagabond King*.

CHAPTER XXIII

DEVIL MACAIRE

One of the real criminals continually used in French and English melodrama is of course that dissipated scoundrel Robert Macaire, who divided his time between highway robbery, unspeakable brutality to the women who had loved and befriended him, and murder, or at all events great bodily injury to his victims, whenever they dared to withstand his assaults.

This favourite French criminal was first dramatically treated for the great melodramatic French actor, Frédéric Lemaître, who seems to have been very magnificent in the part. I say "seems," because Frédéric finished up, as regards his stage work, before my time.

Very speedily this Robert Macaire play, the original title of which was *L'Auberge des Adrets !* was adapted for the English stage by various playwrights.

The first and best English version, one which I have seen over and over again, from my boyhood upwards, was prepared by that excellent player and playwright, Charles Selby. This adaptation, which was first tried at the Old Vic in 1834, was soon brought to Covent Garden, where Robert Macaire was played by the extremely robust character actor, Henry Wallack ; and Jacques Strop, the timid comic colleague in all Macaire's villainy, was enacted by a tremendously popular low comedian and comic

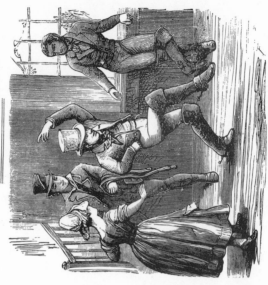

TOM CRINGLE;
OR, MAT OF THE IRON HAND.
A NAUTICAL DRAMA, IN TWO ACTS.
BY EDWARD FITZBALL.
First Performed at the Surrey Theatre, May 26, 1834.

A FAMOUS PIRATE PLAY

THE RED FARM;
OR, THE WELL OF ST. MARIE.
A DOMESTIC DRAMA, IN TWO ACTS.
BY W. T. MONCRIEFF.
First Performed at Sadler's Wells Theatre, August 29th, 1842.

THE FRENCH "MARIA MARTIN" MELODRAMA

Facing p. 129

singer, H. Vale, who was brought over from the Surrey for that purpose.

This version, according to my prompt book, was sometimes called *The Two Murderers*, but as a rule the dramas on this subject have mostly been called *Robert Macaire*, or *Macaire*. One notable exception was the version which I remember being done by the fine actor, Fechter (and a great Macaire he was) ; this was called *The Roadside Inn*.

I have seen Macaire played by all the stars of my time, for in addition to Fechter I saw Henry Irving in a Lyceum version—in which he was not at his best—and of course Beerbohm Tree, who happened to be far worse than Irving. In between I saw more Macaires in London, the suburbs and the provinces than I could very well count.

It should be noted that the character of Jacques Strop, the comic criminal, a very droll character part, has been seized upon with avidity by all the chief comedians ever since the play first come out. For example, in addition to Vale, J. L. Toole made a great hit in the part with Fechter ; Weedon Grossmith failed in it with Irving.

Irving relied upon a re-written version of the old Macaire for his revival at the Lyceum, but in his earlier days he used the one I have started with, and indeed played it much better than he did at the Lyceum. Tree picked a very special version. This was written by no less distinguished persons than Robert Louis Stevenson and W. E. Henley.

Now this version, although of course written in far better or more literary fashion than the previous Macaire plays, proved to be singularly deficient in dramatic force, chiefly because, as in two or three other dramas in which this otherwise great pair collaborated, they went in for highbrow divisions of scenes, as in the old classical method, and omitted the lurid colours of Macaire himself and, strange to say, did not heighten the humours of Strop.

Naturally it was not long before miscreant Macaire and the scoundrel Strop were seen upon the burlesque boards. I have myself seen several of these travesties; in fact I was guilty of committing one myself. It was called *Devil-May-Care*; but no more of mine.

The best burlesque of Robert Macaire of the many I have encountered was the one by that arch-wag, Henry J. Byron. It was entitled *Robert Macaire; or, the Outside of the Inn-side.* Macaire was played by that fascinating actress of her time, Fanny Josephs, and I remember that a very remarkable new comedian came into London to play the character of Marie, Robert's neglected mistress, in this play. His name was E. V. Sinclair.

Jacques Strop was really the leading character, as indeed he has been in many a version; his exponent in Byron's burlesque was that always great character actor, John Clarke, and I can recall even now that woebegone manner in which he addressed his co-criminal in the following couplet :—

Of courage, cully, I have not an ounce,
But you're like an india-rubber ball . . . all bounce !

There were several other burlesques of *Robert Macaire*, one by Lloyd Clarence, called *Robert Macaire Renovated.* There were also at least a couple of comic operas, one composed by George Fox, a well-known musician, who did it about thirty years ago. Moreover the characters of Macaire and Strop have been utilized under other names in many another drama, burlesque, and comic opera.

One of these was entitled *Robert and Bertram; or, The Volatile Vagrants,* and I remember seeing it played at the Artillery Theatre, Woolwich, which then was under strictly military rule. Even now it

is under War Office control over the Lesseeship of
that popular manager and manageress, Mr. and Mrs.
R. D. Littler, but in those earlier days, we who
visited that theatre, or were engaged behind the
scenes, had to pass in and out under military convoy
or guard, and indeed were compelled to give counter-
signs to certain sentries. At that time also the
programmes were handed around by military uni-
formed attendants to the stalls, pit, gallery, etc.,
and the orchestra was composed of players from the
local barracks bands.

Perhaps the most successful " conveying " of
Robert Macaire and Jacques Strop was shown in
the comic opera *Erminie.* In this lively work,
produced exactly forty years ago, the Macaire part,
renamed Ravannes, was played by the recently
deceased comedian and dancer, Frank Wyatt, the
husband of Miss Violet Melnotte. The "Strop"
part was acted by Harry Paulton.

It would be unfair and unjust to finish these
Macaire-full mems., without reference to one of the
most remarkable and most successful versions that
I have ever seen, and I saw this one over and over
again with increasing interest and delight.

This adaptation was a dumb show drama, and
after being called *Robert Macaire* for a while, it was
renamed *Jacques Strop,* for in this version, as in
several others, that character was the leading part.

This dumb show drama was sometimes called a
ballet, and it was toured in theatres and music halls,
especially the latter by that late great pantomimist
and wordless actor, Paul Martinetti. The other
characters were played by sundry members of the
Martinetti troupe, a far-flung family, the chief
members of which were Anglo-Italians, who had been
trained mostly in America and had come here when
they were very young.

Paul Martinetti himself played Jacques Strop, and he played it with such artistically finished dumb show as absolutely to fascinate the onlooker. Night after night have I called at dramatic and variety theatres, on purpose to catch this especial " turn." Paul's impersonation of Strop finished in a manner which had been used in only one of two versions ; that is to say that the hitherto uncourageous co-criminal of Macaire's met his death at the rifles of the gendarmes in trying to save Macaire.

Strangely enough this inclusion of the great performance of Paul Martinetti leads us again to the verge of crime, for it was the widow of that late dear friend of mine who was instrumental in bringing to justice that unspeakable murderer, Dr. Crippen, of whom maybe more anon.

CHAPTER XXIV

Some Fair Female Felons

Among the criminals around whose crimes plays have been written is that fascinating Suffolk heroine and horse-stealer, Margaret Catchpole.

Margaret's real exploits were first spread about, in a literary sense, in a novel written by the Reverend J. Cobbold, and named after her. This clerical gentleman was a fellow-native of Margaret's and he gathered together a mass of interesting matter concerning her.

This Suffolk damsel's chief crime was that in order to reach her lover, who had been arrested on a false accusation, she stole a local steed and, dressing herself up in male garb, rode away at break-neck speed, to find her sweetheart and to save him from his prison doom.

Alas ! Margaret was anon arrested on the charge of horse-stealing, which like so many other minor crimes in those days was punishable by death. The dramatic interest of the story, and of course of the plays based thereon, was much increased by the fact that there was a bold bad smuggler, William Luff by name, who, pining to " possess " Margaret, made things very hot for that heroine for a time.

In the plays, of course, all ends happily—and on the spot—and I will now give you some indication of those dramas.

One of the several *Margaret Catchpole* plays which I used to see in my youth was by J. T. Haines, a very popular melodramatist of the period. Another and perhaps better one was the work of Edward Stirling. His *Margaret Catchpole* play was certainly an effective version and it held the stage, especially of the suburban theatres, for many years. Stirling's *Margaret Catchpole* was first produced at the Surrey Theatre, but years afterwards I saw that one and several others at all sorts of outlying playhouses.

I think I am right in saying that the only *Margaret Catchpole* drama to be produced in the West End was that presented by my widely lamented friend, Laurence Irving. He engaged Walter Frith, usually a very capable playwright, to re-write and polish up one of the old Catchpole plays. " Lorrie " (as most people called him) embarked on this venture in order that his accomplished wife, Mabel Hackney, should play Margaret, the Suffolk horse-stealer. He chose the character of the smuggler Luff.

Laurence Irving, knowing that I had had a great deal to do with such blood-and-thunder plays in general, and with *Margaret Catchpole* in particular (both on my own account and with my stage relations), sent for me to assist him in this production.

Our meetings with regard to this melodramatic masterpiece were of the most interesting and joyous kind. I did not get my own way entirely in per- suading Mr. and Mrs. " Lorrie " to revert to the proper blood - and - thunder " atmosphere " with regard to *Margaret Catchpole*, but I was able to prevent Friend Frith from polishing away too much of that " atmosphere."

The Irvings' production of this more " culchawed " *Margaret* at the Duke of York's Theatre did not succeed over-much, at least not financially. I know that Laurence had a notion, however, of reviving this hitherto exciting drama afterwards, more on the lines suggested by me, and based upon lavish experience.

But alas ! as is known only too well, poor Laurence Irving and his dear wife, whom we all loved dearly, perished in the wreck of the *Empress of Ireland* when they were at the very height of their fame.

Their passing was of the most heroic nature, and rounded off two lives always so full of earnest and enthusiastic endeavour.

As there still seems to be some vagueness as to the actual fate of the real Margaret Catchpole, I may as well make things clear.

More than once of late, and even a few days before writing these statements, I was bombarded with queries regarding Margaret. (1) As to whether she was executed ; (2) As to whether she escaped and died young ; and (3) Whether she did or did not escape to Australia and die forthwith ?

As a matter of fact, this intrepid Suffolk heroine was twice sentenced to death. Once was in 1797, for the hereinbefore-mentioned horse-stealing, and next in 1800, for breaking (Jack Sheppard-like) through her local county jail, and getting away again on horseback, and on the high road to London.

This extraordinary esquestrienne *did* reach Australia, but she was officially transported there, after she had been recaptured. After serving her term of imprisonment " Down Under," Margaret married and settled down in comparative comfort. From information in my possession it would seem that she lived there until nearly seventy years of age, when she passed to " Where beyond these voices there is Peace."

And now for a very strange female felon !

The case in which this lady was concerned is not so much intensely dramatic as insanely erratic. I allude to the celebrated case of the Beauty Specialist who for business purposes called herself " Madame Rachael," but who was really an Israelite named Leverson. She " flourished " fifty years or so ago, and I remember as a youngster that for some time she drew a vast amount of custom from armies of society and other ladies from whom she extracted large and continual fees on the pretence of making them (to use her own advertised words) " Beautiful for Ever."

Even in these days of lipsticks and other " adventitious aids," such as cannot be expected to be described by a mere man, it would scarcely be credited as to what a far-flung extent " Madame Rachael " doctored (and diddled) her fair clients !

Eventually one poor dupe who had been swindled for hundreds (or it may have been thousands) of pounds, brought an action. Then all the legal fat was in the face-plastering fire !

I remember that the trial of this Beautifier for Ever took a long while. Also that the evidence was so full of comic disclosures of the " secrets of the toilet " that the newspapers of the period did a roaring trade. Likewise that the comic journals attained a prosperity of which they had never before even dreamed !

Of course it was not long before this decorator of damsels' visages was seized upon by play-makers and ballad-builders.

A " Madame Rachael " character was introduced into several plays, and of course into all the pantomimes of the period. A full-grown play devoted entirely to Madame Rachael (or rather the script thereof) has eluded my vigilant search up to now, but I well remember a couple of short comedies, or farces, which I saw played, each under the name of *Beautiful for Ever*.

One was by Frederick Hay, a then young rising

and very clever playwright and parodist. The other was by a man named G. D. Hodgson, whom I never heard of before or since. His was a very clever little play though, and I first saw it produced at the Surrey Theatre with a popular low comedian, named Mat Robson, as Madame Rachael herself!

The burlesques, then very numerous, of course teemed with warbles and wheezes concerning this facial impostor, who was severely punished for her fraudulent freaks.

There was, however, one really big song of the times; for a good while it was warbled and whistled all over the town, to say nothing of the country. It was sung by that really remarkable and versatile comic singer (formerly a " regular" theatre comedian) named Arthur Lloyd. Arthur, whom I knew and had a good deal to do with at the halls at that time, was especially noteworthy for his always having very tuneful airs to his songs, especially for the choruses thereof. Arthur, who was one of those actors who would never part with his heavy moustache, made up in this song as Madame Rachael herself in appearance, but was really supposed to be one of Madame's victims. For this female impersonation he contrived to "soap" his moustache over *almost* sufficiently to hide it from view!

Anyhow, he gave a very clever performance of this " drag " part (as the old pro.s used to call such female characters). Having in each verse described the consecutive sufferings of Madame Rachael's victims, he burst forth after each stanza with the following chorus, which was set, I remember, to a very catchy tune. That refrain ran as follows :—

"So all you young damsels take warning from me !
Shall I forget Madame Rachel ? Oh, never !
For, oh, she took from me a very large fee,
To make me a Beauty for Ever."

CHAPTER XXV

PIRATES AND PIRATICAL PLAYS

Doubtless it is true that " All the world loves a lover." It is to be hoped that it *is* so, especially of course when the lover is a proper lover, and not a mere Don Juan-ish skunk. Whether the above adage be correct or not, undoubtedly it is true that all the world (especially the masculine part of it) loves a Pirate ! And I am not so sure that the Dear Ladies also are not enamoured of a bad bold buccaneer when they meet him—I mean, of course, in books or on the boards, and especially do they delight in a pirate "on the pictures."

This being thus, I will now proceed to give some short survey of Real Pirates and of some of the more or less (generally more) strange sanguinary dramas and melodramas written around them.

In proof of the above remarks, I may mention that it is not so long ago that several eminent scientists, painters, poets, and even parsons, to say nothing of sundry lady novelists, were interviewed as to which was their respective favourite pirate or most beloved buccaneer. Even that famous religious savant, Sir Oliver Lodge, hardened spiritualist though he is, confessed that he revels in histories of pirates and such-like. He added, with a kind of pathetic joy, that his favourite desperado of this kind was the bold Captain Morgan. The Honourable John Collier, R.A., also testified to his own admiration, and even affection, for such buccaneers, adding, however, that he had no special "Pet Pirate." The great musician, Josef Holbrooke (whom I well remember graduating from the music halls to his present high position), seems to suggest that Raleigh and Drake were among his popular pirates, but that he preferred Paul Jones. Even the gentle singing actress, Gwen Ffrangçon-Davies, confessed her love for "bloodthirsty, treacherous ruffians, whose rapacity nothing can palliate." Shame upon her otherwise gentle heart!

Merely stopping to state that Sir Barry Jackson and Miss Tennyson Jesse, Lord Dunsany, Max Pemberton, Compton Mackenzie, and his sweet sister, Fay Compton, seemed to select among them Captain Kidd, Morgan, Pew, Captain Avery, and the always popular scoundrel, Paul Jones. I may mention that these pro-piratical interviews appeared in my old friend T. P. O'Connor's *T. P.'s and Cassell's Weekly.*

Strangely enough even the most ardent pirate-lovers whom I have met, or of whom I have read, seem to be ignorant of the fact that the finest, most thrilling, and most realistic stories of real pirates are to be found in the pages of Daniel Defoe. His *Lives of Notorious Robbers,* and sundry other books, especially, of course, *Bob Singleton the Pirate,* teem with dramatic narratives concerning these mostly bloodstained mariners, who "Go on the Account," as D. D. always says, when he means to show that one has gone in for professional piracy.

And who will ever forget Daniel's wonderful character of the Quaker, who didn't want to be a pirate, but who, somehow or other, generally gave the tip when a "Prize" came into view on the high seas!

Undoubtedly this William the Quaker was the basis of our dear old friend the nonconformist pirate

Smee, in *Peter Pan*, a part played for so many years
in succession by Johnny Toole's low comedy comrade,
George Shelton.

But leaving Defoe to take care of himself (as he
always very well could) I will proceed to the Real
Pirates themselves.

With all deference to the above-expressed opinions
of eminent pirate-lovers, or, if you prefer it, eminent
lovers of pirates, I venture to assert that one of the
most popular and unscrupulous of the many men
who "went on the account" was our old friend,
William Kidd.

It is not many months ago that Lord Birkenhead
gave a very detailed and of course deeply interesting
and technically correct account of the trial of this
bold buccaneer. As I have said, however, with
reference to his lordship's account of the respective
trials of "Eugene Aram" and "Deacon Brodie,"
Lord Birkenhead makes no mention of even one of
the several dramas written around Kidd and his
companions.

It is not generally known that Kidd was a Caledonian, a native of Greenock. He was born about
the middle of the seventeenth century. Showing
very early great talents, not only in the navigating
line, but also in that labyrinthine art, diplomacy,
William had a series of Government appointments,
both of a commercial and of a Revenue cutter type.
He also became associated with sundry American
merchant shipping and similar enterprises, and
altogether he promised to prosper exceedingly in a
financial way, even by following strictly honest
courses.

Kidd, however, "acquired a habit" (as Micawber
would say) of dropping into crime of the piratical
type. In order to advance himself in this profession,
William anon took ship to Madagascar, where in

those days buccaneers abounded. Indeed it was the rendezvous for pirates of all nations !

Kidd, however, speedily showed that he could hold his own among all these skull and cross-bone merchants, British or foreign. He soon took many a prize upon the high seas, but, as in the case of so many other similar artists in crime, he took one too many—one which, in point of fact, to use a common melodramatic expression, "handed him over to Justice and sealed his Doom."

There is no need for me to go into all the details either of Kidd's life and adventures, or the long and protracted trial which, after all sorts of evasions and "innocent pleas" on his part, finished up his buccaneer career. All these things are fully set forth in the Newgate Calendar or other annals of crime. It is my duty to supply the omission by Lord Birkenhead and other Kidd chroniclers, by describing in some measure the plays written around that pirate.

As regards William's real self, it is enough to add that he was charged with nine other co-pirates of his crew, and that with three of these he was hanged at the very beginning of the reign of the late Queen Anne, 1701, at Execution Dock down the Thames, not far from Wapping Old Stairs. There he was gibbeted for a long time, plain for all up-river-coming mariners to see !

As in the case of other brutal pirates, I was wont to see several melodramas concerning Kidd : rough-hewn plays, but very effective in their way, at the London and suburban blood-and-thunder theatres. Some of these plays, being of a hackwork type, written often for a couple of pounds or so, by some needy "resident" playwright, have disappeared from public ken. There were several such I remember in the remarkable collection of holograph drama scripts nailed up in the pre-typewriting days and acquired by that late quaint enthusiastic expert comedian, Arthur Williams.

I had several of these strange scripts myself, for, as I may (or may not) have said earlier, part of my work in the theatres in my youth was to copy out these strange sanguifulminous dramas.

A printed copy of a Captain Kidd play, which I still possess, is a fine specimen of the blood-and-thunder drama. But as in the case of so many criminal " heroes," the whitewashers themselves have done their work only too well, or ill. For, of course, in these dramas Captain Kidd baffles his persecutors, or as one may say, in the case of this Greenock native, he gets off Scot-free !

Several of the Captain Kidd plays come from America, perhaps because the more or less gallant Captain had a good deal to do with that then very youthful, and not now particularly old, nation. It does seem strange, however, that several of these American " Kidd " plays also conceal the fact of his punishment and his gibbeting.

What is stranger still, perhaps, is that Kidd has been used on several occasions, both on the American and on our own stage, as the fascinating hero of Comic Opera ! One of these, called *Captain Kidd; or, The Buccaneers*, written by Clare Kummer, of the U.S.A., a cousin of the famous actor-dramatist, William Gillette, was of the wildest comic opera form.

Our own native-made " Kidd " comic operas included a very clever specimen which was written by G. H. Abbott, and had a brilliant score by the late Edward Solomon, one of the most gifted and also one of the most eccentric composers of modern days.

It was this composer who bade fair at one time to rival even the great Sir Arthur Sullivan himself.

But alas ! a carelessly-led life, sandwiched with many matrimonial troubles of his own making, ended his life at a very early age.   Even during that short career little Teddy (whom I knew and collaborated with as librettist from our joint youthhood onward) produced some remarkable comic opera and extravaganza scores, including one which I have mentioned in the Crime Plays and ditto comic operas written around Claude Duval.

Before finishing with Kidd, I might add that a brief but very dramatic play was built up around that buccaneer by a very clever sketch-actor of the theatres and halls, one W. J. Mackay.   I remember this little Kidd concoction very vividly, for though it was crude, it was certainly very convincing.

CHAPTER XXVI

MORGAN THE MARVEL

As was shown in the opinions expressed previously, that bold buccaneer, Captain Morgan, seems to hold the record for affection-inspiring among pirate-lovers.

And certainly much may be said in favour of this view, for Morgan undoubtedly was one of those hearty, breezy, " wind-on-the-heath-brother " kind of sea criminals. At this present moment there are several songs of recent composition setting forth certain deeds of chivalry, helping of lovers and so forth, practised by that pirate.

Moreover, in Morgan there is more than a dash of that virtue claimed for so many of our thieves and blackguards of the so-called romantic days ; that is to say, that very often Morgan seemed to " rob the rich to give to the poor." At all events he and his worshippers said he did.

His adventures, on all the ocean, always make first-class reading, and these adventures have often been utilized and furnished up by our novelists, romancers, and of course playwrights.

Henry Morgan was born in 1645 of poor but honest Glamorgan parents, look you. Like many a Defoe hero of the sort, little boy Morgan was kidnapped at Bristol and shipped to the Barbadoes. There, of course, he fell into bad company, especially of the buccaneering type.

HENRY IRVING
as Vanderdecken in *The Flying Dutchman*

Facing p. 144

HENRY IRVING
as sundry criminals and crooks—Macbeth,
Mathias, Digby Grant, Jingle, etc.

Anyhow he soon joined these murderous mariners, and starting in the guise of a privateer, he went out capturing sundry ships, Spanish vessels for choice. At this behaviour the King of Spain was very much annoyed and set a price on Morgan's head! The bold pirate, however, went on undismayed and became quite a wholesale and ferocious swash-buckler.

Many a crime did Morgan commit upon the high seas, but like most of the plays of an earlier date, he had quite a " happy ending." Further details of Morgan's strange career, which finished at the age of fifty-three (just about the time that William, Prince of Orange, landed here), will be found set forth in more or less detail in my mems. of the plays, etc., written around him.

It may be added, however, that Morgan's exploits in the way of ship-capturing, and even sometimes of squelching other pirates, were similar to the American tactics to-day, within the Twelve Mile Limit, when one party goes out to " squelch the bootleggers," and to get away with what is now called in the American language, " The booze, sonny."

I haste to say that hitherto the plays written around Morgan do not as a rule use his name, but only certain episodes connected with his sea-dog caréer.

This evasion of Morgan's name is probably due to the fact that he ended his stormy career by becoming Governor of Jamaica, which post he seems to have received, together with other Government grants, for valuable services rendered in the cause of patriotism as distinct from piracy.

I am afraid that good old Sir Henry (as he became) was not always so chivalrous as he appears in song and story. There is rather a black mark against him for his behaviour in firing upon certain nuns,

or certainly not preventing such firing, during one
of his many buccaneering bouts ! Still, he wound up
in the odour of sanctity, so to speak, and so we will
pursue that pirate no farther.

Luckily I can conclude these Morganatic mems.
by stating on the best authority, namely, that of
the author, that there is in existence a drama which
this time bears Morgan's own surname.   It is called
at present, *Morgan's Luck*, and a very good drama
it is, as well I know, because I have read most of it.

There was a time when *Morgan's Luck* seemed
likely to see the footlights at one of our leading West
End houses, but a change of management intervened
and this really strong play is still unproduced.

That it is likely to pan out as a work of considerable merit, is shown by the fact that its author is
that clever poet-essayist and dramatic critic, W. R.
Titterton.

CHAPTER XXVII

THE REAL PAUL JONES

Here we have another pet pirate, or privateer, as I believe he preferred to be called. It is usually supposed that Paul was an American by birth, whereas he was born in Kirkcudbrightshire in 1747. His father was a poor but honest gardener named John Paul, and he wanted the lad to till the soil. The boy, however, preferred to plough the seas.

So he ran away from home and made several voyages to America, and some years later, somehow or other, he inherited or took possession of an estate in Virginia.

Whether this was so or no, the boy John Paul started serving five years on the Slave Ships, and anon changed his name to Paul Jones.

It is perhaps no wonder that America has always not only whitewashed but worshipped Pirate Paul (for such he became), for when that certainly then badly served young nation rebelled against the English rule, this bold buccaneer turned renegade and gave his sea-fighting services to the Americans !

Indeed when, about 1775, America resolved to fit out a naval force and fight against us, this Caledonian " Privateer " offered that nation his services ! Even after our regrettable scrap with America was ended, Paul Jones revisited the British shores on several occasions, to blow up places and people. Indeed his raids off the Solway proved very disastrous to that

district.   And I may add even to some of Paul's own
Scottish friends and relations, for whom he did
not seem to care one solitary tinsmith's execration !

Anon the ex-Scotch-American " citizen " nearly
blew up Leith, and also captured and carried off
two British men-of-war.

For performing these exploits against what had
once been his native land, Pirate Paul Jones was
rewarded by the French King, Louis the Sixteenth,
and was made a Chevalier of the Order of Military
Merit !

Later the Russian nation also honoured the Rover
Renegade and he entered the Russian Service as
Rear-Admiral of the Black Sea Fleet !

So you see that this Anglophobe Caledonian had
nothing of that spirit which animated that splendid
tar, Ralph Rackstraw, of H.M.S. *Pinafore*, who
in spite of all temptations remained an Englishman !
No, of Paul it must be said that he—

> Succumbed to *all* temptations
> To fight for other Nations ;
> And though not quite a Proosian
> He did become a Roosian,
> Also *A* meri-*Can*.

The French have had several Paul Jones plays,
for P. J. went backwards and forwards to the French
waters a great deal.   It was one of these Gallic
stage works, *Surcouf* by name, which made Paul
Jones a gallant and gay hero, and very attractive
to Les Belles of La Belle France.

This *Surcouf* drama turned up in London thirty-
eight years ago, two years after its production in
Paris.   It was adapted as a comic opera called
Paul Jones, with English libretto by H. B. Farnie,
and with music by Planquette, a composer whom I
had the pleasure of knowing.   His score, if not so

memorably melodious as that of his *Cloches de Corneville*, was really very " catchy " and clever.

Farnie's book was, as usual with him, a little stodgy, but still it served its purpose dramatically, and the comic opera was a great success at the Prince of Wales's Theatre, London.

It must be confessed that a great deal of its success was due to the performance of a very beautiful and statuesque American contralto, Agnes Huntingdon to wit, in the name part. This was a very fine impersonation, both from the singing and acting point of view. It served to keep Miss Huntingdon in London for some two or three years, during which time she played another comic opera or two, including one called *Blue-eyed Susan*, in which she played William, who married Susan.

In this Paul Jones version a great success was also achieved by the recently deceased, much lamented Miss Phyllis Broughton, and by that other deeply regretted artistic actress, Miss Wadman.

The chief comedy parts in the very long cast were successfully interpreted by those great favourites, Harry Monkhouse, Frank Wyatt, and Henry Ashley, all since passed away.

It will perhaps be interesting to note that this naturally very much whitewashed Paul Jones, in operatic form, did away with not only all Paul's rascalities, but also with all his relations. It added instead a very charming sweetheart of his, to whom Paul was able to bestow a vast fortune, which she had amassed as captain of the U.S. corvette, called the *Bon Homme Richard*.

Something of the Indian or Redskin element of the drama I have described, was infused into the comic opera, for Paul and Co. contrived to disguise themselves as savage chieftains, and with the aid of the American crew, to clear off all enemies.

Paul and his sweetheart arranged, of course, to live happily ever after !

This is perhaps not surprising in such a terrible turncoat.

Paul died at Paris, 1792, at the age of fifty-two. In one of the many ballads which I have concerning him, this so-called " Terror of the English Coast," it states that the Americans, considering Paul Jones the virtual founder of the United States Navy, sent to Paris to bring back his body to America, where it was received with " enthusiasm."

Paul is described as having been " the first sea captain who compelled the British Flag to Strike to the Stars and Stripes Flag." Fancy that ! (as Ibsen says).

One of the many ballads concerning this buccaneer contains the following sea-doggerel verse :—

> The " Zeperous " wove round, our ship fought a rake ;
> When he (Paul) made the proud hearts of the English to ache.
> The shot flew so 'ot, boys, it could not stand it long,
> When the brave British colours from the English came down.
>
> And now, my brave boys, we have taken a rich prize,
> A large forty-four and twenty likewise !
> So God help those poor mothers that have reason to weep,
> For the love of their sons now some fathoms deep.
>
> A brave 'Merican frigate, " Richard " by name,
> Mounted guns, forty-four, and from New York she came
> For to cruise in the channel of old England's fame,
> With a noble commander, Paul Jones was his name.

This is perhaps enough in the song way for Friend-Foe Paul ! Readers of Fenimore Cooper's novels will doubtless agree with me that that American novelist's *The Red Rover* certainly embodies much of Pirate Paul's doughty deeds for his adopted country.

As to the plays written around P. J., undoubtedly in addition to the dramatization of *The Red Rover* (which I saw and gloated over often in my youth) certain of Paul's exploits turned up in sundry other dramas, including that very startling specimen, *The Wizard of the Wave*, in which the dual rôle of a courageous captain hero, and a black-hearted buccaneer who runs an Unknown Schooner, called *Il Malachor*, or the Evil One, was played by that great actor of grim sea and land monsters, " Bravo " Hicks.

CHAPTER XXVIII

THE PRINCIPAL PAUL JONES PLAY

Perhaps the most remarkable of the several dramas concerning Paul Jones which I have seen or read during my extensive blood - and - thunder drama career, is a melodramatic romance in three acts, written by Thomas Dibdin, who was one of the playwriting sons of the great Charles Dibdin, the nautical songster, composer, and playwright.

I caught up this play chiefly in the East End and Surreyside theatres, but its original production was at Sadler's Wells, which was Charles Dibdin's very own theatre, a hundred and thirty years ago !

Happily I still have a copy of this play, and somewhere about I have several others, but doubtless this one will suffice for our present purpose.

This Paul Jones drama opens on Solway Firth, at Mermaid Bay in fact, and several smugglers (with more or less appropriate songs) are expecting the descent of Paul Jones upon that coast, for they (dear good souls !) are in his pay.

Presently Paul's relations, at whom I have hinted before, gather around and describe him in anything but a friendly fashion, for all of them have suffered something or other at his hands—and ships ! One of these relations has a habit of going about as a local ghost ! Her intents are charitable, however, for she uses these uncanny séances to warn all and sundry of Pirate Paul's approach from time to time !

Paul does not make his entrance until rather late in the first act, but when he does, he makes things " hum," despite the denunciations of his wretched mother and sister, and notwithstanding what sporting reporters would call " the adjacent proximity " of that local female apparition !

Paul's duties in this drama are a good deal bound up with what is technically called " business " rather than dialogue ; but when Paul gets alone, or nearly alone, from time to time, he becomes rather loquacious.   Here is a sample.

This is a speech of Paul's which fills the entire scene.   It is what we call technically " a carpenter's scene," that is to say, it is used to "mask" the setting of the next and far bigger "set."

THE RUINS OF PAUL'S COTTAGE

Music. Enter PAUL JONES.

PAUL.   So I plunder others, and when I'd try to make one more
effort at reconciliation with my mother, I find my own home
but a burning waste, as if I were the demon of desolation ?
Prosperity and joy vanish at my approach, and I myself
am sinking from myself.   This 'tis to be a traitor !   In
France they smiled upon me, flattered me and fooled me ;
the gallant veterans of Russian Catherine disdained to serve
with me ; and these Americans . . . I much distrust them !
Well . . . well, action must brace, and stern revenge sus-
tain me !   Rejected here by all, England shall feel me yet.
'Tis but a few hours' sail, and the first port we make . . .
ships . . . harbour . . . town . . . all . . . (*Cannon heard.*)
Hark !   A signal gun !   A signal flag too !   (*Looking out,
whistles.*)   No answer.   Yes . . . a boat approaches.   Now,
England, beware of Paul !   *You* offer five hundred guineas
for his head ; keep it to repair the mischief he intends
ye !

This affords some slight indication of the mental outlook of this sea-going scoundrel !

Anyhow, in due course Paul, having shot down several people, including some conscience-stricken piratical tars who mutiny against him, departs for his beloved America. Also, of course, as is usual in this kind of play, All Concerned find means to go in the same direction.

Again it is some time before Paul enters upon the scene, but when he does, there is a cry of " Here come Paul and the Yankees," and Paul at once, before opening his mouth, shoots down a hostile Indian chief named Pechankanough. Perhaps even an honest Injun with a name like that deserves to be shot, but whether or no, Paul starts off again to fight against the British.

Here I think I must quote a British national outburst which subsequently is given off in the British camp.

BRITISH OFFICER. Our flag's triumphant . . . we have won the day . . . a day truly triumphant, should peace be the consequence, for John and Jonathan are brothers ; and may the time come when the only contest we know shall be who best can serve the other, for neither Yankee nor John Bull have any object in war beyond our general rights and liberties !

Now isn't this utterance, which was given off on the stage exactly a hundred years ago, the same as you have often heard in many a drama and sketch ever since ?

And long may it be so !

Now I am going to finish my extracts from this Paul Jones play simply by describing the finale which, as you will see, is given entirely in dumb show. (I quote from my prompt book.)

(*Music.*) . . . The vessel of Paul Jones is seen coming round a point, and a fearful action immediately commences. The people fire from the top, and are fired on in return, and are seen to fall. The orchestra plays " Stand to your guns, my hearts of oak," which is chorused by the people in action. PAUL JONES is seen everywhere in the fight, and is preparing to board, when CORBIE leaps from his vessel to Paul's. A desperate combat ensues, the Pirate CORBIE is slain, his ship at that moment blows up Paul's, a flag is triumphantly waved, he and his Men give three cheers on the deck, the sails are hoisted, and as the vessel prepares to move, the curtain falls.

CHAPTER XXIX

SOME REAL WRECKER AND SMUGGLER CRIME DRAMAS

Doubtless one of the most fearsome of wreckers ever engaged in that "dreadful trade" was one Coppinger, who ever since he "flourished" was known as "Cruel Coppinger."

Cruel Coppinger had acquired a habit, after the manner of his cruel kind, of showing false lights to lure unwary storm-tossed crews to his dangerous shores, and there to cause their doom and to possess himself of their treasures, cargoes, etc.

So artful and manifold were the crimes of Coppinger that for years after his blood-stained life had finished, he was supposed by superstitious fellow-natives to haunt the coast whereon his crimes had been committed. Indeed many a poor worried mother was wont to hush her fractious children into peace, or better behaviour, by warning them that "Cruel Coppinger would come and fetch them away to his terrible tomb."

As in the case of several, or most, of the other crime dramas I have mentioned in these articles, I happened on plays written around Coppinger in some form or other from my boyhood onward.

Sometimes his real name was given ; in other plays he was called something else, but always he retained his unspeakably terrible attributes. And very impressive and indeed terrifying were the episodes set forth in these stormy and shipwreck scenes of such plays.

Among the dramas of this Coppinger kind which I have seen or studied, I may mention the following.

First of all there is the famous Adelphi drama, *The Wreck Ashore*. This was written by the favourite old comedian and theatrical manager, J. Baldwin Buckstone, who as a matter of fact wrote two hundred plays, comic and serious. I am proud to say that I have most of them in my possession !

My chief copy of the *Wreck Ashore* is a valued prompt copy with many illuminative notes, melo-dramatic music cues, etc. Its Coppinger character is one Captain Grampus, and a terrible fellow he is right through, until he is overtaken by an abstract personage very much quoted in the blood-and-thunder plays, namely, Retribution !

This play was founded upon a novel based upon such real criminals as Coppinger. Another version of this especial set of episodes is a still more startling but cruder one. This drama is called *The Rover's Bride; or, The Bittern's Swamp*. It was vamped up by a less polished playwright, namely, George Almar, who was not only a blood-and-thunder playwright, but a ditto player.

He is best known perhaps by those extreme gorio-dramas, *The Tower of Nesle; or, the Chamber of Death*, a terrible play with a sinking bed, on which you dropped your somnolent victim bang into the river below ! Also by a still more terrible melo-drama called *Pedlar's Acre; or, the Wife of Seven Husbands*.

I will merely add in connection with the Pedlar's Acre play that that Acre, on which a pious pedlar found, through a vision from angels, a vast treasure, which he afterwards dedicated to the poor and to the

Church, is now occupied by the County Council Hall on the south side of Westminster Bridge.

Also if you want any further verification of that treasure-finding pedlar's real existence and how he came into the play named after him, you will find such additional proof on one of the stained glass windows in old Lambeth Church, which adjoins the Archbishop's Palace hard by Lambeth Bridge.

But to continue our Coppinger. The other plays obviously written around him, and sometimes taking in other well-known real Wreckers and such, include the following.

The Wrecker, a very strong drama written by two first-class melodramatic actors, namely, Fred Marchant and Cecil Pitt, and produced at the Britannia, Hoxton, in my presence forty odd years ago. Also *The Wreckers*, an early eighteenth-century play (the script of which, alas! I have not yet recovered). *The Wrecker's Daughter*, a somewhat poet-ized drama, by the Irish actor-dramatist Sheridan Knowles, and produced at Old Drury nearly a hundred years ago, and happily here at my hand in " prompt " form.

I should also mention that the late Rev. Baring-Gould, who was a great authority on Wreckers and Smugglers, besides being the author of the famous hymn, " Onward, Christian Soldiers," wrote several novels concerning such criminal gentry as Coppinger and Company. One of the most striking of his Reverence's wrecker-smuggler romances is undoubtedly the one called *Mehalah*.

Now it is obvious that the leading desperado in this story has been based upon that great artist in crime, Coppinger himself. This *Mehalah* romance of Baring-Gould's was dramatized in due course and I saw it in several stage guises. Each of these plays was named *Mehalah*. One was dramatized by another clergyman, namely, the Rev. J. Whitley, and I caught this around the provinces a little over a quarter of a century ago.

An earlier production prepared by W. H. G. Palmer and W. Poel (who is now known everywhere as an Elizabethan drama expert) was seen and criticized by me forty years ago, at the Old Gaiety.

Another *Mehalah* Coppinger-like melodrama I saw at the Grand Theatre, Croydon, twenty years ago. It was certainly the best of the three dramatizations I have mentioned. Its dramatizers were respectively Actors A. E. Anson and Matheson Lang. The latter gave a very fine performance of the Coppinger character !

And now comes the latest play that I can call to mind that was named after this unspeakable skunk.

It was called *Cruel Coppinger* and was written, produced and played in by that remarkable protean actor and entertainer R. A. Roberts, who, as I have mentioned in an earlier series of these Dark Deeds, played for a long time all the parts (except Bonnie Black Bess) in his own dramatization of *Dick Turpin*. As in that *tour de force*, my friend Roberts played all the characters from Coppinger upwards—or downwards ! And a very striking specimen of amazing versatility it was.

Short as this Coppinger drama was, it was full of melodramatic " meat " and indeed showed that diabolical wrecker in his true colours.

The last time I met with Coppinger the Cruel, he was utilized by that brilliant lady dramatist, Clemence Dane, for her powerful tragedy entitled, *Granite*, which was produced not long ago by Sybil Thorndike. In this drama, full of the atmosphere of wrecking and smuggling, and laid on Lundy Island, one of the characters, a sort of local *ingénue*, songfully murmurs, half in horror, a snatch of the old ballad which starts thus :—

> Will ye hear of Cruel Coppinger?
> He came from a foreign land . . .
> He was brought to us by the salt water.
> He was carried away by the wind!

And then the poor little girl goes on to tell how Cruel Coppinger came up naked out of the sea, startled a girl who had been praying for her lover, sitting on her horse, jumped up behind her, rode away and married her! The Devil was in him, and he robbed and burned and killed!

And then this fine play goes on to state that when at last they came to take Coppinger and punish him, he went out to the Gull Rock, waved a sword at the sea, and a ship came up out of it and took him away—no one knew where. That came of praying to the Devil!

And so you see, so cruel was Coppinger that in the local legends he is identified with his Satanic Majesty himself! When you read about him, and see plays about him, as much as I have seen, you will not be surprised at the demoniac associations.

That famous Cornish parson-poet, Hawker, seems to have known intimately the fiends who " possessed" Cruel Coppinger!

Another " Wrecker " drawn from real life is the famous character known as Matt Ironhand in the nautical drama, *Tom Cringle*, by the enormously popular blood-and-thunder merchant, Edward Fitzball, and also produced first at the Surrey. This play, which contains several other smugglers and wreckers, had for its two chief players the great T. P. Cooke and the equally great O. Smith.

Cooke, of course, was the original William in *Black-eyed Susan*.

Paul Clifford.

ONE OF THE EARLIEST OLD "VIC"
HIGHWAYMAN DRAMAS

Facing p. 160

THE RED ROVER;

OR, THE MUTINY OF THE DOLPHIN.

A NAUTICAL DRAMA, IN TWO ACTS.

BY EDWARD FITZBALL.

A PHENOMENALLY SUCCESSFUL ADELPHI
"SKULL AND CROSS BONES" PLAY

I don't think that I have mentioned before that Smith, who played this notorious wrecker, Matt of the Ironhand, was labelled " O " because of his having made his first great hit in the drama entitled *Obi* ; *or*, *Three-fingered Jack*, which is also really one of the most shudderful sanguifulminous melodramas, as I can well testify from experience.

Further details of the story concerning the Wrecker, Ironhand Matt, and his equally base collaborators in crime, can be found in the wonderful old romance from which the play is taken, namely, *Tom Cringle's Log*.

Perhaps one of the most fearsome of all stage pirates " taken from life " is the terrible Mark Ambrose, the bloodthirsty buccaneer of that once famous nightmarish dramatic concoction called *Alone in the Pirate's Lair*.

I had the good fortune to begin my intimate knowledge of this marrow-freezing melodrama when it was first produced at the Old Brit. in Hoxton, for which huge playhouse it was written or nailed up by my esteemed old one-time employer, Colin Hazelwood, who was that theatre's resident dramatist at three pounds a week ! Certain of his plays at that early period it was my duty to transcribe for public performance !

At the Brit., Pirate Ambrose was mostly played by a towering-figured actor named Cecil Pitt, who had also another claim on fame, in that he was the younger brother of the actor-author, Dibdin Pitt, who was a relation of the sea songster, Dibdin. Above all, D. P. was the author of the first play written around " Sweeney Todd, the Barber Fiend of Fleet Street."

On my veering to the Vic., somewhat later, it was again my good fortune to be associated with *Alone in the Pirate's Lair*. There Pirate Ambrose, with his awful pistols and still more awful oaths, was played for us by that great " villain of the Vic." whom I have named in connection with *Guy Fawkes* at that theatre, namely, the grim and gory John Bradshaw.

The story of *Alone in the Pirate's Lair*, which was dramatized immediately after its appearance in the then *Penny Blood*, as it was called, namely, *The Boys of England*, does not call for special description, as to its various ship-stealing, mariner-murdering and powder magazine explosions.

I should like, however, to quote one little gem from the dialogue, an outburst which never failed to bring down the house.   It ran thus :—

MARK AMBROSE (*in deep sonorous tones, to* JACK RUSHTON, *a very young sailor hero whom he had persecuted, and at whom he is now presenting a brace of pistols*).   Backa . . . boy ! Drrread thy dooom ! for English Jack . . . is a name I . . . er hate !

JACK (*in high-pitched voice, snapping his fingers at both pistols*). And fear, too ! . . . my bold black-hearted señor !   (*Crash of music. . . . Ditto applause . . . and what Thunders of Applause !*)

CHAPTER XXX

A good many other pirate plays, dramas of wreckers, etc., which I have perused or have played in, the main characters, although bearing different names, have all been based upon real desperadoes, whose dark deeds may be found in the Newgate Calendar and other Chronicles of Crime.

Among these borrowed-from-life bloodthirsty bandits one might mention that terrible pirate, Black Brandon, the bushy-browed, wolf-jawed miscreant, in the famous melodrama, *My Poll and My Partner Joe*, based by the long popular melodramatist J. T. Haines, upon Charles Dibdin's ballad of the same name.

Black Brandon has a habit, or hobby, when anyone annoys him ever so slightly, of drawing forth a huge pistol from a pair thereof in his belt, and presenting that weapon at the head of the annoyer, male or female, and shouting, " I never-r-r-r for-r-r-give an injur-r-r-ry."

Of course, at the end Black Brandon is, as the low comedians say, " Bowled over," or, as he himself would say, " K—rushed ! "

I do not propose to enter further into the plot of this semi-pirate—semi-Thames waterman drama. It is enough to add that in my boyhood's time I used to shudder at it a good deal, especially when Brandon the Black was played by one or other of the great " heavy villains " of my time.

It may be interesting to add that *My Poll and*

My Partner Joe, on its first run at the Surrey
Theatre, drew £80,000 !

Undoubtedly one of the most awful, because
perhaps to me more personal, buccaneer dramas I
ever met, was one which appeared in two or three
different forms in certain outlying theatres, with
which I had to do, in some form or another, as a
youngster.

These melodramas were based upon a series of
most revolting murders and other crimes, committed
by a band of pirates who, having mutinied upon the
ship upon which they were engaged, namely, the
Flowery Land, at once made arrangements, as per
the before-mentioned Defoe, to "go upon the
account."

Their manifold crimes were at last brought home
to them, and I remember, as a youngster, reading
with horror of their crimes and with a kind of
fearsome delight of their subsequent collective arrest.

After an intensely dramatic trial these *Flowery
Land* pirates, or rather five of their ringleaders,
were sentenced to death ! So appallingly interested
was I in their career and their ultimate doom, that
I walked all alone by myself (as the Irishman says)
to gaze upon their gallows, then being erected outside Newgate, the night before their execution.

I had intended, like the rest of the vast throng
collected and queue-ing up, to see the execution
itself ! But suddenly my youthful pluck dwindled
to such an extent that I walked back home, went to
bed and dreamt of that execution instead !

Thus, you see, for me the *Pirates of the "Flowery
Land"* had a special personal interest apart from
what I must really call a terrible drama written
around their fearful exploits.

I will conclude my present series of Volcanic
Pirate, Wrecker and Smuggler plays by giving you

some account of a very strange and absorbing drama taken from real crimes (in America chiefly) and entitled, *The Pirates of the Savannah*.

The old prompt book of this play in my possession is a copy which was much used originally in the East End theatres. It started at the Royal Effingham, a Whitechapel Road playhouse, which afterwards became a pugilistic rendezvous called Wonderland, and is now a picture theatre called the Rivoli.

The full title of the play then presented, and since revived all over the British Isles, was, *The Pirates of the Savannah; or, The Tiger Hunter of the Prairie*.

Ah me! how I have palpitated and perspired (after I had been made to shudder and to shiver) over this very " busy " blood-and-thunder crime drama.

The villains of the play are numerous, and all based upon real criminals of about sixty years ago. For this play's purpose they are named and described as follows :—

DON SALVATORI (The Pirate Chief of the Savannah . . . a man of desperate means).

GONZALES (His Lieutenant . . . ever ready to second the cause of his commander).

PEDRO, OCTARO, TONIO, VAREZ (Pirates of the Savannah).

These blackest-hearted bandits, among their other crimes, persecute all sorts and conditions of honest folk, especially " virtuous females." In those days playwrights and fiction-mongers always used the word " female " instead of woman or lady. These unspeakable scoundrels also contrived to carry off the heroine, Leonora Petralba (" shipwrecked on the coast of Mexico ") and also her little daughter Julia (the heiress to the Petralba estates).

But these desperadoes have reckoned without

thinking of the intervention of at least three straight
and noble characters.   One is—

NICK LIVELY (a man of the world . . . studied as a medical
practitioner . . . with a heart to feel and a hand to assist).

Another is—

PETER PICKLE (a faithful low comedian of the firm of Pickle,
Grubb, and Pickle, London).

And especially have the villains taken no account of
the probable advent in their midst of a couple of very
courageous tiger hunters of the Savannah, namely :—

PACHOSKY (true to his trust, vigilant and watchful) and
FABRICIO (the Tiger Slayer who makes sure of his aim . . . a
staunch and noble friend).

This marvellous hero pursues the persecutors and
their gang in and through sundry remarkable places.
These include a Ruined Temple of the Sun ; a
Plateau of the Savannah and a Foaming Torrent ;
the Pass by the Torrent, and the Savannah on Fire !
This episode ends with a terrific leap by the hero
into the Foaming Abyss.

But all is not yet well !   The chief villain has
still in his possession the juvenile Rightful Heiress,
whom next he seeks to slay with poisoned wine.
Being foiled in this, he finds means to place that
heiress under a Terrible Tree, from which he knows
there will presently be what is described in the play,
the " Terrific Descent of an enormous Boa-Con-
strictor " !

Down, down looms the awful reptile !   He fixes
his baleful eyes and darts out his fearful fangs and
prepares to envelop in his fatal coils the unsuspecting
heiress !

But lo !   that also unsuspecting Satanic serpent
has reckoned without our hero Fabricio.   Swift as
lightning that dauntless Tiger Slayer fires one dead
shot in the nick of time, and into the python's brain !

This marvellous rescue drives the chief villain and company into such a frenzy of disappointed rage that he and two of his vile confederates throw themselves upon the hero. Then ensues what is described in this marrow-freezing melodrama as " An Exciting Death-Duel of Four " !

A "duel" of four will seem to many a strange thing, but the world of melodrama, especially of the blood-and-thunder type, is nearly as full of strange happenings as Real Life !

Anyhow, so ends *The Pirates of the Savannah*, which, I feel sure, if revived with a proper cast at the present day, would coin doubloons and pieces of eight for its revivers.

" The merest schoolboy knows " (as Lord Macaulay was so fond of saying) the story of the Inchcape Bell ! Apart from sundry narratives concerning this, the said schoolboy, not to mention whole regiments of school-girls, have had this tale driven into them by reason of the poem by Robert Southey. This piece of work, being far better than most of Bard Bob's poetic efforts, was for many years, and still is in some places, a famous recitation at " Penny Readings," school treats, and such-like festivities.

These stories and this poem deal with the real fact that a certain wrecker caused the displacement or destruction of a warning bell, fastened to a buoy, near the dangerous coast, a signal whereby many thousands of lives were saved yearly from shipwreck !

The dastard who did away with this beneficent Bell did so, of course, in order that all sorts of unfortunate storm-tossed vessels and their brave crews might be wrecked and drowned, in order that he might profit by such wholesale maritime slaughter.

In the sequel it is shown that the destroyer of the Bell anon was himself wrecked, and sent to Davy Jones's locker, for want of its very necessary warning! "And serve him right" is, of course, the verdict of all who have read or will yet read that fascinating narrative.

A Deep Doom Drama

As might well be imagined, this crime was soon seized upon for stage treatment, and I have seen some few of such melodramas, which follow the story more or less closely, varying it in accordance with this or that playhouse, or popular player.

The best specimen of these plays, however, is one which is called *The Inchcape Bell*, and it was founded by the famous melodramatist, Fitzball, on the best-known story-variant of the subject, namely, *The Bell Rock*. In Fitzball's really excellent specimen of blood-and-thunderism, the Wrecker (or Rover, as he is called) is one Hans Hattock, and a terrible fellow he is, I assure you!

There is also, as in so many of these dramas of the period, a dumb boy, a juvenile mariner, who is cruelly ill-treated by Hattock and his co-smugglers and wreckers. After the villains have "removed" the noble Bell, which was placed there by the good monks of the neighbouring abbey, the Wrecker (or Rover), regarding the dumb boy as a kind of Jonah and spy, draws a knife from his belt with intent to slay the little lad.

But of course the faithful hero, who is at hand, rescues him. The faithful one also shoots the horrible Hattock, who sinks down in agony among his own loose rigging!

At that moment a thunderbolt strikes that pirate vessel, which goes down—down—down—into the boiling ocean, with the Wrecker and his confederates aboard her! All the virtuous *dramatis personæ*, however, escape into a convenient boat, and the curtain falls amid general joy!

CHAPTER XXXI

SOME REAL CRIME DRAMAS OF "DOWN UNDER"

With the exception of mentioning the fact that the English "Gentleman Pickpocket," George Barrington, was transported to Botany Bay, I have not at present given my readers any description of great crimes or great crime dramas of the Australian kind.

Doubtless the biggest set of crimes, certainly the biggest ever committed "Down Under" by one felonious firm, were those with which the Kelly Gang of Bushrangers made havoc of parts of that magnificent country.

Forty odd years ago the world rang,and the world's newspapers teemed, with the daring exploits of the Kellys in the way of bank-robbing, gold-stealing, and murdering. These Kellys were Irish born, and their chief, Ned by name, was one of the finest-looking men, and one of the most fearless horsemen, that ever dashed across that land of dauntless equestrians.

Day by day, and especially night by night, these Kelly criminals robbed, gagged, bound, and slew victim after victim and got away with the booty or what their criminal prototype, Paul Clifford, would call "the bustle." (N.B.—It was Paul, indeed, who invented, or anyhow passed on, the famous thieves' slang axiom that "he who misses the chance to accumulate bustle is no better than a buzgloak.") Buzgloak, I may mention, is what Shakespeare calls "a blinking idiot."

Overhaul your *Merchant of Venice*—and when found, make a note of it !

For some years these bloodthirsty Kelly bush-rangers spread terror and dismay " Down Under." I should add that what our modern newspapers are so fond of calling " a romance " (when it is nothing of the kind) was connected with the Kelly gang by reason of the fact that these Kellys had a big bouncing, beautiful sister who herself became very proficient as a bushranger-ess. Her sweetness of appearance and studied grace of behaviour did not prevent her from joining in the most awful plots of her bandit brethren !

Well do I remember following these bushrangers' exploits with bated breath, while perusing accounts of them, alike in the Antipodean and London journals of the day.

So recently, however, in story books and things of that sort, have these desperadoes been depicted, that perhaps I have said enough to indicate their general form of "industry," and their sanguinary style of warfare.   Therefore I will now proceed to give some account of sundry dramas based upon the real Kellys and their real crimes.

I am sure the Gentle Reader will be glad to learn that the Kelly Gang was eventually run to earth, thanks to the continuous, courageous pursuit thereof by various Boundary Riders and other officers of justice.   Some of these Boundary Riders I knew in England, both before and after their exploits, but of these more anon !

The Kellys were arrested and tried and some of them were executed.   Ned, the chieftain, was hanged in chains on a gibbet, which soon, either by accident or design, was burnt down and the gibbeted corpse was reduced to ashes.

I fancy that the sister contrived to escape.

Anyhow, I have heard it said by certain experts who were connected with the chase of these criminals, that it was not Captain Ned himself who was gibbeted, but a similar rotter put up in his stead!

Whether this be so or no, I must leave to future history to discover, for it is now time that I proceeded to give you some account of the dramas based upon the Kelly gang's crime plays presented all over Australia, and throughout the British Isles.

One of the most important dramas based upon the terrible deeds of the Kelly gang was entitled, *Robbery under Arms.* Indeed several plays of this named cropped up in due course, and they were all based upon that strong novel of the same name, which was written by a noted Australian Judge, whose pen name was Rolf Boldrewood.

I did not see any of these Kelly plays in Australia, but I soon saw in old England the principal plays and several of the imitations or variants thereof.

It was at a time when the Judge's novel was arousing tremendous interest in the Antipodes and the British Isles that these dramas of the same and similar titles began to permeate the playhouses. The best known, and indeed the best written, *Robbery under Arms* drama, was the work of an actor-author named Alfred Dampier, and a journalist named G. Walch. After doing big business in Australia, this drama was brought to England by the said Dampier (who was an old actor-friend of mine) and was produced at the Princess's in October, 1894.

Several of the other versions, mostly using the same title, bobbed up in our provinces, but another and even better version than Alfred Dampier's turned up about eight years later than the Princess's specimen, and was played, strange to say, at the famous comedy house, the Vaudeville in the Strand.

This version was in four acts instead of five, and it was the work of Bernard Espinasse and H. Leader. I remember being very much struck with this drama, and with the candour of its title, for it was called *Ned Kelly ; or, The Bushranger.*

Whether some influence had been brought to bear by the Censorship, or by somebody else interested, I don't quite know, but this *Ned Kelly* play afterwards had that name taken out of it, and went into the suburban theatres under the title of *The Bushrangers.* Lyn Harding was one of our best impersonators of Bushranger Kelly.

KELLY PLAY BY A BOUNDARY RIDER

Concerning this drama it may well be said, in Shakespearean lingo, that " hereby hangs a tale."

This play, which had originally had a name which suggested the Kelly business, was brought to England from Australia by its author, Charles Haddon Chambers to wit. Although he was young when he arrived on these shores with the script, Charles (who became a firm friend of mine, and remained so until the day of his death) had been one of the Boundary Riders who, as indicated before, had helped to run down and to capture the Kelly gang.

Many a time and oft did C. H. C. relate certain of these and like exploits to me, holding me spellbound by his powers of crescendo construction in narration as he could also show in playwriting.

Incidentally it might be interesting to some, especially to those readers of a religious turn of mind, to know that Chambers's two Christian names were bestowed upon him by his parents in honour of that marvellous preacher, Charles Haddon Spurgeon, whose sermons (as many of us know) spread very early all over the world, and especially among our colonies. But this by the way.

The tale that I am about to tell concerning Chambers's Bushranger play, which was eventually called *Captain Swift*, deals with the great difficulty he had in getting a hearing for it in London.

At length he was introduced to Beerbohm Tree, afterwards Sir Herbert. Chambers soon found, as many of us found, that good old Tree, then very young, had a very evasive habit. It was always difficult for any of us to catch him, even when he had made special appointments. Chambers, however, who had been promised by Tree that he would hear him read *Captain Swift*, continually waited on Sir Herbert, begging him to keep his promise.

Tree, however, with his well-known airy persiflage, contrived from time to time to put off his pursuer. As a matter of fact Tree told me himself that from what he had heard of Chambers's play, he was rather afraid of it, and did not seem to " see himself in it," as actors say.

Naturally a man who had from his boyhood burst through the Australian bush, living on horseback, and chasing Kelly desperadoes, and indeed fighting bravely against the very elements themselves, was not to be daunted, not to say browbeaten, by a mere actor-manager, however " stellar " his rank might be.

So presently Chambers contrived, by a subtle subterfuge, to chase Tree into a Turkish bath, and there, while Tree was naked and helpless, to force him to hear and listen to the script of *Captain Swift* !

This play was duly produced in 1888 by Tree at the Haymarket, where it achieved a very great success, bringing Tree in a lot of money and founding the dramatic fortune of Boundary Rider Chambers.

Tree himself played the bushranger indicated by the title, who under another name got himself introduced into society and eventually so gave himself away that it led to his tragic end.   Many of the Kelly features of this sometimes swallow-tailed bushranger had been softened in order to make the play more a drawing-room drama than a blood-and-thunder melodrama.

But there unmistakably was the Kelly original. There is no need for me to describe the actual story of this long-popular play.   I may add, however, for historical reference in the future, that it was in connection with this debonair bushranger that Chambers invented a phrase which has passed into the language, namely, "The Long Arm of Coincidence."

A KELLY DRAMA BY A FAMOUS DRAMATIC CRITIC

I suppose it will be conceded by most people that there never was a dramatic critic who so belaboured and belittled melodrama as my late friend, William Archer.

That sometimes subtle, but always sincere, highbrow critic seemed to lose no opportunity in his criticisms of sneering, or of implying a sneer, at this flamboyant kind of stage work.

It was a surprise, therefore, to all who knew him or had " read " him, to find him, at what unhappily proved to be the close of his busy life, coming out as an unabashed melodramatist, in that polished but nevertheless blood-and-thundery drama, *The Green Goddess*.

This play brought a long-delayed fortune to its author, and a still larger one to the distinguished actor, George Arliss, who produced it originally in America some few years before he brought it over to our St. James's Theatre.

Surprising, however, as William Archer's sudden playwriting adventure with *The Green Goddess* may

seem to some, here is another fact, which I venture
to think will be still more surprising to a large
number of my esteemed readers.

It is not generally known that about forty-five
years ago Archer came to a theatre with which I
had had a good deal to do from my earliest childhood
days. That theatre was the famous Grecian in
Shepherdess Walk, City Road. It was formerly
known as the Eagle Saloon, and was connected with
that strange but always widely popular snatch of
song, which runs as follows :—

> Up and down the City Road,
>   In and out the Eagle.
> That's the way the money goes.
>   Pop goes the weazel.

This stanza certainly sounds rollicking, if it isn't
rhyme !

To the Grecian then came the afterwards critic
" W. A.," and prevailed upon the management to
produce a Ned Kelly-ish melodrama in five acts,
written by himself and A. G. Stanley, and entitled,
Australia ; or, the Bushrangers.

I ought to add that Archer's full name did not
figure on the Grecian playbills. Indeed I used to
find in after years that he rather resented any
mention of this play, either from myself or the few
others who happened to know it. Archer's attitude
in this respect has always seemed strange to me,
for really *Australia* was not a melodrama at all
unworthy of that famous home of examples of
the sanguifulminous stage !

A startling real crime " Bushranger " melodrama
called "Van Diemen's Land" (I have a scarce
prompt copy) was produced at the Surrey a hundred
years ago. It dealt with Michael Howe, whose
execution was regarded as stopping all Bushranger
crimes ! And yet—

CHAPTER XXXII

THE FRENCH JACK SHEPPARD AND DITTO JONATHAN WILD

Every nation, of course, has its crimes and criminals. Therefore it is not surprising that La Belle France soon gave birth to her own Jack Sheppard kind of desperado. The only surprising thing about the matter is perhaps that this criminal, Louis Dominique Cartouche by name, made his appearance on the stage of life about the same time as the English Jack did.

Strange to add it was about the same period, within a year or so anyway, that Jack Sheppard was hanged at Tyburn and Louis Cartouche was broken on the wheel in Paris.

Good old Daniel Defoe, always a reliable as well as realistic chronicler, especially of rogues and robbers, describes this execution with gruesome detail, thus ending up what is absolutely the best life and adventures of this French criminal.

Some of the chief editions of Defoe have special engravings and plates depicting this horrible execution of Cartouche, who after having become at an early age the head of a Paris slum band of robbers, met this awful fate at the age of twenty-eight!

The English Jack Sheppard was only twenty-one when he was taken to Tyburn, and indeed, in looking back through the careers of criminals of this sort, it seems that they end up for the most part in very early manhood. My previous remarks concerning

TURPIN'S RIDE TO YORK;

OR, BONNY BLACK BESS.

AN EQUESTRIAN DRAMA, IN TWO ACTS.

BY H. M. MILNER.

First performed at Astley's Amphitheatre, on Whit Monday, 1836.

The Most Popular Dick Turpin Drama

THE DUMB MAN OF MANCHESTER.

A MELO-DRAMA. IN TWO ACTS.

TRANSLATED FROM THE ORIGINAL MS. OF "UNE CAUSE CELEBRE,"

BY B. F. RAYNER.

The Drama with the Fiercest Fight
(Acted at Astley's and the Adelphi)

Claude Duval, Paul Clifford, Dick Turpin, and Co.,
are proofs of this early doom to cut-throats, bandits,
pirates, etc.

That there is nothing new under the sun, even in
crime, is shown by the fact that young Cartouche
was so agile an acrobat and gymnast, such a climber
over housetops, and up drain pipes, and so forth,
that he was really one of the first of the now rather
common cat burglars.

And here kindly permit me to make a digression
concerning this kind of feline felon.

In all the accounts of the many cat burglaries I
have read of late years, I have found no mention
whatever of an extraordinary play which I used
to see in my younger days, at the Old Vic., and
similar blood-and-thunder theatres. It was a housebreaking melodrama entitled, *The Man Cat.*

Stranger still there is no mention of this play (by
this name) in any of the chronicles of play productions. And lucky as I generally am in possessing,
or in tracing, such scripts, I have never been able
up to now to find one of *The Man Cat.*

From what I remember of the play, which I used
to see acted by such enormously popular transpontine
and East End favourites as Louis Nanton, Edward
Fitzdavis, and that remarkably clever actor-author
Fred Marchant, I feel inclined to state that *The
Man Cat* was a kind of modernized, Londonized
version of the " Cartouche " dramas and made to
fit an epidemic of such cat burglaries as broke out
over this metropolis about that period.

Leaving this remarkable Cat-Burglar drama to
take care of itself (anyhow until I can find out more
about it), I will now proceed to give some account
of some of the many strange mixtures constructed
around Cartouche.

In these discourses I have given many instances

showing how swift or topical the playwrights of each period were in providing dramas on real crimes for the melodramatic market.

It was so in the case of the French Jack Sheppard. Hardly had the mangled remains of crib-cracker Cartouche been huddled away from the gallows for shameful burial, when lo ! writers of plays about him began to arise both in France and in England.

One of the earliest of such plays on the British boards was produced at the quaint old Lincoln's Inn Theatre, within a year of that criminal's execution ! It was a translation of a French play, called *Cartouche.* In the English version it was named *Cartouche; or, the French Robbers.*

I have said that some of these Cartouche plays were very strange ; here is a case in point. This first version was described as a three-act farce, and it really pans out as a kind of Criterion go-as-you-please piece of extravagance, with Cartouche darting in and out, to help the lovers and of course, whenever he sees a lucrative chance, also to " help himself."

It is by no means so good a play as several of the dramas concerning this felon. Certainly Cartouche himself for the most part is a very pantomimic character. Once or twice, the bold robber does a few sensational stunts, such as fighting his pursuers with pistol and sword, creeping up the chimney here and there in his shirt, compelling innocent citizens to change clothes with him, and finally going so far as even to defy an army of one hundred archers ! (" Without "—of course !)

There is, however, a great " let-down " in interest in this early play, for it ends with the bald statement that the courageous Cartouche has been arrested in an adjacent auberge !

Perhaps the strangest thing in connection with this anglicized French farce is the fact that bound up with my ancient printed copy is the following semitragic account of some part of his career.

It is an advertisement of a book concerning this cat-like criminal, and it runs thus :—

> The Life of Cartouche, the famous French robber, who was broke alive upon the wheel at Paris the 24th of November last, giving an account of his education in the College of Jesuits, and the pranks he played there ; of the several robberies he committed alone, and of his turning thief taker ; how after several and various escapes, he put himself at the head of a gang, which defied the publick justice of France above 7 years ; with a particular relation how he was apprehended, and the manner of his execution ; also an account of his bold and undaunted behaviour under confinement and upon the scaffold ; the whole being a series of adventures and incidents, remarkable, entertaining and full of variety . . . translated from the original just arrived from France.

Characteristically French though this biography of Cartouche may be, it is obvious to me, as a continual devourer of Defoe, that it was based very largely, if not entirely, upon Daniel's splendid monograph concerning that criminal in the book entitled, *The Lives of Six Notorious Robbers*.

Leaving that, however, for criminologists to settle to their own satisfaction, I will now proceed to tell you of some other dramas, written or nailed up, around this French Jack Sheppard.

One of the earliest Cartouche concoctions with which I became personally acquainted (in front and behind the scenes) was entitled, *Cartouche, the French Robber*, and was produced some little time before I was born. I caught it up, however, when I was a young lad at the City of London Theatre, Norton Folgate. At that long-defunct resort the criminal hero was played by the adapter of the piece, a very powerful and fine actor named William Travers, whom I grew to know in those early days and to become very fond of. Travers was an old friend of my pantomime-actor uncle whom I have mentioned before, and the said uncle on many occasions played in *Cartouche* a very peculiar loathsome villain, called Red Judas. It is this very foul felon who gets to know all Cartouche's secrets, both of the love kind as well as the larcenous, and eventually betrays that " hero " to Justice !

I saw Travers's drama played at several other theatres such as the Old Brit., the Marylebone, the Pavilion, the Effingham, etc., when it was generally called *Cartouche, the French Jack Sheppard.*

Other plays of the sort followed from year to year, and one of the most recent was the drama produced in the Provinces first, about forty years ago. It was adapted from a fifty-year-old melodrama by D'Ennery and Dugué. Other variants of this version have cropped up from time to time, but I think that this production by W. R. Waldron, a very well-known provincial actor-manager of his time, was one of the latest.

And now I have a confession to make of my very own concerning Cartouche.

Shudderingly I will reveal to you the awful fact that I wrote a burlesque (and so far as I know the only travesty of the kind) around this French Jack Sheppard.

I perpetrated this parody for my (and everybody's) beloved friend, Vesta Tilley, who is now Lady de Frece.

I did it because that brilliant variety artist had only appeared on the regular stage as principal boy in pantomimes, and it was her wish to tour around the country in some stronger form of character written for herself.

The fair Vesta and her husband, Walter de Frece (now Sir Walter, Colonel, and M.P.), commissioned me to do this dark deed. The music was by that late very melodious composer, George le Brun, and it was produced at the Theatre Royal, Birmingham (also one of my boyhood's playgoing haunts), in 1892.

The vivacious Vesta made a great hit as the French Jack Sheppard, and the late very popular comedian, Edward Lewis, did ditto in the chief low comedy part.

Whatever else I may think myself about this burglarious burlesque, I am rather proud of its title. It was *Cartouche and Co.; or, The Ticket of (French) Leave Man.*

I may add that in this topsy-turvy travesty of mine I followed, of course, in satirical fashion the great sensational " stunt " of all the Cartouche dramas for the last two hundred years. That is to say, my chief scene showed Cat Burglar Cartouche climbing up walls, over roofs, and so on and so forth. For indeed no Cartouche play which I have ever seen, if minus this acrobatic episode, would, as certain slum-dwellers say, be " worth twopennurth of the coldest gin."

CHAPTER XXXIII

THE FRENCH JONATHAN WILD

This rascally rotter was Eugène François Vidocq, and I have often wished that the good old Daniel Defoe had lived to put Vidocq into a volume, in his own matchless realistic way, but alas! Daniel died nearly a quarter of a century before E. F. V. was born.

Vidocq was a baker's son and was born at Arras in 1775. Very early he showed what Turf reporters would call "a liking for the course," meaning in this case the Course of Crime. Little boy Vidocq began his nefariousness by stealing money from time to time out of his father's till!

So increasingly frequent did this unfilial practice become that naughty lad Vidocq was sent to prison. On finishing his term in what the romantic fictionists delight to call "durance vile," young Vidocq joined a circus troupe as an acrobat, when also he soon got into trouble for fraudulence. Being nothing if not a patriot, this juvenile criminal joined the Army. But alas! he was speedily dismissed therefrom for illegal behaviour of various kinds, "filching," or "pinching," being among them.

Looking about him for fresh felonious scope, Vidocq took to forgery and he became an expert thereat. Being caught at this, however, our busy friend was sentenced to eight years' servitude at the galleys, but he anon resumed his "Jim-the-Penman"-ship.

By perseverance the young forcat contrived to escape. Then he went in for crime in rather a wholesale line, by joining a band of most notorious highwaymen. And here at last we come to the versatile Vidocq's plunging into Jonathan Wild-ness.

Vidocq started this form of crime by betraying the whole band to the local gendarmes. Receiving official praise—and pay—for this " peaching," he set up business as a Government spy on the criminal classes. In connection with this spy-ness, Vidocq started what he called a " Brigade de Sûreté," and with himself as Chief, it soon proved a really marvellous organization, and did a roaring trade !

But alas ! it had always been the fate of felons and such-like fearful wildfowl to overdo things, and to give themselves away. So it was with Vidocq, for soon the Government discovered that the burglaries and other crimes concerning which he gave information which led to the arrest of the criminals of these respective " joints," were really organized and instigated by himself ! Also that he was really taking fees and royalties (as one might say) on both sides. Thus you see the French Jonathan Wild now boldly adopted the method of the English Jonathan who had happily been executed some fifty years before.

It was no wonder that Eugène François Vidocq was presently superseded and escaped by the skin of his teeth, as Job puts it.

He then started a paper mill which was in effect a factory for coining and other crimes. After a little while, however, the Government of the day raided the establishment, and once more Vidocq was thrown upon the world like that other often dramatised "smasher"—namely Suil Dhuv, the Coiner.

Thanks to sundry little flukes and fakes, this remarkable many-sided malefactor contrived to get a dishonest livelihood for many years longer, dying in 1857, at the ripe old age of eighty-two.

So you see that whatever else may be said against this desperado, he was in any case a man of colossal diligence in his business.

Once again in this case, as in so many instances of real crime dramas, it was my good fortune (if one may say so) to be concerned with various Vidocq dramas from my early youth. One of the first plays of this sort which I saw was a remarkable, intricate melodrama called *Vidocq, the French Jonathan Wild*, and it was played at the Old Brit., in Hoxton, where I saw it on several occasions with different Vidocqs. These included Joseph Reynolds, a fine actor who was leading man at the Brit. for over forty consecutive years, and Cecil Pitt, one of the most sanguifulminous of the Sweeney Todds of my time.

At the Surrey, the Standard, Shoreditch, and other outlying playhouses, I saw other plays revolving around this wholesale scoundrel. Their titles varied, coming out for example as *Vidocq, the French Thief Taker* (which brings us, of course, near Jonathan Wild again), *Vidocq*, with no subtitle, *Vidocq, the French Police Spy*, and so on.

One of the most notable impersonators of Vidocq in my time, and indeed an impersonator of famous criminals of all kinds, was that remarkable actor, J. B. Howe, whom it was my privilege to know, to watch, and to listen to, from my earliest boyhood, until he died a few years ago at King Lear's age, " four score and upwards."

J. B. Howe, whose front name was really Tommy (and he never allowed me to call him anything else) was one of the many very lovable, blood-and-thunder villains I have known. He was a man who thought nothing of playing Richard the Third and

Rip Van Winkle in one evening, and I have often seen him do it. Or, when he was on a more virtuous job, I have also seen him take on Hamlet at 6.30 p.m., and William in *Black-eyed Susan* at 9.30, and scoring in both. Yea, he even played the fiddle and danced the hornpipe in the character of William that married Susan.

This kindly stage scoundrel, who was also a very clever oil painter, and a writer of plays, including one on the *Pilgrim's Progress* if you please, was one of the most impressive Vidocqs, Jonathan Wilds, Sweeney Todds and William Corders I have ever seen. I could tell many a quaint story of " Tommy " J. B. Howe, but perhaps I have said enough about him at present in this Crime Play collection.

It will doubtless give you gladness when I tell you that a new Vidocq melodrama is about to loom large upon the London stage. It has already been produced in Australia and South Africa, and if I remember rightly it had a " try out " some time ago in Birmingham.

This Vidocq drama was written by that lovable and loyal friend of everybody, the lamented dramatist, Arthur Shirley. Dear old Arthur went through the details of this Vidocq play with me, which he had based upon that varied criminal's autobiography, a very remarkable book indeed.

Shirley and I, both being lovers of the blood-and-thunder drama, not only of the criminal, but of every kind, revelled over the script of this new Vidocq drama. And when you come to see it, you will, I feel sure, be deeply interested in Vidocq's new impersonator who is no other than the famous actor and Dickens mimic, Bransby Williams.

CHAPTER XXXIV

Some Real Slavery Crime Dramas

Of course we all know there was a time when Slavery was not regarded so much a crime as a comparatively honest industry. In fact it is not more than a hundred and fifty years ago when the outcry for the abolition of Slavery was first aroused through the sufferings of the poor devils of slaves, male and female.

It is also well known, or at least it should be, that it was England who set this outcry afoot, and it was this nation who, under the influence of Clarkson, Wilberforce, John Howard, and sundry famous Quakers, such as the Frys and the Buxtons, set its own slaves free all over the world at the cost of untold millions ! Indeed, all Britain determined that the Accursed Thing should cease anyhow, so far as this nation was concerned.

It was not until over half a century later that the Slavery Abolition movement awakened in America, under the leadership of John Brown, after whom the famous " John Brown's Body " song is named. It was also fomented by the great Channing (Unitarian leader), the Poet-Politician Russell Lowell (otherwise " Hosea Biglow "), Nathaniel Hawthorne, the great romantic novelist, Henry Wadsworth Longfellow the poet, and of course the dear old Quaker poet, John Greenleaf Whittier.

There is abundant proof, both literary and commercial, that almost up to the time when England resolved to give up Slavery, the Churches embodying millions of so-called Christians held that Slavery was a perfectly legal business, because it is mentioned without disapproval in certain parts of the Old Testament !

From Abraham onwards the ancient patriarchs, Hebrew and otherwise, had their thousands of slaves apiece, and treated them for the most part as they treated their cattle and sometimes not quite so kindly as that.

It was indeed not until the more humane brotherhood kind of teachings in the New Testament began to permeate the up to then religious folk, that Slavery was seen to be an unthinkable thing for any nation professing and calling itself Christian.

I assert, however, that it was the Stage which started, or at all events which first helped to push along, the Anti-Slavery Movement in the British Isles.

And here is the earliest slave play in proof thereof.

This was a tragedy entitled *Oroonoko*, and it was a more humanized variant of a kind of " shocker " novel, or romance, written by Mrs. Aphra Behn, who, as all who know her books and plays will remember, was perhaps the most indecent of all the disgusting dramatists of the Restoration period.

It was the poet Pope who, referring to Aphra, under her pen name of " Astrea," wrote those biting lines :—

> The Stage how loosely does Astrea tread
> Who fairly puts all characters to bed.

Mrs. Behn's *Oroonoko* novel was plentifully sandwiched with her usual salaciousness, but it possessed a kind of nucleus of a story showing something of the sufferings of a colony of slaves held by Dutch and English owners in Surinam. The play had for

its hero a negro Prince, who had been captured
and put into slavery in this colony, and whose
name gave the book and the subsequent play its
title.

By the time *Oroonoko* reached its acting form,
much of its nasty material had been scrapped,
though quite enough remained and was utilized by
the dramatist concerned. This partial purifier of
Mrs. Behn's book was that popular dramatist,
Thomas Southerne, who gave the stage some dramatic
and often pathetic plays. His best work of the sort
undoubtedly was that great tear-extracting drama,
Isabella; or, The Innocent Adultery, the title of which
was afterwards softened to *Isabella; or, The Fatal
Marriage*.

This was the play in which Sarah Siddons is said
to have made " strong men sob in the pit." So you
see the recently published disclosures of First Aid
being required by sobbing and hysterical playgoers
of the present day is by no means a new occurrence.

Oroonoko, as dramatized by Southerne, is really a
workmanlike affair, and has given scope to fine actors
from Betterton down to Macready and Phelps. I
have seen myself this play with lesser stars, but it
has not been revived for a good many years. Undoubtedly its episodes of Slave suffering helped to
wake the National Conscience in this matter. For
many years, for this reason, and also for its dramatic
and romantic interest, *Oroonoko* was continually
revived for a hundred and fifty years !

Briefly its story may be indicated by stating that
into the midst of several pathetic scenes, showing
the ill-treatment of the dusky victims, there is
brought the lately captured slave, this West Indian
Prince, the black Oroonoko. He is a noble-minded
negro, who with topical appropriateness gives off
from time to time some very scathing remarks on

so-called "Christians" who, as compared with pagan savages, are, or can be, monsters of cruelty.

Stagy as some of these exclamations come out, they are always truly dramatic, and have a real religious fervour. The more romantic side of this really touching if occasionally turgid tragedy, shows that the princely Oroonoko has been torn from his similarly dark-skinned bride, the Princess Imoinda, and, as poor Othello once was, "Sold into Slavery."

To the poor Prince's horror and increased suffering, presently he beholds this beautiful black bride of his, who has been snatched from her equally beautiful black baby and is brought in as a slave like himself.

Their joint sufferings arouse the spirit of revolt, not only in themselves, but in a tribe or two of their fellow-suffering, lower-born slaves.

The black Prince will not countenance any actual treachery or bloodshed even against his oppressors, stating that if there is anything in the so-called Christian creed he will show that spirit at its noblest —pagan though he be !

Eventually the hapless pair, so full of wonderful love for each other, in order to save their rebellious fellow-slaves from further punishment, elect to commit suicide together ! Poor Imoinda beseeches Oroonoko to stab her to the heart. He, however, on attempting to do the deed, breaks down and arranges to slay himself. His Princess, however, will not hear of this, and after a most poignant scene (an object lesson to far greater dramatists than Southerne) the faithful Imoinda stabs herself ! She is speedily followed by her husband, who turns the fatal poniard against himself, first taking care to slay the wicked governor of the slave colony.

After a brief discussion between the chief slave-owners, virtuous and villainous, the play of *Oroonoko* ends with a sort of forecast that some nobler form

13

of religion and civilization will yet take into account
the unspeakable sufferings of the slaves of divers
nations.

One of the virtuous officials ends the play with
the following tag :—

> I hope there is a place of happiness
> In the next world, for such exalted virtue !
> Pagan or unbeliever, yet he liv'd
> To all he knew ; and, if he went astray,
> There's mercy still above to set him right.
> But Christians, guided by the heav'nly ray,
> Have no excuse if we mistake our way.

It may surprise some to learn that the Epilogue
to Southerne's *Oroonoko* was written by no less a
literary light than the great Mr. Congreve himself !

The witty William, although unable to conceal
the fact of the play's inherent teaching, managed to
get in a bit of characteristic satire on the Sex, quite
on the lines of some of his matchless, but not too
moral, comedies.   Here is Congreve's tag :—

> Forgive this Indian's fondness of her spouse ⎫
> Their law no Christian liberty allows :   ⎬
> Alas, they make a conscience of their vows ! ⎭
> If virtue in a Heathen be a fault,
> Then damn the Heathen school where she was taught.
> She might have learn'd to cuckold, jilt, and sham,
> Had Covent Garden been in Surinam.

Southerne's *Oroonoko* came out in other dramatic
forms as time rolled on.   His was produced at
Drury Lane in 1696.   Sixty years later a version of
Southerne's play by Doctor John Hawkesworth was
presented also at Drury Lane.   Another version of
the same name was produced (apparently at Covent
Garden) the following year, when the adapter was
simply described as " Anon."

Very soon another version of the same play, but
renamed *Victorious Love*, was produced at one of

the outlying theatres.   Yet another called *Oroonoko;
or, The Royal Slave,* adapted by Francis Gentleman
and acknowledged as " altered from Southerne,"
was produced in Edinburgh.

The Oroonoko character continued to be selected
by all the best " stars " and that of Imoinda by all
the best actresses of tear-drawing capacity.   So
much for all the Oroonoko plays, or at all events
all that I know up to now.

CHAPTER XXXV

OTHER FAMOUS SLAVE DRAMAS

The next Anti-Slavery drama of renown was one called *The Slave*, written by Thomas Morton, author of (among other popular plays) the comedy called *Speed the Plough*, wherein he invented the since famous Mrs. Grundy with the exclamation, " What will Mrs. Grundy say ? "

The Slave was produced at Covent Garden a hundred and ten years ago with the then twenty-three-year-old tragedian, Macready, as the Slave, named Gambia. It followed much on the lines of the character of Oroonoko, except that Gambia managed to conquer his persecutors and to live ever after in England, which nation at Curtain Fall he describes thus :—

> " England ! shall I behold thee ? Talk of fabled land or magic power ! But what land, that poet ever sung, or enchanter swayed, can equal that which, when the Slave's foot touches, he becomes free ! His prisoned soul starts forth, his swelling nerves burst the chain that enthralled him, and in his own strength he stands, as the rock he treads on, majestic and secure ! "

I saw the last revival of *The Slave* ever given in London. Strange to say, that revival—which was at the Old Vic in the early 'seventies—is not mentioned in the usual dramatic chronicles. Yet it had a very strong cast, and proved very successful not only dramatically, but also as regards its

JONATHAN BRADFORD;

OR, THE MURDER AT THE ROAD-SIDE INN.

A MELO-DRAMA, IN TWO ACTS.—BY EDWARD FITZBALL.

THE REAL CRIME DRAMA WHICH DREW £80,000 TO THE "SURREY"

Facing p. 192

PAUL JONES.

A MELO-DRAMATIC ROMANCE, IN THREE ACTS.

BY THOMAS DIBDIN.

First Performed at Sadler's Wells Theatre, September 3, 1827.

A STARTLING PIRATE DRAMA OF THE "WELLS"

original music, which was by no less a composer than Sir Henry Bishop.

The Slave Gambia was then played by T. C. Burleigh, an excellent all-round actor and producer. The splendid low comedy character, Fogrum, written for the great Liston, was very cleverly acted by a youngster who had just joined us there, namely, James Fawn, afterwards the popular comic singer on the "halls." I may add that Fogrum had a catch phrase which spread all over the Metropolis, suburbs, etc. It was, " York, you're wanted ! "

It was in the midst of the earlier-mentioned anti-slavery rising in America, the rising which led to that country's Civil War, that there arose that long-famous champion of the Slaves' cause, Harriet Beecher Stowe. Her novel, *Uncle Tom's Cabin*, was then, and has since been, read by millions of people all over what Mr. Micawber calls "The Habitable Globe." There is therefore no need for me to give any details of its story, or that of the many plays which soon grew out of that world-famous book.

So numerous were these " Uncle Tom " dramas, that were I to enumerate all of the many dramatizations which I have seen and been concerned with (to say nothing of the others) it would take up large masses of space.

Naturally several of the early plays of this kind came out in America, and indeed they continue to be played all around the still happily United States and the British Isles. Negro actors, either born black or blacked up, appeared there and in England in the name part, in the comedy character Topsy (who " 'spects she growed ") and in the speaking or " thinking " slave parts which abound in that often mixed but always moving drama !

I think I am right in stating that it was the late

actor-manager, the extraordinary and eccentric John
Coleman, who prepared the first full-sized dramatization for the English stage. At any rate John
always told me so.

Coleman's version was called *Slavery*, and John
used to say that to his great surprise—after starting
tamely—it crammed the theatres and brought him
much unexpected money at a time when he was at
his lowest ebb in such necessary material.

Soon Charles Dillon, Creswick, and others brought
out other versions, Dillon's being a kind of rival to
Coleman's. Anon came to the certain West End,
and to many outlying theatres, all kinds of *Uncle
Tom's Cabin* plays, and I sampled most of them
from my earliest boyhood until the present time.
I say the present time because a few months ago
still another version was produced in the suburbs,
and, as I write, yet another " Uncle Tom's Cabin "
is being built.

This dramatization was peculiar in many effects,
for it contained not only the usual negro sentimental
and comic songs, which were always used in the
previous versions, but also sundry interpolated
numbers of a musical comedy or even Jazz type !
Even one or two original characters were dropped
in. Whether this vandalization (as I may call it)
was justifiable or not, this latest of all *Uncle Tom's
Cabin* plays is still careering around the provinces
strong in cash-drawing properties.

Indeed I have never known an *Uncle Tom's Cabin*
play, especially the versions run for years consecu-
tively by Charles Herman and Charles Harrington
respectively, that did not draw crowded houses.
This, of course, is due to its always moving story
and to the big scenes affecting poor Uncle Tom and
his fellow-slaves, and the villain Legree's terrible
whip-slashing, slave-driving pursuit of the poor

quadroon Eliza Harris across the ice. Also that other wholesale tear-drawing episode, the death of Little Eva, who, in most of the versions that I have seen, is shown to be received at Heaven's portals by a couple of glittering angels !

It may be interesting to note that " your Little Eva " (as the dying child always calls herself) was played seventy years ago by a tiny five-year-old actress named Madge Robertson, who happily is still with us, as the world-renowned Dame Kendal.

I have known all sorts of stars figure as Uncle Tom and all sorts of low comedians as Lawyer Marks. My aforesaid uncle played, in turn, every male character in these Uncle Tom dramas !

Poor Uncle Tom, in most versions, dies at the end with visions of angels also in view. In some cases he lives on, but in very few.

While writing these nigger-drama memories, I met my old friend, Alfred Denville, the runner and proprietor of so many stock companies in the Provinces¯ and London, as well as occasionally putting on productions of higher note. Also Mr. Denville has of late become deservedly historical as having founded and endowed a beautiful Haven of Rest for aged actors and actresses at Northwood in Middlesex.

Now it so happened that Actor Denville, some years ago, was playing Uncle Tom in a version in which that long sufferer has to die. He had already sung the usual songs, including one which I used to hear separately given in the music halls and entitled, *Pity Poor Uncle Tom*. At length the Death Scene arrives and Uncle Tom Denville laid down and prepared to depart out of all his persecutions to " Another and a Better World ! "

He began his last dying speech when a voice from

the prompt box whispered, "Spin out the dying, Alf—
give us a little more time to set the next piece."

Uncle Tom began to " gag " his moribund mono-
logue, and again prepared to die. Once more,
however, and still again, he was implored from the
wings to " keep it up a bit longer " !

At last this Uncle Tom, at his wits' end to know
how to delay his dying any further, arose, and said
to the assembled weeping crowd, " But now, white
and black folks, before I pass away, I will sing you
de dear old song, ' Good old Jeff has gone to rest,'
and then I shall die happy."

He gave this famous Christy Minstrel ballad as
promised, and finding that even then he was ahead
of time, he added :

" And I feel that I could even do de good old
plantation dance, which you kind folks always loved."
And then the dying Tom did the dance, and having
had the tip that all was well, the anguished Uncle
laid down again and "passed away" most pathetically to appropriate music !

Although Uncle Tom usually died in these numberless dramas built up around him, I may tell you
that, as a matter of fact, the real Uncle Tom, thanks
to the unceasing efforts of his Abolitionist Friends,
not only escaped and regained his freedom, but even
came to England on more than one occasion.

The last time he visited this land, and he was then
getting very old, I saw him, his ebony-black head
surmounted by a ring of snow-white hair. He had
become a travelling preaching evangelist, and when
I saw him he had come to preach at Spurgeon's
Metropolitan Tabernacle near the Elephant and
Castle. And placards were all around billing him
by his real name, which was " The Reverend Josiah
Henson."

CHAPTER XXXVI

MANY MORE AVUNCULAR SLAVE DRAMAS

As a specimen of the sensational stuntful manner in which *Uncle Tom's Cabin* was always billed, I append the scene-plot of one of the chief West End revivals which I saw with a big company of English and American stars.

Here starts the amazing synopsis :—

Mr. Shelby's Plantation—Sold in Bondage—Tavern on the Banks of the Ohio—Uncle Tom's Cabin—Negro Devotions—George Harris determines to Escape to British Soil—Choral Hymns by the Jubilee Singers—The Slave Catchers—Pursuit of Eliza—Splendid View of the

OHIO RIVER IN MID-WINTER.

ELIZA'S ESCAPE ACROSS THE FLOATING ICE.

St. Clair's Mansion and Grounds on Lake Pontchartrain—Yankees in the South—Topsy's History—The child that never was born—Song and Breakdown, " Golly, I'se so wicked "—Tavern by the River—The Ohio Senator and the Quaker.

ROCKY PASS AND CASCADE OF REAL WATER !

Escape of George and Eliza—Uncle Tom and Eva. " I see a band of Spirits bright "—Topsy and Aunt Ophelia—Eva's Bedchamber, Love, Joy, Peace.

DEATH OF EVA.

TABLEAU : SLAVE MARKET IN NEW ORLEANS.

Slave Melody, " Mother, is massa going to sell us to-morrow ? "—Uncle Tom sold to Legree—Courtship of Aunt Ophelia and the Senator,

GREAT PLANTATION FESTIVAL,

INTRODUCING SCORES OF JUBILEE SINGERS. THE LOUISIANA
TROUBADOUR QUARTETTE.

ARRIVAL OF THE FLAT BOAT WITH THE NEGRO SLAVE MELODISTS.

THE FOUR JOLLY COONS.

Horace Weston, the Champion Banjoist of the world.
Sarah Washington, the Inimitable Camp Leader and Shouter.
The Slidel Children, Dancers.

CROWDS OF REAL AMERICAN FREED SLAVES.

REALISTIC STEAMBOAT RACE.

Chants and Shouts. Concluding with a Characteristic Slave
Dance, entitled

THE HARVEST HOME.

LEGREE'S PLANTATION.

The Poor Old Slave—Song, " Uncle Tom's Lament "—Flog that
Woman ! " I'll die first ! "

THE FLOGGING ! !

Street in New Orleans—George Shelby looking for Uncle Tom—
A Lawyer's Information never Gratis—Legree's House—The
Workings of a Guilty Conscience—The Fatal Blow—Arrival of
George Harris.

CASSY COMPLETES HER VENGEANCE.

DEATH OF UNCLE TOM.

BEAUTIFUL ALLEGORICAL TABLEAU.

EVA IN HEAVEN.

NOTICE—The Performance is over in time to see ZAZEL in the
Aquarium.

The other *Uncle Tom's Cabin* plays which I have
seen or read (or both) include versions respectively
named as follows :

Uncle Tom, by Leonard Rae (from a French
dramatization), at the Standard, Shoreditch ; one with

the usual title, by George Fawcett Rowe (a popular impersonator of Micawber), at the Princess's; another by an unnamed adapter at the Kennington Theatre, and the really first, but by no means the worst one.   This was by the popular melodramatist, Fitzball, and was brought from Drury Lane all around the so-called "minor" theatres.   It was entitled, *Uncle Tom's Cabin*; *or, The Horrors of Slavery*.

Other versions were called respectively, *The Slave Hunter*, *The Slave Girl*, *A Slave's Ransom*, *Slave Life*, and *Blackbirding*.   The last-named was a kind of Slavery "mixed grill."

CHAPTER XXXVII

THE GREAT RIVAL SLAVE PLAY TO " UNCLE TOM "

I suppose that the greatest and most enduring Slave drama competitor to *Uncle Tom's Cabin* is the late Dion Boucicault's four-act sensational but very human melodrama, *The Octoroon; or, Life in Louisiana.*

Apart from this play's thrilling Slave auction scenes and similar slavery horrors, it also possesses several other stupendous " appeals." These include the relentless persecution of the pathetic octoroon heroine by a double-dyed villainous slave-driver ; the foul murder of a half-breed little Indian boy by that brute ; the snapshotting of the murderer doing the deed, by a crazy old-fashioned derelict camera, and the relentless pursuit and righteous slaying of the murderer by a stalwart and almost silent Redskin who loves the half-breed boy.

Many a time and oft have I seen *The Octoroon* since it was brought from America to our Adelphi, Princess's, etc., and around the suburbs and the provinces. I have seen all sorts of stars and staresses respectively as the chief villain ; the " Weenie " Paul (as the avenging Indian calls him), the Nigger Pete (a fine serio-comic " Uncle Tom " part), Salem Scudder, a gum-chewing but golden-hearted Yankee (who helps all the persecuted), and as the splendid Indian Wah-no-Tee.

One especial thing, however, will ever be memorable to all of us who saw the early London productions of *The Octoroon*, and that is the thrilling, heart-gripping performance of the almost dumb Wah-no-Tee by the play's author, the elder Boucicault, usually a comic-stage Irishman !

My list of anti-slavery dramas is by no means exhausted in my previous survey. Even the great Mrs. Beecher Stowe herself achieved universal popularity for many years with a similar story called *Dred*. This was speedily and numerously dramatized from about seventy-five years ago onwards. A good many years after that, when I was a very young fellow, I caught up all sorts of what any more frivolous person than myself would call Dred-ful dramas.

These dramatizations which I saw so often played by many stage favourites, including some of my own relations, were mostly entitled, *Dred, a Tale of the Dismal Swamp*. I have even known big stars of my earlier period play the character of Dred, including that fine melodramatic actor, but not so fine a tragedian, William Creswick.

This hero, Dred, a kind of negro-monarch, like Eugene O'Neill's Emperor Jones, went about delivering slaves by means of his deadly rifle and revolver.

Deservedly great as was Mrs. Beecher Stowe's renown for her story championing the cause of the oppressed slaves, sometimes of the almost equally oppressed Red Indians of America, it is certainly interesting, if it is regrettable, to note that, to put it Shakespeareanly, she unlaced her literary reputation some twenty years after her first great success, by writing a very sensational and unnecessarily unhealthy book. This dealt with the many amours of that wonderful poet but by no means worthy man, Lord Byron.

But it has always to be remembered that this

misguided Poet-Peer who died at the age of thirty-six
undoubtedly sacrificed himself in the cause of the
Freedom of Greece.　So it may be said of him, as of
Macbeth's predecessor in the Thaneship of Cawdor,
" Nothing in his life became him like the leaving
it."

Unfortunately Mrs. Stowe, like so many delvers
into such ghoulish details, did not give poor Byron
the credit which was his due, either as Poet or as
Patriot.　Therefore, it was perhaps not surprising
that during the rather vicious vogue of these Byronic
revelations I heard the late famous comedian, David
James, sing a song in an old Strand Theatre burlesque
in which he referred to the great lady novelist
thus :

> She put her Beecher's foot in it—
> I mean her Beecher's toe.

Two other anti-slavery plays really call for some
attention.

One of these was played at the Surrey, also by
Creswick, and was entitled, *A Woman of Colour; or,
From Slavery to Freedom.*　Unfortunately, unlike
previous examples I have given, I have not by me
a copy of the play itself, but I remember seeing it
at certain revivals.　It was a very effective and
often pathetic drama, setting forth the terrible
sufferings of slaves in general and the Eliza Harris-
like character of the heroine in particular.　This
heroine was finally rescued by, and wedded to, an
English Peer !　The slave girl was played at first
by Emily Sanders, who really did marry a Real
Nobleman, who was also an actor, namely, Sir
William Don, Bart.

The only other play of the sort now to deal with
is one of the latest anti-slave plays within my
experience.　You see it must be remembered that
with the abolition of slavery in America, nearly

seventy years after England had set all her slaves free in all her Dominions, the need for anti-slave plays had died out, and any revivals thereof were regarded in the nature of historico-theatrical curios.

Now the other play in this slavery series was entitled *Blackbirding*. It was written by that long-popular ex-low comedian and prolific playwright whom I have mentioned before, namely, Colin H. Hazelwood. Hazelwood wrote this drama fifty odd years ago for the famous Britannia Theatre, at Hoxton, where (as I think I have stated) he was resident dramatist, at a salary of about three pounds a week. For this sum very often he wrote a new play every fortnight!

When I say that Hazelwood "wrote" these plays, of course it was hardly to be expected that he would be able to sit down and work out such new dramas in any pronounced literary fashion for such a weekly wage.

He had a very good method, however. He used to take in the popular periodicals of the time, such as *The London Journal, The London Reader, Reynold's Miscellany. The Welcome Guest*, and other such publications, alas! long since defunct. To these Hazelwood added all the "penny bloods" of his young days, and later of mine, such as *The Boys of England, The Young Men of Great Britain*, and all the highwaymen stories and similar cheap books.

Hazelwood, or one of us working with him, would run through these periodicals, jotting down the main incidents in the stories thereof, and scissoring out here and there sundry aphorisms, axioms, and moral sentiments and so forth. These were docketed alphabetically, and when Colin (a dear old fellow) was engaged in writing, or in sticking down, a new play for the Brit, etc., he or his assistants would take down from the shelf sundry envelopes contain-

ing these aphorisms, such as "Ambition is," etc.,
or "Kindness of heart," etc., and so forth, and would
pop these moral, patriotic and other reflections into
the play-script then under way.

"Blackbirding," as some may know or may not,
is a term applied, especially by professional pirates
so often engaged in this pursuit, namely, that of
hunting down, capturing, and selling into slavery
at great profit, any capturable negro, male or
female, likely to be saleable in the slave markets.

I do not disguise the fact that this *Blackbirding*
melodrama owed something to previous plays of the
kind, especially perhaps to the *Octoroon* and *Dred*,
to say nothing of *Uncle Tom's Cabin*. Still, it was
a very interesting and useful play. Moreover it was
interesting in a dramatically historical sense, for it
formed one of the last, if not the very last, drama of
the sort, at that great Hoxton Gold Mine of a playhouse, where I myself had seen, back and front of
the stage, all manner of anti-slavery and of war
dramas. Also I had heard there all sorts of songs
concerning that never-to-be-forgotten American up-
heaval which was ended by Lincoln's great victory
for the Slaves.

It was at the Brit., for example, during the then
customary singing "between the pieces" that I
heard several leading lady vocalists, including the
afterwards great Gaiety favourite, Constance Loseby,
sing that stirring American patriotic ditty, "General
Stonewall Jackson," which started thus :—

> On a bright May morn in '63,
> And ready for the action !
> On the battlefield for Liberty
> Fell General Stonewall Jackson.

Also it was at the Brit. that some of my earliest
impressions of the sufferings of the negro slaves in
America were indelibly imprinted on my youthful

memory by means of certain " Negro " melodies. These included that very touching, if crude, old ditty, " Poor Ole Jeff has gone to rest, We know that he is free," " Poor Old Joe," and especially a nigger warble which, throughout the four or five years of the American War, was one of the most successful songs that I have ever heard in my life.

I should add that *Blackbirding* was based by Hazelwood, *not* on " penny bloods " this time, but on a series of then recent real and awful negro-stealing crimes in the South Seas !

The strangely moving " Uncle Sam " ditty was sung there chiefly by a very versatile actor and character singer, who used to be billed as the " Great Maclagan." This song was called " Pity Poor Uncle Sam," and started thus :—

> White folks, I've just come over
> To tell you who I am.
> I am a poor slave nigger,
> And my name is Uncle Sam.

It then went on to detail some of the horrors of slave life at that time, and always, the many times I heard it, drew thunders of sympathetic applause. Often when this comic and character singer had finished his " Uncle Sam " song, he would wash off his " black-up " and be off to another theatre, sometimes in the West End, to play the tenor hero, in a selection (and sometimes the whole of) the grand opera *Faust.*

14

CHAPTER XXXVIII

TREASON CRIMES AND DRAMAS THEREON

Treason doth never prosper; what's the reason?
When it doth prosper, none dare call it treason.

Another proof of the unvarnished truth of this couplet is found not only in the result of this or that treasonable plot, but even more so in the case of plays based upon such conspiracies.

It is very rare to find the dramatist or playwright putting forth any special outspoken view of his own, with regard to any historical rebellion against the monarchy of any nation which he happens to treat. Indeed very often the author emphasizes the pro-monarchical side and proportionately belittles the rebel faction, however earnest and however necessary that faction may prove to be in historical fact.

Before proceeding to some very marked, and indeed often very strange, dramas of this kind, I might mention, for purposes of future reference, that perhaps the most glaring examples of whitewashing of notoriously bad Kings and Queens was carried to its height by W. G. Wills. This undoubtedly gifted and almost genius of a dramatist belittled any historical value which the plays might have had by his special pleading on the Royal side.

For example, the aforesaid William Gorman Wills makes his Charles the First in the famous Irving play an exceedingly saintly angel of light, and his Cromwell a low-life slum bully whom he describes as "Judas, a mouthing patriot with an itching palm."

Wills's specimen of the almost numberless plays written around Mary Queen of Scots shows that lovely but scarcely loyal lady of so many husbands and lovers, as quite a spotless goddess ! Per contra the whitewashing Wills turns the black-wash very lavishly on John Knox, making him not only a foul-mouthed, self-seeking, canting skunk, but also actually showing him as being desirous of becoming one of Mary Stuart's very own paramours !

Similarly in other historical dramas, including a very peculiar one called *Sedgemoor*, the brilliant but untrustworthy play-historian, Wills, was so partisan as to become ridiculous. This was, of course, to be deplored, for our late old friend was undoubtedly a real poet, and when not hampered by his piled-up partisanship, left us some very fine plays.

The author (or adapter) as he was of dramas of such commanding merit as his version of Goethe's *Faust* and of Goldsmith's *Vicar of Wakefield*, in the matchless play *Olivia* made famous by Ellen Terry and Irving, is certainly a dramatist for whom the English stage should be grateful in spite of all his idiosyncrasies.

MONMOUTH TREASON PLAYS

In William Gorman Wills's rebellion drama entitled *Sedgemoor* he was assisted collaboratively by his brother, the Reverend Freeman C. Wills, whose playwriting and parsonic qualities I have described in connection with *The Only Way* and *Eugene Aram*.

Sedgemoor was produced at the famous Sadler's Wells Theatre, in the early eighties. It had the advantage of the leading female character being played by the great actress, Miss Marriott, who for so many years ran that renowned playhouse, and was one of the best of the eighty-five Hamlets which I can claim to have seen.

Other clever important players appeared in this drama. They included Richard Edgar, a son of Miss Marriott (Mrs. Robert Edgar), and a young grotesque actor-player, stage-named E. J. Lonnen, who afterwards became such a great Gaiety favourite and burlesque actor. The cast also included a strong leading man of the time, George Warde, and a very statuesque beauty, stage-named Marie De Grey, a young actress who possessed some financial means, which she spent in using to " back " sundry theatrical enterprises in which she figured.

Miss De Grey was one of the tallest actresses I have ever met, taller even than Miss Viola Tree, and like that lady she was also a very loyal and delightful friend.

Sedgemoor, in spite of some beautiful writing and its excellent cast, was so hampered by the Brothers Wills's historical freaks that it faded out very speedily so far as London was concerned, although later in a revised version, and renamed *Loyalty*, it did very well on tour.

Not long after the failure of our old friend the enemy, Guy Fawkes, and his fellow-conspirators, Treason Crimes began to increase and multiply. Those plots which were involved in the Cavalier *versus* Roundhead Period are perhaps sufficiently indicated in what I have just said concerning the *Charles the First* plays.

I ought to mention, however, that, alike in Carolian days and on through the eighteenth century, until my own times in the theatres, there were several other *Charles the First* plays, including one which was written by an actor named W. Havard, for the great David Garrick, if you please !

WHITEFRIARS;

OR, THE DAYS OF CLAUDE DU VAL.

A DRAMA, IN THREE ACTS.

FROM THE CELEBRATED ROMANTIC NOVEL OF THE SAME TITLE

BY W. THOMPSON TOWNSEND.

First Performed at the Royal Surrey Theatre, April 8th, 1844.

THE MOST BLOODTHIRSTY DRAMA OF THE
RESTORATION PERIOD

THE BEGGAR'S PETITION;

OR, A FATHER'S LOVE AND A MOTHER'S CARE.

A DRAMA, IN THREE ACTS.

BY GEORGE DIBDIN PITT.

First performed at the City Theatre, Monday, October 18th, 1841.

THE MOST STARTLING SOB-STUFF PLAY OF THE
SUBURBAN STAGE

Facing p. 208

I have a copy of this scarce and somewhat strange play which I do not think has been reprinted for at least a hundred and fifty years. Considering the tempestuousness of the period, player Havard's drama of the Cavalier–Roundhead time is rather placid and plaintive. Even Mary Russell Mitford's *Charles the First* tragedy, refined as that is, is a little more ruffled than Havard's.

Coming to my own time, the plays dealing with those unhappy Civil Wars, and all embodying as the previously named plays did a good deal of the plots and counterplots concerned therewith, have included some strong and strange specimens.

Among these is another extremely scarce tragedy of which happily I possess a prompt copy.

This play is called *Cromwell*, and it was written by that late brilliant journalist, Colonel Bate Richards, who was at the time Editor of the *Morning Advertiser*. I may say that I am one of the very few who saw that play when it came out, for although it possessed great merit in its blank-verse writing, it was not dramatic enough to carry itself into financial success.

Perhaps another reason for its financial failure was that, unlike nearly every other play of the sort up to the time, Colonel Richards's specimen was nearly as bad as Wills's for extreme partisanship. In the Colonel's case, however, he poured bucketfuls of whitewash upon Cromwell and pailfuls of black-wash upon poor King Charles.

It so happened that the good Colonel, who wrote some very clever plays which do not come within the scope of these crime or treasonable series, intended his *Cromwell* play as a sort of counterblast to Wills's *Charles the First* which Henry Irving had just begun to run, and did long run with such tremendous success at the Lyceum. The Colonel's

Cromwell had a powerful representative in that powerful actor, George Rignold.

The soldier-dramatist showed his extreme partisanship of Oliver still more in the preface of this play. While Wills's drama ran on and was always being revived, Colonel Richards's polemical play sample soon dwindled out of sight.

I might add that there was a real crime play written by the Colonel, and I remember seeing it at Drury Lane. It was called *The Prisoner of Toulon*, but although I have also a copy of this, inasmuch as I cannot trace the real crime on which its galley-slave story is based, I shall leave it at that.

Another pro-Cromwell specimen which also emphasizes King Charles's more or less alleged treason against the State and his people, was called *Colonel Cromwell*. It was the collaborative work of a very clever literary man and poet named Arthur Patterson and that late fine " villain " actor, Charles Cartwright. Now mayhap it was that playgoers then especially preferred the pro-Stuart to the pro-Protector sort of drama, anyhow this rather partisan Cromwell play likewise failed to attract.

One of the greatest, if also partisan, pro-Oliver dramas is, of course, the one written by our old friend, Poet-Patriot Victor Hugo. Nowadays when you read it in its original form you certainly are driven to the conclusion that the eminent Victor was extremely verbose. Still it has its vivid and dramatic qualities, and these I remember were brought out very well indeed in a translation or adaptation by a very diligent playwright named Frederick Phillips, whom we shall meet anon in sundry crime plays.

Phillips's version was produced at the Surrey Theatre when I was a little youngster, but was revived on several occasions as I was growing up.

One of the latest *Cromwell* pieces which have come my way was one described as an historical episode. It was written by a now prosperous variety agent, named Warland S. Wheeler, and was produced at the Paragon Music Hall in the Mile End Road.

I found this playlet a very dramatic and interesting piece of work, although almost as pro-Stuart as dear old Wills's *Charles the First.*

One of the most important as well as one of the latest *Cromwell* plays (at least of those produced) was Poet John Drinkwater's *Oliver Cromwell,* dedicated to Bernard Shaw as " Master dramatist of his age," and presented at His Majesty's Theatre about a couple of years ago, with that fine actor, Henry Ainley, giving a very impressive and artistic impersonation of the name part.

Despite the distinction of the writing of this *Oliver Cromwell,* its financial success was not equal to its artistic ditto. This regrettable result may have been due to the fact that like Colonel Bate Richards, friend Drinkwater stressed too much his partisanship of the Protector and made it a bit too hot for Charles.

This character, however, although shown to be quite shifty, on the usual Stuart lines, had some really beautiful things to say. It is more than probable that the comparative failure of Drinkwater's beautifully written play arose to some extent from the still current habit of playgoers leaning always to the Cavalier rather than the Roundhead side, in plays dealing with the time, when as Hudibras says :

> Civil Dudgeon first grew high,
> And men fell out, they knew not why.

A very recently written *Cromwell* play, penned with great distinction, literary polish, and real fervour, was by a very gifted poet and essayist, Edward Willmore, who, strangely enough, was also a very keen business man, prosperous in various undertakings. Some of the ventures were of a cinematic kind and were run by him in and around South Wales.

I had the privilege of knowing Mr. Willmore for many years, and I always enjoyed my chats with him upon Literature and the Drama, yea even when he drifted (as was usual with him) into a profound or Swedenborgian mysticism.

Mr. Willmore, moreover, brought me his Cromwell play before it was published, and I had the pleasure of making sundry technical and dramatic suggestions which he carried out in the printed book.

Mr. Willmore's play was for some time earmarked by Sir Frank Benson, but up to now nothing has come of that earmarking. I regret deeply to add that Mr. Willmore died a few months ago while waiting and hoping for the production of his *Cromwell* play which, I may mention, was quite as pro-Cromwell as Drinkwater's or any other such drama that I know, and perhaps even more so. If literary merit and poetic vision count for anything, however, Mr. Willmore's *Cromwell* should yet see the footlights.

Shocking as it may be to some who hold, and often hold rightly, that there are some historical personages and ditto events which should not be parodied and held up to ridicule, even the Civil Wars, together with their protagonists (as the Highbrows say), have been travestied a good deal.

It has to be said that the first or certainly the chief offender in this regard, was the author of the above-mentioned " Hudibras " poem, for that great satirist, Samuel Butler, poured forth volume after volume in this epic burlesque. Samuel, however, like so many of the poets and playwrights then and

since, showered all his vitriolic satire upon the
Puritan side, and upheld the Royalists, with
undoubted humorous strength.

Butler, as we know, was very much subsidized to
take this violently anti-Puritan view, by Charles
the Second himself, who promised (after the fashion
of that sovereign) to provide evermore for the poet
concerned.

As usual the " Merry " Monarch broke his
promises and poor Butler was left to starve. So
sad indeed was his fate that when a marble bust
was erected over his tomb a good many years later,
the Poet Pope, himself no mean satirist, wrote that
memorable couplet :—

> The poet's fate is here in emblem shown,
> He asked for bread, and he received a stone.

As the gist of these articles is chiefly dramatic, I
ought to mention that the poem of *Hudibras* itself
has been dramatized a good deal. In one form it
came out on the stage as an opera parody called
Hudibrasso. In another form it was travestied by
some few early eighteenth century stage scribes.

The most striking stage form, however, of Butler's
matchless skit was that it provided the subject for
the first of the forty pantomimes, which our late
beloved friend, E. L. Blanchard, wrote for Drury
Lane.

That pantomime was entitled *Harlequin Hudibras ;
or, Old Dame Durden and the Droll Days of the Merry
Monarch.* I was not born in time, alas ! to see this
Hudibrastic pantomime myself, but I am thankful
to say that I have a very nice copy thereof. All I
will add concerning it is that I wish most heartily
that any of the pantomimes produced in recent
years had a tithe of the artistry, quaint humour and
polished rhyme of this old Drury Panto.

Oliver also appeared in a farcical extravaganza which was produced at the Queen Theatre, Long Acre. This little *Cromwell* play, the author of which did not state his name, was a pleasant trifle, I remember, but not strong enough to live long.

Perhaps the most successful burlesque of the kind was a very smart, but not too happily named one, entitled, *Oliver Grumble*. This was written forty years ago by a then very young Midland visitor to London, one George Dance, who then (like me) was earning a bit here and there by song-writing for sundry music-hall stars, including Arthur Roberts and Vesta Tilley.

This was Dance's first London production of a regular stage type, and was most humorously put over by those two not yet replaced delightful comic players, Willie Edouin and his brilliant and beautiful wife, Alice Atherton.

This George Dance afterwards became author of many stage successes of a musical play type, includ-ing musical farces and extravaganzas, notably, *The Lady Slavey, The Gay Parisienne, Ma Mie Rosette*, and that extremely long-running musical mixture, *A Chinese Honeymoon*.

G. D. also became a wholesale theatrical manager and producer, making a good deal of money, out of which he gave £30,000 in order to " save the Old Vic."

For this and for other good-hearted unselfish services, my friend George was knighted.

CHAPTER XXXIX

SOME TERRIBLE TREASON DRAMAS

One of the most striking of the more blood-and-thundery specimens of the real Treason dramas of Charles the First's time was a melodrama by one of my early stage employers, the skilful manager, Edward Stirling. This play, which I used to see pretty often at the Standard, Shoreditch, Astley's Theatre, etc., was entitled, *The Three Black Seals*.

The conspiracy depicted in this play is headed by John Felton, a neglected and much persecuted lieutenant in Charles the First's army. Poor John, like so many others, had been misled, not so much by the monarch himself as by certain of his courtly unprincipled advisers. In this case the chief persecutor and neglecter of certain of the soldiers, driving them not unnaturally into rebellion, was the Duke of Buckingham of the period. Felton placed himself at the head of these rebels and extracted promise after promise from Buckingham, who characteristically took care to keep none of them.

Eventually Felton waited for Buckingham at a meeting in Portsmouth and stabbed him to the heart!

King Charles was so upset at the death of his favourite Buckingham that he flung himself upon his royal bed in a passion of tears!

Outside the Court, however, as historian John Richard Green shows so graphically, John Felton's assassination act was welcomed with unbounded joy. Indeed Oxford undergraduates and grave and reverend London aldermen, etc., went in for drinking toasts to Felton.

That long-suffering assassin was of course arrested, but on passing on his way manacled to the Tower for execution, the crowds en route shouted, " The Lord comfort thee." Anon, many of the slain Duke's men-at-arms, then about to embark from Portsmouth, yelled to the King who had come to see them off, " Save John Felton, our sometime fellow-soldier."

You can imagine what a sympathetic character could be made of Felton as it certainly was made by Playwright Stirling, a man who knew his business well. I saw several leading actors, mostly local favourites, play Felton with great power and pathos. I have marvelled more than once why so strong a real-crime drama as *The Three Black Seals* has not been recently revived on the London boards.

Now, with one other specimen, I think I can conclude with the Charles the First plays.

This additional drama was written by those then very successful and very artistic authors, Robert Buchanan and George R. Sims, both, alas! since passed away. This drama, called *The White Rose*, was founded on Sir Walter Scott's Cavalier–Roundhead romance entitled *Woodstock*, and was produced at the Adelphi Theatre thirty-five years ago.

I remember arguing a good deal with these two old colleagues of mine regarding certain things which I thought overdone, on both sides of the political or State question involved, but Sims was always obstinate in an English way, and Buchanan was also ditto in a Scottish. So after an argument or two at rehearsals I left George and Robert to " gang their ain playwriting gait."

It will be interesting to add, however, that the political sympathies of these two dramatists were opposed to each other a good deal. Thus in some parts of the play the sympathy was bestowed upon Charles, and in other parts Cromwell had the sympathetic " pull." Cromwell was again played by Charles Cartwright, and Charles the Second, then struggling to reach his throne, was enacted by Fuller Mellish, a very clever son of that artistic actress, Rose Leclercq.

The young Royalist heroine was played by the still beautiful Evelyn Millard. The Royalist soubrette and the Roundhead sweetheart were represented respectively by the late Lionel Rignold (of the famous theatrical family) and the still surviving smart soubrette Clara Jecks.

Perhaps the most interesting feature of this cast was that Oliver Cromwell's daughter Elizabeth was acted by that still strong favourite, Mrs. Patrick Campbell.

Some Strafford Plays

The real treasonable act here indicated, a treason to the nation—it was little else—was that which the Earl of Strafford was incited by Charles the First to organize and to carry out.

This " unspeakable job " roused the nation to frenzy and to rebellious utterances throughout the British Isles.

King Charles, finding himself in a cleft stick, so to speak, did what so many Stuarts did before and since, that is, he left his dupe Strafford in the lurch. Poor Strafford was impeached and speedily executed. At the carrying out of that dread sentence the nation shrieked with joy, and all around London in particular, the joyous cry went up, " His head is off ! . . . His head is off ! "

There were many pictures of the episode showing Strafford at his trial and execution. Also, of course, the dramatists were soon busy writing around that much misled and foully-treated statesman.

One of these plays was by John Sterling, concerning whom Carlyle wrote one of his best biographical volumes. I don't think that poor Sterling's " Strafford " play found its way to the " boards," but several dramas and melodramas written around him did.

Undoubtedly the most important " Strafford " tragedy was the one by Robert Browning, "you writer of plays," as he called himself in a certain poem. Browning's " Strafford " play, although not always so dramatic as might be wished, is full of beautiful blank-verse lines.

The last scene has a very poignant finish, and indeed much of the piece is in Robert's best and most observant vein. I am afraid that Browning, like Tennyson, is not regarded as he should be, in these days of very exalted highbrow criticisms. Whatever else Browning has written, however, even that mighty dramatic performance, *The Ring and the Book*, with its 21,000 lines, is not better work than his " Strafford."

It is not generally known, I think, that Robert Browning wrote this " Strafford " tragedy for Macready ; and, especially that R. B.'s contract stipulated that he should receive £12 per night for twenty-five nights, and £10 per night for any subsequent performances.

CHAPTER XL

Treason plots grew very lively (if I may say so) in the time of the so-called " Merry " Monarch.

There were Catholic plots, Protestant plots, Nonconformist plots, and all kinds of political, besides the usual religious and other plots, and counter-plots.

In fact, all sorts of people and personages seemed to come down to posterity as being among the champion plotters of the period.

These included the Monmouth Rebellion adherents, namely, Lord William Russell, the Earl of Shaftesbury, Colonel Blood (who did a little side stunt by stealing the Crown Jewels), and that very " spotted beauty," Master Titus Oates, who was not only a " Mr. Facing-both-ways," but a Mr. Facing-everyway—wherever there was a chance of a bribe.

The wicked Rye House Plot loomed large at this time. Among the conspirators concerned were the aforesaid Lord William Russell, the Earl of Essex, and in the more or less background, the Duke of Monmouth, the illegitimate son of Charles the Second by Lucy Walters.

Of Monmouth's own Rebellion and its result more will be said anon. For the present I will confine myself to the Rye House Plot which was organized in order to capture the King, who, having arranged to come from Newmarket Races to London, via Rye House on the River Lea, was to be kidnapped and sent away, or, if necessary, "removed" by assassination!

I count myself fortunate in having both seen and read among my many real crime plays, some four or five dramas based upon this Rye House Plot. The most striking of these is perhaps the so-called historical drama written by the once renowned melodramatist, J. T. Haines, and entitled, *The Rye House Plot ; or, The Maltster's Daughter.*

This three-act play, a very thrilling affair, was produced at the Sadler's Wells Theatre ninety years ago. It was therefore a good age when I caught it up in my youth, and saw several very popular players in the principal characters both on the Middlesex and the Surrey side.

The peculiar thing, or rather one of the peculiar things, in this play, was not only its plenitude of sword fights and secret poisonings, but also the fact that the perfectly innocent hero and heroine, dwellers at the Rye House, get very much mixed up with the conspiracy, and are compelled to adopt all kinds of subterfuges and to face many dangers per scene before they can properly clear themselves.

During the working out of the plot or conspiracy, the Papal password of which is, "The old man's still at Rome," sundry murders are committed *coram populo*! What is more extraordinary still, is that the low comedy character, Simon Stagg, described as "a gentleman in easy circumstances," becomes so involved in the Rye House Plot that he is taken by the conspirators for a spy and is stabbed and dropped down a well, and there left to perish miserably!

After the traitors have set fire to the Rye House itself, and have daggered, poniarded or poisoned all and sundry, somebody happens to go to that well to draw water. When the bucket reaches the top it is found to contain not that refreshing liquid, but the ghost of the said Stagg !

But as Mr. Puff warned his friends at his rehearsals, " not to be sure that the Beefeater just entered was a Beefeater," so I warn you not to be too sure that the contents of that bucket was really an apparition.

As a matter of fact, this comic personage was not quite dead when brought to the surface. Moreover, he was found to have upon him certain " papers " which proved handy in bringing to justice all those traitors against the " Merry " Monarch. I may mention incidentally that His Majesty was not above lending a hand in drawing up the bucket which contained the alleged " ghost " !

I have said that the Duke of Monmouth was implicated in this conspiracy. Indeed, in this play he bobs in and out, to lend assistance that may help to further his own special rebellion. But here again, as in so many of these dramas of real criminals, the whitewash brush is brought into play. And perhaps because the Rebel Monmouth was really of royal birth (on papa's side, anyhow) it was deemed advisable by dramatists to let him off lightly.

It is only fair that I should mention that this drama, *The Rye House Plot*, like several others of the time, is based upon a long romance written by that most gory or sanguinary stuntful novelist, G. W. M. Reynolds.

This voluminous author, who was going strong when I was a youngster, did perhaps more harm to the rising generation of his time than any other writer that might be mentioned. Like Mr. Silas Wegg, he even " dropped into poitry " ever and anon. For example, on one occasion, when he was advocating the unexampled violence of the Chartists and even more rebellious rioters and rick-burners, Bard Reynolds broke into the following couplet :

> You cannot snatch the lucifer match
> From the hands of the labouring poor !

It may be added more or less to the credit of G. W. M. R. that he founded *Reynolds's Newspaper*, which was for a long time a very gory and grimy sheet, but of late years has become quite respectable among such crime-purveying newspapers.

I did not have the honour of knowing G. W. M. R. himself, but I did have the pleasure of knowing and sometimes working for his son, who was then an eccentric but very rich old bachelor. Reynolds Junior had one very strange hobby, I remember, that was to collect and to keep around him every kind of monkey and ape ! So much for Reynolds *père et fils*.

In this drama, *The Rye House Plot*, instead of being executed on Tower Hill, three days after he was sentenced (as we know to have been the case), His Grace of Monmouth is pardoned by the King, immediately after one of Monmouth's chums has emptied a large horse-pistol full on His Majesty's manly chest.

This politefully pardoning Sovereign now also pardons the innocent hero and his ditto sweetheart for crimes they have never committed (mainly because the hero threw up the horse-pistol as it was fired). Then the shielded monarch, telling Monmouth that he feels deeply what it is to have a thankless child, adds :—

> Now, gentlemen of the City, to your business ! Even then in the midst of rejoicing will we offer prayers that England's Peace may ne'er find ruin from Rebellion's arts.
>
> (*Music . . . with Grand Flourish . . . firing of cannon . . . waving of flags . . . presentation by the Lord Mayor . . . blessing of the hero and heroine. . . . Shouts. . . . Tableau and* CURTAIN.)

The treasonable practices and Royalist and other conspiracies involving our old friend the enemy, Oates, and bringing in the infamous Colonel Kirke, and the still more infamous Judge Jeffreys, turned up in many a play, both in that period and much later.

One of the most renowned stage works of the sort (certainly of the nineteenth century) was that remarkable little drama written by the skilful Tom Taylor, and entitled, *A Sheep in Wolf's Clothing*. Brief as this play is, running for about an hour, it is most full of dramatic "meat," especially of the plot and counterplot kind.

The Sheep in question is the splendid young wife named Anne Carew, who after the Battle of Sedge-moor, at the collapse of the Monmouth Rebellion, manages to conceal her valiant but fugitive husband in a kind of cupboard, or cabinet, for a long time.

In the process the brave Anne contrives to "vamp" (in a virtuous fashion) even the great Colonel Kirke himself. In fact she brings all her husband's enemies to her feet, bluffing them entirely until she gets her husband, not only free—but pardoned !

This very English play was, like Taylor's fine drama, *The Ticket of Leave Man*, adapted from the French, but no one would ever guess that fact, so utterly racy of the soil is *A Sheep in Wolf's Clothing*.

Although this play has not been revived for many years now, it was often revived in my time. Indeed I have been known to play in it myself the part of the faithful but illiterate Somersetshire yokel, Kester Chedzoy. Every leading lady from the time of the original English impersonator of the part, namely, the great Mrs. Stirling, has played or sought to play the magnificent character of Anne Carew.

Among these impersonators I may mention two

more of the greatest, namely, Dame Ellen Terry and Dame Madge Kendal.

The Doone Dramas

Among the most recent treason dramas of the time of Charles the Second, and his wretched brother, James the Second (previously Duke of York), it is necessary to mention at least about half a dozen picturesque dramas based upon Blackmore's great romance, *Lorna Doone.*

These plays, all dealing of course more or less with the wretched Judge Jeffreys, the pestilential Colonel Kirke, and other traitors and time-servers of the period, included dramatizations by the brilliant comedy actress, Annie Hughes (the original Little Lord Fauntleroy) ; another actress named Mildred Dowling ; one by the late South African actor, Leonard Rayne, and Mary Ford, and a very dramatic five-act version by the now well-known novelist, Horace W. C. Newte.

In one of these (I forget which it was) the great character of John Ridd was played by the popular singing actor, Hayden Coffin.

In the case of so thoroughly well known a novel, it is unnecessary for me to give any details of these Doone dramas. It is perhaps enough to add that in most cases these dramatizations gave emphasis to the statement quoted in the preface of that Blackmore story, a statement by a Devonian, that " *Lorna Doone* is as good as clotted cream a'most."

UNCLE TOM'S CABIN.

A DOMESTIC DRAMA, IN SIX ACTS.

DRAMATIZED BY GEORGE L. AIKEN.

THE ORIGINAL DRAMATIZATION OF THE SCORES MADE
OF MRS. BEECHER STOWE'S FAR-FLUNG SLAVE-STORY

Facing p. 224

Descart, the French Buccaneer.

A POPULAR PIRATE PLAY OF THE COBURG
(AFTERWARDS THE "VIC")

CHAPTER XLI

A Most Daring Drama of Treason

By this label I allude to one of the most extraordinary, certainly one of the most shudderful
melodramas about traitors ever seen on any stage,
a play which, when I first used to meet it, was wont
to make me tremble with terror.

Certainly I grew up rather to " guy " some of its
extreme episodes, but even now I have never quite
got over being thrilled by its audacious and indeed
nerve-shaking situations and speeches.

Not to keep you waiting too long for some samples
of this highly-seasoned dramatic dish, I must tell
you that it was called *Whitefriars ; or, The Days of
Claude Duval*. It was adapted by that once very
popular resident playwright, Thompson Townsend,
and was first performed at the Surrey, in the early
forties. That was a good many years too early
for me to have had the privilege of attending its
first night. But, thank Thespis, I have oftentimes
witnessed it since, and I have also a strange copy or
two in my possession.

This drama was based on the romance called
Whitefriars, the author of which remained for many
years anonymous. The writer proved eventually to
be a lady named Symons, and she was in effect the
nameless Ethel M. Dell of her period.

Now *Whitefriars*, which is in three acts, has for
its chief characters our old friend the " Merry "

Monarch, Colonel Blood, Titus Oates, the Duke of
Monmouth again, Sir Edmundbury Godfrey (whose
awful murder is depicted very early in the play) and
Highwayman Duval, whom Playwright Townsend
has whitewashed even more than usual.   In fact he
makes that High Toby merchant a constant protector of the hero, Mervyn, and of that hero's
sweetheart, Aurora Sydney.

The intrepid Mervyn (who has no other name)
for some time is shown to be the illegitimate and
previously baby-farmed child of Lady Howard,
than whom a more villainous vamp never appeared
even in film dramas !

This poor noble lady has really been the secret
mistress of the fearsome Colonel Blood, who throughout the play gloats over having stolen the Crown
Jewels and on having been foolishly pardoned by
the King, as was indeed the case.

Charles, of course, as usual, had his own secret
reason for this extraordinary act of forgiveness.
But strange to say, that King in this play, *Whitefriars*, is by no means the whitewashed monarch of
so many Carolian dramas up to and including
that Julia Neilson and Fred Terry perennial
success, *Sweet Nell of Old Drury*.   (N.B.—This is
an American-made Charles the Second play, but no
matter.)

No, the *Whitefriars* Charles is shown to be anything but a gentleman.   Among other things, with
all his light o' loves hanging around, he endeavours
to seduce and eventually tries to capture the sweet
maiden heroine, Aurora !   Here a daring thing
occurs, for her sweetheart, Mervyn, goes for the
King, and fells him to the ground !   There's Treason
for you !

Charles, struck with the audacity of Mervyn's
wicked act, lunges at the youngster, inflicting with

the royal sword a wound in the right arm. (Kindly keep your eye on this wound, it means much later on.)

After the murder of Sir Edmundbury Godfrey by Blood, Oates, and Co.—a deed witnessed by our hero, who is unable to prevent it—there are some awful goings on between Blood, Titus, and the wicked Lady Howard, who now is consumed with a passion for having her alleged illegitimate son the hero " removed " at all costs !

For lo, that hero is continually " recalling her sin " to her, and Blood and his minions continue to "make a bit " throughout the play by their attempts, real or pretended, to " remove " the moral Mervyn !

The unfortunate Lady Howard, finding these efforts at son-slaying all in vain, eventually bribes a Jewish Alchemist, one Elkanah, to do away with the unsuspecting boy by poison. And how do you think that poison is to be administered ?

It is a happy thought on the part of Alchemist Elkanah to apply to the afore-mentioned wound an ointment which he has prepared for the nonce, an unguent, which will infect the spot.

Elkanah really has very strong reason for loathing Lady Howard, because once upon a time she dared to call him " A Dog of a Jew," but, for certain gold, he undertakes to apply the Fatal Ointment, and this is how the precious pair allude to the matter :—

ELKANAH. Bah ! Dead men tell no tales. His wound is a mere scratch yet it might be made mortal. No gate of death is without a little creaking on the hinges. 'Tis but dressing the wound with a peculiar ointment and on a sudden the blood is tainted into a plaguelike mass . . . the man dies !

LADY HOWARD. I do not bid thee do it, yet would I give a hundred crowns to any man who told me it was done.

ELKANAH.   A hundred crowns! Every ounce of the precious drug is worth its weight in gold. Delude the searchers with a tale of the spotted fever . . . bury him too . . . all for a hundred crowns. . . . Not for King or Kaiser! [*Taking a light and holding it before Mervyn's eyes.*] See, he sleeps soundly.

LADY HOWARD (*gazing upon him*).   He is the very image of the unhappy man, his father! Oh Elkanah, what a son were he to a mother who dared love and dared acknowledge him. Away! it kindles hatred in my heart to see how like he is. He *shall* die! Elkanah . . . prepare the ointment for the wound, and look to me for thy reward. (*Exit.*)

I may inform you that in the original cast this vampire mother was played by a great Surrey favourite, Mrs. Henry Vining, who was the mother of the late great comedy actress, Mrs. John Wood.

I may add that Claude Duval, after helping all the virtuous, goes off singing the couplet which I have quoted as sung by Jack Sheppard. Claude, however, is something of a prophet, for it is when on his way to Newgate that he sings the couplet which runs thus :—

> When Claude Duval was in Newgate thrown,
> He carved his name on the dungeon stone!

I must not forget to tell you that *Whitefriars* also contains a Fatal Well! Poor Lady Howard, being detected in enacting still more villainy, is denounced by her ex-paramour, Colonel Blood, now swearing to prove that hero Mervyn is indeed legitimate, and "shall be restored to his rights."

At that instant the guilty mother gives a piercing shriek, and rushes to the well, the planks of which give way and she falls down—down—down, to be dashed to pieces!

"Ah, ha!" exclaims Blood, who then, seizing his sword and fencing imaginary pursuers, falls dead!

And here we bring in Monmouth again, for that

brave but base-born son of Charles rushes in at the moment followed by Titus Oates, who is waving a warrant to seize Mervyn and Aurora.

OATES (*breathlessly*). " Behold the King's Warrant ! "

Whereupon Monmouth exclaims :

" Which is useless, villain . . . the King is dead. Seize the traitor ! "

Monmouth and his party then capture all the villains who are not dead, and the soldiers, with Monmouth, wave torches victoriously as the curtain falls !

There's a thick and slab Real Crime Drama for you !

CHAPTER XLII

MORE MERRY MONARCH REBEL MIXTURES

I feel it necessary to state that numerous as these Carolian Treason plays and such may seem to be in these essays, I am leaving out large numbers of plays of Charles the First and Charles the Second period when, as so often happens, they do not touch on any special conspiracy and therefore do not come within scope of my Treason Crime Series.

There are, however, certain plays of a lighter form which do touch upon one or other of the many conspiracies that blossomed so lavishly in Merrie England in those strange and stirring times.

One of these pieces of a comedy mixture is *Nell Gwynne*, written by that illustrious but mostly ill-paid satirist, Douglas Jerrold, whose great-granddaughter, Mary Jerrold, is one of the artistic ornaments of the present-day stage.

Jerrold's *Nell Gwynne*, which I have known intimately from my boyhood's days both before and behind the curtain, is still, in my opinion, the best play concerning that actress out of large numbers I have met.

I say this although, as in the case of Jerrold's hundred other plays, all written for a mere pittance, the action is cut up into several changes of scene, as was then necessary owing to the scanty stage equipment of the period.

There wasn't much that Jerrold didn't know about the Merry Monarch time, or anything else for the matter of that, and this especial play, although on the lighter side, as I have said, contains many a strong dramatic touch concerning the eminent Eleanor and her Royal " Protector."

Another very popular play of the period, one with which I was also very familiar, although it has not been seen on the stage for many years, was a serio-comic drama in two acts called *Charles the Second ; or, The Merry Monarch.* This piece, although containing a very fine couple of acting parts in Charles and his favourite chum Rochester, is still stronger in the " character " part called Captain Copp. He dominates the action both in dramatic business and in song. In fact the captain is largely instrumental in developing or in preventing certain plots and schemes which permeate the play.

I have seen all manner of eminent leading men, even tragedians like John Ryder, and others of the kind, " take the stage " and conquer the audience in impersonating Copp, who was in effect a variant of those Elizabethan roysterers sometimes known as Copper Captains.

Merely pausing awhile to marvel that this really clever Charles the Second play has not been revived of late years, I pass on to tell the sad story regarding its author. This was none other than John Howard Payne, an American-born player-playwright who visited England and figured ever and anon upon the London stage, a little over a hundred years ago.

Among the old prompt books which I have mentioned more than once, I have several plays, mostly domestic dramas written by Payne, in the intervals of his taking up from time to time a Consulship here and there.

During his early time in association with the British boards, Howard Payne wrote a somewhat

crimeful domestic drama. It was entitled *Clari ;
or, The Maid of Milan,* and in it among other ditties
is the world-famous song, " Home, Sweet Home."

I have a first-night criticism of this play, which
scarifies the " book," but speaks with some mild
approval of the musical score by Sir Henry Bishop.
The critic was kind enough to say that he thought
perhaps one or two of the songs " might achieve
some temporary popularity " !

What the interpolated ballad, " Home, Sweet
Home," achieved in the " popularity " line, need
not be stressed here.

But one thing, and that a dramatic and sorrowful
thing, remains to be added. It is that John Howard
Payne, the author of that famous ballad, thanks to
many adversities (some caused by himself) died
penniless and without a home in the world !

CHAPTER XLIII

PLOTS AGAINST THE PRINCE OF ORANGE

It is now time for me to speak of the conspiracies against William the Third, otherwise known as "The Dutch Orange."

Of course some are familiar with sundry stage versions of Dumas's famous romance, *The Black Tulip*, which deals with sundry conspiracies, plots, etc., against William and Company.

One of these dramas, the most striking of any such produced on the London stage, was brought to the Haymarket some years ago under the Dumas title. The dramatization was by that very skilful adapter and smart writer of dialogue, the late Sydney Grundy. Other versions had cropped up before then, at more or less outlying theatres.

Undoubtedly, however, the very best drama which I have met in connection with the conspiracies against William, formerly Prince of Orange, was one by Tom Taylor.

This play of plots was entitled *Lady Clancarty ; or, Wedded and Wooed*, and was described on the playbills as "a tale of the assassination plot of 1696."

This play is quite good enough for me to give you a précis thereof. Here it is.

Constructing his drama, as his custom often was, from a few historical details, Tom Taylor showed how Donagh Macarthy, who is really Earl of Clancarty, has dared to come from Ireland to England without a Royal Licence, as was then necessary for such Irish and other visitors. He becomes by no means malignantly mixed up with the aforesaid assassination plot. The doughty young Hibernian is at first pursued by King William's men for being in England at all, and afterwards he is hunted down because of his supposed complicity with the conspirators.

After several exciting episodes the impulsive young Irishman, in flying from his persecutors and while intending to prevent Royal bloodshed, takes refuge in a chamber of a house in St. James's Square. This proves to be the bedroom of a beautiful young lady of the Court. Presently the fair occupant is startled at seeing the intruder, discovers that the fugitive is really her own husband, and that she is in fact Lady Clancarty!

They have never met since they were children, when, as was not uncommon in those days, they were betrothed by their respective parents. They are, therefore, really bona fide husband and wife, and it is within the range of practical domestic politics anyway that the lady should shield her husband and even desire him to stay!

He, however, although volcanically Hibernian (or perhaps because he is such), acts as the very pink of Chivalry. Rather than force himself, as a sort of rebel, on his Royalist-minded bride, he elects to go forth and face all dangers in order to save her from any trouble or implied dishonour.

The courageous Donagh passes through many a trying time, and being anything but a sanguinary traitor, suffers a good deal from the assassination plotters. These include Cardell or " Scum " Goodman, who, as students of the stage will remember, was a very popular actor with the great Mr. Betterton at Old Drury. " Scum " was in the habit of filling

in his time after the show, by going out on the road
at nights to take a purse ! Ay, and e'en to slit a
throat or two in the process !

The sweet Lady Clancarty gradually learns to
love and to yearn for her fugitive young lord, and
after Clancarty's Earl has been discovered in King
William's private chamber in Whitehall, not with
intent to assassinate that monarch, but really to
shield him, all ends happily for the virtuous and
otheiwise for the vicious !

This really powerful, not to say instructive, drama
had its production by Henry Neville at the Olympic,
with that beautiful actress, Ada Cavendish, as Lady
Clancarty, and the late Charles Sugden, actor and
sportsman, then about twenty-one, giving a fine
performance of King William.

This play was revived by Mr. and Mrs. Kendal
at the St. James's some ten years later, with themselves of course as Earl and Lady Clancarty respectively, and with that remarkable, but too seldom
seen actor, William Mackintosh, as William the
Third. I saw both productions several times.

A play which I saw on its first night at the old
Princess's Theatre in Oxford Street at the beginning
of the seventies was called *The Rapparee; or, The
Treaty of Limerick.* It was by the late extremely
skilful and artistic dramatist, Dion Boucicault, and
although not quite equal to his usual form, was
really a very interesting drama. So much so that I
wonder it has never been revived since that production.

The real treason involved in this case might be
called " double," for it involved conspiracies against
both the new English (or Dutch) King, William the
Third, and the still " holding on " James the
Second. The action started immediately after
the signing of the Treaty of Limerick, which is

commemorated on a huge stone which you may still see on the chief Town Bridge spanning the Shannon.

Limerick, I may remind you, was the last stronghold of the then fast-fading James Stuart, and it was there that various Irish bands collaborated, as one may say, in fighting his Catholic Cause, against the Protestant William.

One of these bands ran a kind of guerrilla warfare against William and were called " Rapparees," from that Irish word which means the haft of a pike, that being the kind of weapon that these Rapparees mostly used.

Mostly they were what Hamlet calls " a sharked-up set of resolutes," but being Irish, naturally, they had their humorous and pathetic uses, especially for the dramatic stage.

Boucicault played a sort of sympathetic comic Irish peasant with of course a love interest of his own. The big acting opportunities, however, I remember, were shared by that fine actor, Hermann Vezin as the Rapparee Chief ; by the powerful villain representative William Rignold (who, alas ! became totally blind for some years before he died) ; and by Shiel Barry the elder, who that night, in playing a scoundrelly cow-doctor, made his first appearance upon the London stage.

Many will remember that this powerful and intense Irish actor subsequently made his greatest and most enduring success as the wretched miser in *Les Cloches de Corneville*, of which character.he was the original representative in England. Also that his bright young son of the same name was one of the first stage players to give his life in the Great War.

The Rapparee is well worth mentioning here, for I do not remember a play so full of what the gentleman in *The Merchant of Venice* calls "Treasons, Stratagems and Spoils."

An osculatory Treason drama was also written by Dion Boucicault the elder and was entitled *Arrah-Na-Pogue.*

This title means "Arrah of the Kiss," and it is worked out by showing that a certain treasonable secret sign in a conspiracy against the English Rule is "passed on" by the heroine kissing the hero!

Arrah-Na-Pogue was a very delightful drama, and its rollicking humour, blended with its really romantic and charming love story, plus the sensational escape for the hero down a very high ivy-mantled tower, really obscured, to a large extent, the real treasonable undercurrent of the play.

Some few years after his original production, Boucicault brought this, with other plays of his, to the Gaiety Theatre, a house with which I have been concerned for many years. On reviving *Arrah-Na-Pogue* there, the author-actor, again playing the hero, Shaun, the Post, did what he had not done for some time. That is to say he dropped in for himself that melodious but rebellious Irish ballad, *The Wearing o' the Green.*

Unhappily for Dion, there had just been trouble again between the English Government and the Fenians, and so it happened that Boucicault had hardly got beyond the first verse of this treasonable ditty when the entire audience arose in its wrath and hissingly "ballooned" him from the stage!

So popular an actor and so brilliant a dramatist was the otherwise eccentric Dion, that I would not have believed that any audience would have treated him in this summary sibilant fashion had I not, as the noble Horatio says, had "the sensible and true avouch of mine own eyes."

16

DION'S LAST REBEL DRAMA

This was *The Shaughraun*, which he first produced in America in 1875 and brought to England in the same year and presented at Drury Lane with a very remarkable cast.

I remember the first night well and how enormously popular were the chief members of the company, especially the author, in that wonderful character part, Conn, who is described as " The Shaughraun, the Soul of every Fair, the Life of every Funeral, and the First Fiddle at all Weddings and Patterns."

Some may remember that in this piece Conn has to pretend to be his own corpse at a wake ! Eventually he gets out of his coffin and walks off ! That is when he has discovered all the " evidince " he requires for his plotful purposes.

The other chief players comprised Shiel Barry as a scoundrel named Harvey Duff, and the wonderfully handsome and attractive, but ill-fated, William Terriss as a chivalrous but duped English Captain, a character originally acted in New York by our first English matinée idol, namely, H. J. Montague. Mrs. Boucicault played the heroine Moya. This drama is always being revived somewhere.

Without going into details with regard to *The Shaughraun*, it may be mentioned that unlike other of Boucicault's Irish Rebellion dramas, this one deals with certain episodes in the Fenian Uprisings.

In certain scenes *The Shaughraun* bears some resemblance to Sean O'Casey's Irish 1916 Rebellion plays, *The Shadow of a Gunman*, and *The Plough and the Stars*, both very recent successes on the London stage, but each causing a great deal of rioting when produced in Erin's Isle.

Now *The Shaughraun*, like Boucicault's splendid drama, *The Colleen Bawn* (in which I often acted), had the "honour" of being burlesqued. Undoubtedly the best specimen of these travesties was one written by a playwriting confrère of mine, Frank W. Green, who, alas! died young. His burlesque had the happy title of *Conn ; or, Out of Sight, Out of Erin.*

By the way, *The Colleen Bawn* was chiefly burlesqued by the irrepressible Henry J. Byron.

His Boucicault-ian burlesque was called *Miss Eily O'Connor,* and in the great Water Cave scene, when that heroine is thrown by Danny Mann into the fearsome flood below, she bobs up in this case, exclaiming, " I roises 'cos I'm Eoily."

It may seem strange, but I saw the great Edward Terry play this heroine once, with a tiny but tiptop Myles Na-Coppaleen, namely, the still surviving little Jennie Lee, the great " Jo " of our earlier playgoing days.

It might be interesting to add with regard to *The Colleen Bawn,* which has more love than treason in it, that old Boucicault took the play bodily from the romance entitled, *The Collegians ; or, The Colleen Bawn,* written by that neglected genius, Gerald Griffin. Poor Griffin, after many struggles with poverty, died in a monastery, leaving behind him two sisters, charming colleens, who lived on in destitution.

Old Dion made £45,000 out of the first run in England of *The Colleen Bawn,* but I am unable to find any record of his ever having given anything of this good round sum to the brilliant Gerald's ill-fated sisters or to any of Griffin's family.

CHAPTER XLIV

These three plays, all treating more or less of the Irish Rebellion of '98, were written by Edmund Falconer, a very fine actor who was the original London representative of that fine character, the hunchback Danny Mann, in the above-mentioned drama, *The Colleen Bawn*.

I have seen many actors play Danny since the original production, but Falconer was certainly the best. He was not always so happy in other impersonations, especially when he took, as he sometimes did, to playing " coat and trouser " parts.

One of these characters he enacted in a play of his own entitled, *Extremes*, a modern satire which failed, as so many of Falconer's plays did, on account of the extreme voluminousness of its dialogue.

But to our Irish plays. The first of these Treason dramas, written by Falconer (soon after he penned that beautiful ballad, *Killarney*, to the lovely music of Balfe) was *Peep o' Day*, a drama in which all who beheld it, indeed supped full with horrors. For example, in a big quarry scene, where several murders were planned and some committed, the chief villain, Black Mullins by name, dug a grave in full sight of the audience and gloatingly deposited the corpse of his victim therein !

Sandwiched with murders and other crimes, this drama had a kind of oscillating or undulating

"MY POLL AND MY PARTNER JOE."

A NAUTICAL DRAMA, IN THREE ACTS.

BY JOHN THOMAS HAINES.

First performed at the Surrey Theatre, September 7, 1835.

ONE OF THE MOST FAMOUS PIRATE PLAYS

(It drew £75,000 on its first run at the Surrey)

VANDERDECKEN;

OR, THE FLYING DUTCHMAN.

A LEGENDARY DRAMA, IN FOUR ACTS.

BY T. P. TAYLOR.

ONE OF THE EARLIEST DRAMATIZATIONS OF THIS
WEIRD STORY

(This play influenced Wagner—per Heine, who saw
it in London)

Facing p. 240

rebellious sub-plot in the doings of the *Peep o' Day* boys of more or less happy treasonable memory.

This extremely blood-and-thundery melodrama was first produced at the Lyceum, but I caught up several revivals, especially one at Old Drury. Poor Falconer, just before had been associated with the management of that theatre for some years, with the famous F. B. Chatterton, who subsequently ran the "Lane," finishing up about 1880 with debts to the amount of £36,000 !

I ought to mention that, like all of Falconer's other plays, the sanguifulminous *Peep o' Day* had a very idyllic, Cornfield scene. This was utilized for the exploitation of certain popular Irish ditties and dances, especially, of course, the infectious " Jig " of that glorious Emerald Isle.

Another of the Falconer Irish plays dealing with more or less treasonable matter, was one called *Eileen Oge*. This phrase, which means " Eileen Darling " (or something of that sort) is, as students of Irish Minstrelsy will remember, part of the " Keen "-y treasonable ditty, "Savourneen Deelish." In fact the subtitle of *Peep o' Day* was, *or, Savourneen Deelish*, which of course is a term of endearment for " the disthressful Counthry."

When I saw the first performance of *Eileen Oge* at the Princess's, I couldn't help smiling when about the middle on came the inevitable Cornfield scene, and on came the Hibernian hero holding forth in endless loquacious platitudes. Even this play, although not quite worthy of Falconer, had a great deal of charm and beauty. It had but a short run, however, and I don't think it was ever revived, not in England anyway.

Now for Edmund's disastrous drama.

Alas, this is the third Falconer treasonable drama included in my previous headline. I say alas, because it really led to a memorable stage disaster, as will be seen. This Irish drama was entitled *Oonagh*, which was the name of the persecuted heroine. Falconer, who always, as I have indicated, ran to great length in his plays, this time mapped out his story in seven acts !

The treasonable part of *Oonagh* dealt with the conspiracies of that very secret Hibernian brotherhood known as the Ribbonmen. It was based upon a story of one of the famous Irish novel-writing brothers, the Banims, a narrative entitled *Fardougha, the Miser*. This time Falconer played that character instead of his usual hero.

There was a great deal of talk about Erin and her wrongs, so much talk in fact that the performance which took place at Her Majesty's Theatre (now His Majesty's) lasted from 7 p.m. until the small hours of the morning !

As in all his other plays, Falconer kept coming on and holding forth at all sorts of times more or less inopportune, although he had already before the curtain rose delivered a very lengthy Prologue !

At the approach of midnight *Oonagh* had not finished the third of its seven acts, and the audience grew very restive. By about 1 a.m. they began telling poor Falconer to " shut up," " go home," " leave off," etc., but the actor-author still kept ladling it out, with no uncertain ladle ! At last, about half-past two that morning, when the audience grew more and more incensed, the stage hands and scene shifters, scenting a riot afoot, seized Falconer, then in the middle of another long speech, rolled him up in the theatre carpet, and trundled him off the stage !

Thus ended *Oonagh*, or so it left off, for not more than four and a half acts had been reached by then, so this disastrous drama never finished at all !

One of the chief lyrical questions put to all and

sundry, in Hibernian treasonable minstrelsy, runs
thus : " Who fears to speak of '98 ? "

Whether one fears to speak of that year of Irish
Rebellion or not, I do not see why I should fear to
speak of plays of '98, and its sometimes very sincere
plotting patriots, and also its sometimes very
insincere schemers who indeed proved to be traitors
to both sides.

This double-dyed treachery element crops up in
several treason dramas of that period and others.
Like the previously-mentioned plays, *The Shaugh-
raun, Arrah-Na-Pogue*, and such-like, each of
the plays written around those real patriots,
Grattan, Lord Edward Fitzgerald, and above all
Robert Emmett, possesses a " facing-both-ways "
Irish villain, usually a very fine acting part.

As to Lord Edward, I remember a very striking
drama written around him by J. W. Whitbread, and
entitled, *Lord Edward ; or, '98.* This drama, in
five strong acts, was produced in dear dirthy Ould
Dublin just over thirty years ago. It was brought
to London first at the Mile End Pavilion Theatre,
which ancient playhouse Gentile and Yiddish is—sad
to say—closing down to be delivered over mostly to
the cinema, even as I am writing these lines.

This and several other Fitzgerald plays, mostly
previous to Whitbread's, of course treated that
Irish hero in a very sympathetic light. Thus poor
young Edward was really an object of sympathy
rather than of execration.

Robert Emmett, being of a very high and lofty
personal character, soon attracted the dramatists
and playwrights, not only of his own but of the
English nation, plus (not unnaturally) some
American playmakers. An American-made specimen called *Robert Emmett*, written by one James
Pilgrim (U.S.A.), was not only popular in America,

but was, I remember, played a good deal in our own country, alike in London and the provincial theatres.

I have here a very scarce prompt copy of this *Robert Emmett* drama, and with all its long speeches (nearly as long as poor Falconer's) it is nevertheless a strikingly dramatic work. The chief villain, a very fine character named Kernan, described simply as "traitor," is one of the best of those double-dyed villains who join, and give away their fellow-conspirators, for "greed of gold."

The character of Emmett in this play has in his loquacious speeches sundry very interesting dramatic and illuminative utterances. They are sometimes very sesquipedalian. Here is an extract wherein, after advising cautious proceedings to his fellow-rebels, Robert hold forth as follows :—

EMMETT.   The children of '98 paid dearly for their hasty movements. Then, as a boy, my blood rose indignant, and I longed to revenge them ; the scenes of that period can never be erased from my memory. The blood-smeared soldier hanging up the poor defenceless peasantry, even in the streets of Dublin ; wives lamenting their husbands, children their parents. Fellow-countrymen, look at our present condition ; our soil uncultivated, our manufactures crushed, and we all subservient to the caprice of a foreign power. Upon the day the brave Fitzgerald died in his country's cause . . . may every Irishman venerate his name . . . upon that day, boy as I was, I swore to devote my life and fortune to the relief of a suffering people ! That vision of my childhood is never absent from my thoughts. I saw the pampered lords of another soil gormandizing upon the hard-earned labours of the poor peasant. I heard the merry song from the thatched cottage. But the tax-gatherers came, and all was gloom ; O, that we had another Cincinnatus, or some godlike Washington, to rise up, shake off our servitude, and hail the natal day of Irish liberty.

The vile Janus-faced Kernan, who manages to escape after being arrested by both sides for treachery to each, contrives to wreak his vengeance upon Emmett, and is mainly the cause of that patriot's arrest, trial, and sentence.

There is a long trial scene in this play of Citizen Pilgrim's, and of course in this scene Emmett, between bursts of Irish music, gives off several very stirring speeches. One of these runs thus :—

> I appeal to the immaculate Maker, I swear by the throne of Heaven, before which I must shortly appear . . . by the blood of the murdered patriots in the time before me, that my conduct through all this peril has been governed only by the conviction I have uttered, and I confidently and assuredly hope that there is still union and strength in Ireland to accomplish this noble enterprise !

At this the Judge, Lord Norbury, exclaims :—

> I do not sit here to hear Treason.

He has to listen, however, to several more long speeches from Emmett, including one nearly a page long which I shall not inflict upon you. Anon, to the music of " Exile of Erin," with a snatch of " The Harp that once through Tara's Halls," Emmett is sentenced. After a quick change of scene we see Robert on the gallows tree ! His wife Maria is watching him in anguish, exclaiming that " the rope waves to and fro in the clear wind, with at hand the hangman, the coffin and the strong and gaping multitudes."

And then come these words, for Robert :—

> Forget this awful hour, and think only of the halcyon days we have enjoyed together ; but if hereafter my name should be used as a ribald mock by those in power, say, he died in transport of his country's cause.

The bell tolls and Emmett is executed !

I have given this somewhat copious extract from the Emmett drama because the hero's utterances show in effect what is the real substance of all these '98 and similar dramas, whether they deal with

Peep o' Day Boys, Rapparees, Ribbonmen, or *Moon-lighters.*

It is not generally known that among other Emmett dramas one was written by a journalist and essayist, indeed a brilliant man of letters, named Frank Marshall, who was the husband of Ada Cavendish, whom I have mentioned as the original Lady Clancarty. Marshall wrote this play for no less a star than the then " Mr." Irving, who often discussed this Emmett drama with me, as I had had a good deal to do with such plays, and, in fact, am not altogether un-Irish myself !

Marshall's was a very fine play, for while embodying much of the historical part of Emmett's doings, it was also written in distinguished literary fashion. Whether it would have succeeded in public we had no chance of learning, for lo, the play licenser of the period intervened, and forbade the public performance thereof. This Emmett play is, I believe, now in the possession of Mrs. H. B. Irving, to whose lamented husband it descended with all his distinguished father's play scripts.

I ought to add that among the many Irish treason and Fenian plays were two or three dramatizing the unspeakable Phœnix Park murder, embodying the assassination of Lord Frederick Cavendish and Mr. Burke in 1882—" The Accident "—as that awful deed was called by the foul assassins !

CHAPTER XLV

AND NOW FOR THE FENIANS

Here we come to the period well in my own time. Even at the present we are not without such Fenian plotters, by whatever label they may nowadays call themselves.

This Fenian rising gave opportunities to sundry playwriters ; indeed, as we have seen, Boucicault's *Shaughraun* was somewhat concerned with that movement.

One of the most successful dramas of the kind, especially in the sense of touring for many years, was one written by a very quaint old friend of many of us, the late humorous character actor, Hubert O'Grady. It was called, quite boldly, *The Fenian*, and it arrived at the Standard, Shoreditch, about thirty-six years ago. It was a very artless Irish stage play which wobbled a good deal on both sides, English and Irish, but it afforded Hubert and his also strong character-actress wife, good scope for popular acting and " natural " appeal.

Several other Fenian dramas of more or less intrinsic value (generally less) bobbed up upon the boards from time to time. Being mostly of one pattern, there is no need to devote more space to them. Instead of that I will come at once to a very powerful drama which was based upon one of the most dastardly deeds that even the worst of the Fenian brotherhood ever conceived or carried out.

Towards the end of the sixties, the Fenians quartered in London (where I used to see a good many of them) had an idea of extracting from Clerkenwell Prison certain of their fellow-conspirators then lying under sentence there.

Irish-like, they adopted the notion of blowing up the prison " intoirely," and this vile, unspeakable deed they executed, regardless of the lives of all other people concerned with that " stone jug," as the crooks always call such abodes.

As it happened I saw this explosion, with my own eyes, happily (for me) at a safe distance, which safe distance, however, I enjoyed by sheer accident, and not by design.

I was about fourteen, and I was engaged in certain work (between my youthful stage experiences) at this time in the office of a huge factory called " The London Zinc Mills." One side of these extensive premises, full of roaring engines, etc., lay on the banks of the Regent's Canal Basin, a huge sheet of water, extending from this factory to the City Road Bridge.

At the corner of this bridge, by the way, stood the famous vast Dodd's Dust Yard. The owner, Mr. Dodd, whom I used to see when he was very old, was the original of Charles Dickens's Mr. Boffin, in *Our Mutual Friend;* but this by the way.

Even in that early boyhood of mine I had a quenchless mania, one which I have retained to the moment of writing, that is, of watching and following all kinds of streams, rivers and canals. Whenever I could leave my office at the other side of these zinc works, I was either engaged in looking at, or sometimes falling in, the Regent's Canal Basin.

It so happened that on the very day when these desperadoes carried out their dastardly plot, I, then balancing on the timber logs on the canal, saw this

very explosion at the prison which lay, plain to
see, across the Basin some little distance inland.

The terrific explosion, beside the vast damage it
did at and around the prison, was so violent that it
agitated the waters of the Canal Basin and even
shook that zinc factory to its foundations!

So much for that explosion. Now for the play
founded upon it.

This was a four-act drama written by that splendid
constructor of melodramas, the late Henry Pettitt.
It was entitled *Taken from Life*, and was produced
at the Adelphi a little over forty years ago (about
fourteen years after the explosion), with Charles
Warner as the persecuted hero.

The title took its rise from the fact that early in
the play this hero, an artist by profession, painted
a portrait of one of the characters from life, and this
picture subsequently formed a valuable link in the
chain of evidence to bring the two chief villains to
justice. Another meaning of the title was that the
hero himself, being falsely accused of complicity in
the Fenian conspiracy, was arrested and " taken
from life " for a long period, by being put in the
aforesaid " stone jug."

The whole play led up to a most realistic repre-
sentation of the Clerkenwell Prison Explosion, as I
was able to prove in my *Referee* notice at the
time. One other point, interesting to criminologists,
with regard to this Fenian explosion and the play
based thereon, is the fact that the chief Fenian
concerned in that explosion, one Michael Barrett by
name, was executed at Newgate. That doom proved
historical in this regard, for Barrett was the last
criminal ever executed in public in England!

CHAPTER XLVI

TRUE TALES OF THE TERRIBLE TODD

In submitting a story or two of Todd the Terrible (meaning of course the sanguinary Sweeney, otherwise the Demon Barber of Fleet Street), I suppose I ought to walk, or write, warily.

For, look you, it has become the vogue of late to treat that criminal coiffeur as though he were a kind of Mrs. 'Arris and to assert that " There ain't not no sich person." Such scepticism as this need not disturb us, however, when we come to remember that even such old favourite heroes as William Tell and even Dick Whittington (to say nothing of his Felix friend) have also been regarded as merely legendary characters.

I have met, and read, of some disbelievers who dared to suggest that this barbarous fiend is based only on a character in a French melodrama. Nay more, some of these sceptics have even combated with me in print on this great question !

Having studied Sweeney Todd, however, ever since I could read or sit at the play, or toddle behind the scenes, I have come to the conclusion that the story of *Sweeney Todd ; or, The String of Pearls*, is really based upon a real criminal of the time, who operated on the very spot where Sweeney's shop was supposed to be.

Having been brought up, as it were, to regard this bloodthirsty blackguard as a real person, naturally I too made it my business to find out the site of the emporium wherein he committed his dark deeds.

Now this shop site was, I found, that which became utilized in after-times and up to a few years ago as Craigs' fish restaurant, a few doors on the City side from the Church of St. Dunstan's, Fleet Street. That site is now partly occupied by the offices of the *Weekly Telegraph*. It is in effect about a couple of hundred yards westward from the hairdressing saloon which now bears the name of Sweeney Todd, a shop close to the old Cheshire Cheese.

It is not generally known that some years after the first Sweeney Todd drama was produced—that is to say at the Brit in Hoxton, eighty-six years ago—no less a literary personage than George Augustus Sala wrote a kind of " penny blood " serial all about that sanguifulminous shaver. From this other dramas of the sort were extracted and soon spread all over the country. I have seen and read, I suppose, all the many versions, and in the process I have been thrilled by all the most famous Todds of the times.

I first saw the Sweeney Todd drama when I was a little boy at the Brit in Hoxton, and on the first occasion I remember I saw it from the front and was so terrified that I tried to hide under the seat ! A little later I got more used to this terrible tragedy ; and from that time I often saw it from behind the scenes, that is from the wings or the prompt box.

The Todd drama which I saw in those early days was the above-mentioned nearly ninety-year-old specimen which had been played over and over again up to the time I caught it.

This version was the one by George Dibdin Pitt, and our picture of Todd and his fatal revolving chair is taken, by permission, from that remarkable series, " Dicks's Penny Plays," which (alas !) since the war have risen to twopence !

The Sweeney when this play was first presented in 1841 was an actor named Mark Howard, and according to certain of my relations who played with him in that and other dramas, he was a very appalling Todd indeed.   When I first met "Todd " he was acted by an enormous figured " Brit " heavy villain named Cecil Pitt, who was a much younger brother of the author of this piece, who had died before I was born.   The other principal cut-throat razor-stroppers and fiendish exclaimers of " I'll polish 'em off ! " seen by me included such other East End heavy villains as T. G. Drummond, Edwin Drayton, Wilton B. Payne, and of course the often herein-before-mentioned Shakespearean and sanguifulminous star, J. B. Howe.

More than once have I seen this short but powerful actor enact Sweeney after having just given a capital performance of Hamlet, Othello or Richard the Third, and sometimes William in *Black-eyed Susan*.

Undoubtedly, however, the greatest Sweeney Todd within the memory of living playgoing man was little George Yates of the Pavilion Theatre, Mile End.   Like Howe, Yates was an exceedingly powerful actor for his size, and he had one of the finest voices ever heard upon the stage.   To see little George play Todd with his large-sized wife, Harriet Clifton, as Sweeney's co-criminal, Mrs. Lovett, the mysterious pie-maker, was to see a couple of performances and to hear a couple of voices memorable ever after !

Their combined vocal vigour has descended in a great measure to their son, the fine young baritone singer, Clifton Yates, who is heard in sundry concert parties beside the rolling sea, as well as in town.

I knew this apparently fiendish couple, George
Yates and Harriet Clifton, many years during my
association back and front with the East End
Theatres, and although I saw them always enacting
the most unspeakable villains, they were, I assure
you, the most kindly and hospitable couple.

And thereby hangs a tale.

After many years of Sweeney Todd-ery, George
Yates had a special Benefit night in which my
aforesaid acting uncle was largely concerned, for he
played several parts that evening.   Yates, of course,
elected to appear, during the performance, as the
terrible Todd.   At the end of the show some of his
associates told him that they had formed a little
presentation for him, and presently they handed
dear old George a beautiful morocco case, inscribed
" To George Yates, Esq., with the Love and Affection of his Comrades at the Pavilion Theatre."   On
opening this case, Yates discovered a series of
smaller cases, and each one of these contained a
beautiful razor.   On one side of the blade was
inscribed " To George Yates," and on the other
side was Todd's famous ferocious catchphrase,
" *I'll* polish 'em off ! "

This presentation rather disappointed the little
heavy villain, as from the appearance of the case,
as he confessed afterwards, he expected " something
in the silver way."

For the information of those unfortunate folk
who have never seen *Sweeney Todd*, I may just
mention that it was that bloodthirsty barber's
homicidal hobby to send out boy scouts of a sort
to inveigle to his shop any wayfarers who seemed
likely to possess what Dickens's gentleman calls
" portable property."

Once within the barber's fatal revolving chair, he
took care to cut their throats, and to precipitate

17

the victim down . . . down . . . down . . . down into his sanguinary cellar !

At the time the play opens, Sweeney has had the tip that a certain sailor named Mark Ingestre has landed at Temple Stairs ; and soon that unancient mariner makes his appearance on Sweeney's premises. The reason for luring this honest tar into the toils is that he is said to possess (and it is soon proved that he does) a priceless string of pearls. It is noteworthy that throughout the play whenever the word " pearls " is mentioned, it serves as a special music-cue, music of a most thunderous crashing nature. This outburst is accompanied by an exclamation of Todd's, " Pearls ! . . . he has pronounced his doom ! " Another crash of music !

In this case, although our hero is precipitated below in the usual Todd fashion, yet thanks to the plots and plans of his faithful sweetheart, Johanna Oakley, and other virtuous folk, Mariner Mark is eventually rescued and Todd and his fair but frail confederate, Mrs. Lovett, are slain in their attempt to escape Justice !

But mark you, not before Sweeney has added to his mass of crimes an attempt to have one of his boy assistants or scouts who " knows too much " sent to a most terrible madhouse to be tortured as a mopping, mowing idiot.

[N.B.—I have purposely avoided, in the account of the Todd drama, the under-plot which alleges that Todd's pie-making paramour, Mrs. Lovett, used some of the bodies of her victims for her pies ! I believe this allegation to have crept into the Todd dramas from sundry very extreme French versions. Anyhow, let us hope that it wasn't true !]

The last of the many, many times I saw *Sweeney Todd* was only a few weeks before writing these mems., and then I saw that grim goriodrama twice in one week !

The first of these revivals was given by sundry Cambridge Undergraduates, assisted by several professionals, at that beautiful little playhouse, the Festival Theatre, which has been made out of the old-time Barnwell Theatre, where many ancient blood-and-thunder players strutted and fretted for so many years.

On that occasion, besides writing my usual London criticisms, I was honoured by an invitation to write a Sweeney Todd and general article on S.T. for that popular Cambridge Undergraduate Journal, *The Gownsman*.

The second revival was given at the Prince of Wales's Theatre, when it formed part of a very varied programme which was put forth in aid of the Sadler's Wells Restoration Fund. On that occasion the Barber Fiend was enacted by Andrew Melville, the actor-lessee of that popular twice-nightly playhouse, the Grand Theatre, Brighton. This player is a son of the late clever actor-manager of the same names, who used to bill himself as " A. Emm."

That remarkable man made a large fortune at first out of fitting blood-and-thunder dramas with certain startling posters and wall printing. This fortune enabled him to run several important theatres, including the huge house known then as the National Standard Theatre, Shoreditch, a playhouse which has since become the twice-nightly variety house known as the Shoreditch Olympia.

Hard by is a picture of young Sweeney Todd, as played by young Andrew Melville, who, it may be added, is brother of the Walter and Frederick who run the Lyceum and Prince's Theatres.

Before finishing with Todd the Terrible, I have to make another little confession of the kind I have been compelled to make earlier in this volume. That is to say, that once upon a time I was commissioned to write a burlesque of *Sweeney Todd, the Barber Fiend of Fleet Street; or, The String of Pearls.* The commissioner was none other than George Edwardes, for whom I had already written for the Gaiety several such plays in collaboration with Richard Butler, when we collaboratively called ourselves " Richard-Henry."

We worked a good deal on the Todd travesty, but had to keep delaying submitting it to Edwardes. As last he grew impatient, and I went to him and had to admit that, to my great sorrow, we had torn up the script when nearly finished because we found it utterly impossible to make a burlesque of that Demon Barber anything like as funny as the serious melodramas written around him !

" AHA ! I'VE POLISHED HIM OFF ! "

Here, however, is my epic poem (or part thereof) concerning—

THE TERRIBLE TALE OF SWEENEY TODD

List, oh list, to a story of deep demoniac dread,
A narrative heaped with horrors, all piled upon horror's head ;
Such a terrible tale you'll never discover where'er you plod. . . .
As this, of a Demon Barber, whom people called Sweeney Todd.

His emporium stood in Fleet Street . . . where the Law
    Courts now loom large,
And his motto was " Easy Shaving " at quite a normal charge.
But he made it pay, did Sweeney, yea ; he at bad biz could
    scoff,
For whene'er he'd a wealthy client he'd mutter, " I'll polish
    him off ! "

And he managed this polishing neatly . . . just as he trimmed
    their hair.
For, lo ! in his Lather Depôt there stood a revolving chair,
And he'd touch a spring while shaving, and over the client
    would go,
Into a deep dark dungeon . . . yards upon yards below !

It happened thusly : one evening, when the sun was sinking E,
In walked an unshorn sailor, whose name was Mark Ingestrie ;
His beard had been some days growing ; his love, though,
    was longer grown,
And he longed to be shaved in order to ask HER to be his own.

The HER was a beauteous damsel, who pined for her Jack Tar's
    sake,
And long ago would have wedded, if she could have taken
    the Cake.
But though he could hire a ring, he no wedding-cake could
    afford,
For cakes weren't lent out in those days . . . so again did
    he go aboard.

So, alas, to Todd's Easy Shaveries Mark bent his steps that
    day,
And with many a " Your turn next, sir," Todd's lather boy
    lathered away.

And oft 'twixt the lather splodges Mark gazed at those pearls
with pride.
" He pronounces his doom ! " quoth Sweeney, as the Pearls
he well eyed aside !

Anon, Todd stropped his razor with care . . . and a cautious
cough.
Then, *sotto voce*, he muttered, " Aha ! I'LL polish him off ! "
Then, anon, as he scraped our hero, he clutched at the Bay
Rhum spray . . .
A spray which was dosed with drugs upon Jugginses' Mugs
to play !

Then approaching his heedless victim, who thought he'd had
lather enough,
Todd punched his pronounced proboscis . . . just so . . .
with the powder puff.
Then the wheel of his Patent Brusher he whirled with a few
wild whirls,
And down, down, down to that dungeon went Mark and his
String of Pearls !

The remainder is too marrow-freezing for
quotation !

CHAPTER XLVII

A Batch of Bloodthirsty " Bungs "

Having finished with the bloodthirsty barber, let us now consider some ditto " bungs," meaning, of course, publicans or licensed victuallers, all of whom figured in real crimes before they reached the stage.

The first of these, as regards period of play production, was Jonathan Bradford, who figured in a melodrama written by prolific Edward Fitzball and first produced at the Surrey Theatre, Blackfriars Road, nearly a hundred years ago.

The real crime on which this drama is based is set forth fully in the Newgate Calendar and other annals of crime. It was a very peculiar murder case, and it really happened in this wise. Jonathan Bradford, a very poor tavern keeper, was in the throes of debt and in the meshes of duns, when temptation came in his way by reason of the coming of a customer who soon gave proof that he carried a large sum of money and other valuables about him.

The wretched Jonathan, driven to desperation by his own and his family's necessities and by visions of the debtor's prison, suddenly decided to go to this customer's bedroom and to murder him while he slept, for the sake of his riches!

It so fell out that when Jonathan, armed with a terrible knife, crept into the room and was about to plunge the weapon into the breast of the sleeping man, he saw that the wretched victim was already " weltering in his gore," as the penny showmen and booth actors used to say.

As a matter of fact, someone had forestalled Bradford only a few moments before, and had got away with the plunder. The affrighted innkeeper, in his terror and amazement, dropped his awful knife into the pool of blood then soaking the bed of the unhappy stranger !

Before Jonathan could find means of concealment, he was arrested, and in due course he was tried, and despite his protests of innocence of the deed, though confessing his intent, he was hanged.

It was not until some few years later that the real murderer was caught, and then the Government made what reparation it could to Bradford's widow and children by giving them a grant of money for their maintenance.

As in the case of the *Lyons Mail* plays, and several other crime dramas I have mentioned, the criminal " hero " was saved at the finish in this Jonathan Bradford drama. In this case the actual murderer was caught and shot down just in time for curtain fall. It is interesting to note that *Jonathan Bradford*, which was produced at the Surrey Theatre, drew the large sum of £80,000. Of course I was not born in time to see that drama then, but I am proud to say that I saw it as soon as I could go to the play, and that I have often seen it since, with sundry stars in the name part !

This character was originally played by the famous actor-manager Osbaldiston. A comic character called Sally Sighabout was acted by that tremendously popular, usually sentimental heroine, Miss Vincent.

To give you some idea of the moral attitude of

audiences in those days, at the blood-and-thunder theatres, I may mention that when, as afterwards happened, Manager Osbaldiston eloped with leading lady Vincent, he leaving behind a wife and family, the audiences, especially the pit and gallery, for many years afterwards, roundly hissed and execrated that guilty couple whenever they appeared on the Boards! This sibilant punishment, which took place alike at the Surrey and at the old Old Vic, etc., was often described to me by my uncle and aunt, both of whom often acted with those two stage favourites.

I may also add that, strange as it may seem in these days, even the dramatic critics of the period (and I have their criticisms at my elbow) also, in their respective notices of Osbaldiston and Miss Vincent, took every opportunity to work therein furious denunciations of the "illicit relations" between that actor-manager and his leading lady!

I am especially proud of an old prompt book of *Jonathan Bradford* which contains a full description of how to work a very wonderful set scene for the murder episode. This scene shows four rooms, in full view of the audience at the same time. The exterior of the inn, divided into four compartments, is thus described in the stage directions, and with of course sundry prompter's marks which cannot very well be reproduced here, unless one photographed the entire page. Here is a short description :—

No. 1.—A two-bedded room opening to a tiled roof. One bed or sofa (practicable) the other just on ; a chair L. ; table near bed with newspaper on it.

No. 2.—A two-bedded room with the window opening to the same tiled roof. Table R. and chair.

No. 3.—Little back parlour ; table and two chairs in centre seen through window.

No. 4.—The Bar seen through window, Punchbowl . . . glass of brandy and water, etc., on Bar ; in centre of all a door and sign of " The George Inn."

It is difficult to describe, without actual acting, to the reader, the extraordinary effect of the " business " worked from each of these four apartments to the other. I have seen players of Jonathan Bradford and of the real murderer (in this case named Macraisy, alias Gentleman O'Connor, alias etc., etc., etc.) hold vast audiences spellbound during the action leading up to the murder at this roadside inn.

Several versions of this story have appeared on the stage, but the best is the original Fitzball one which I have chosen for my purpose.

And now for the other sanguinary publicans.

The second specimen of murderous licensed victuallers I shall quote is one called Clauson in the drama (also by Fitzball) entitled, *The Innkeeper of Abbeville; or, the Ostler and the Robber.*

In this French drama the inn, or auberge, is the Henri Quartre and the tavern keeper is a veteran soldier also very hard up. He too, like Jonathan Bradford, is intent ever and anon of getting a little wealth by murderous means, and it so happens that he, also like Jonathan, is forestalled in one or two such matters. He is, however, charged with having stabbed a visitor named Baron Adenberg. As a matter of fact, the crime is really committed by a tramp, who not only uses the innkeeper's own dagger for the purpose, but after the dastardly deed, wipes that gory weapon upon a cloak belonging to Mine Host !

To cut the story short, it is perhaps enough to add that although several other people are killed in this play, the Baron himself turns out to be not mortally wounded, but to have been dragged to a barn, then into a thicket, and thus led to recovery.

The Innkeeper of Abbeville is just a hundred years old and was also produced at the Surrey a few years before Jonathan Bradford came out there. Eventually the play was brought to the West End, where it had quite a vogue.

The third and, of course, most famous of bloodthirsty bungs is our old friend Mathias in *The Bells*, a play also based upon a real French crime utilized by the collaborative fictionists, Erckmann and Chatrian, for their renowned novelette or shocker called *Le Juif Polonais*.

The best-known dramatic version of this thriller was the aforesaid drama, *The Bells*, prepared by a Jewish ex-solicitor named Leopold Lewis for Henry Irving, who on first acting it at the Lyceum in 1871 at once leapt into fame as the head of the British stage.

Perhaps one might say " the potential head," for a far greater actor, Samuel Phelps (the dramatic god of Irving's idolatry and of mine), went on for another seven years or so before ending his marvellous career.

The Bells was so often played by the late Sir Henry and subsequently by his son " H. B.," and of late years by our young tragedian Henry Baynton, etc., that there is no need for me to give details of that drama. It is enough to remind readers that this gory licensed victualler, Mathias, was also very hard up. Also that after murdering the Polish Jew who had sought shelter at his inn during a terrible snowstorm, the wretched murderer for ever after, and especially at certain music cues, heard the jangling of the bells of the sleigh on which the Jew was departing from the tavern, when the murderer smashed him down with a domestic axe !

The awful, mysterious, and uncanny hypnotic trial scene of this otherwise ordinary blood-and-thunder melodrama, will always be remembered by those who saw Sir Henry play the part right up to his death, twenty odd years ago.

I have seen many Mathiases (including H. B. Irving and Henry Baynton) besides those mentioned above, in all sorts of West End and suburban theatres, but perhaps the most extraordinary exponent I ever saw (beside Sir Henry) was the French original, the great Coquelin.

No two performances could be so opposed to each other as Coquelin's and Irving's. Irving gave a romanticized and inescapably magnetic performance that haunted one for many a day and night after seeing him. Coquelin made this innkeeping murderer a bullet-headed bully of the most matter-of-fact criminal description. The Irving " Mathias " was in continual terror at the idea of detection, whereas Coquelin gloried in his gory crime and laughed and chuckled over it.

I remember that Irving and I talked to Coquelin about this strange disparity of view concerning this homicidal licensed victualler. Coquelin, admitting that Irving's was a very great, penetrating performance, asserted roundly that nevertheless it was totally unlike the French murderer that he represented. Coquelin added, " I play Mathias as I know such murderers to be in parts of my country ; Irving's is a great assumption, but not a bit like the real thing."

With this strange contrast I conclude my descriptions of terrible tavern keepers and their real crimes.

CHAPTER XLVIII

SUICIDE AND INFANTICIDE UPON THE STAGE

Real cases of self-slaughter (as Hamlet calls it) and of the doing away with infant babes have from time to time appeared in drama form. In many cases, of course, the real persons or criminals have appeared under disguised names, but there are several plays with the real persons' names figuring therein.

One of the most important suicide tragedies, especially in literary history, is that of the poor boy-poet, Thomas Chatterton, whom his brother bard Wordsworth so finely described as—

> " the marvellous boy,
> The sleepless soul that perished in his pride."

Not long after poor Chatterton's hasty suicide at the age of little more than seventeen, plays of various sorts began to appear. It was not, however, until Henry Arthur Jones and Henry Herman wrote their play called *Chatterton* for Wilson Barrett that the " sleepless soul " began to be largely dramatized.

Barrett (whose Chatterton picture is included among our illustrations) made a great success in the character, and indeed the play was altogether a very worthy specimen. In it W. B. had, I remember, a very striking but over-long speech with the kind of refrain, " What's the use of Poetry ? " That being in reply to a question put to him by a very prosaic person.

This little drama showed the boy-bard at the end of his resources and at the dawn of a little love affair, and ended with the unhappy lad poisoning himself and dying just as a tap came to the garret door, bringing help and hope.

This Princess's Theatre play was speedily followed by several other dramatizations of this historic suicide. Among them was an adaptation of a French drama on the subject written many years before by the famous playwright, Alfred De Vigny. Also there came a four-act piece written by a German, translated into English and set forth with a prologue by that experienced Shakespearean commentator, Edward Dowden.

Likewise we had even a little grand opera called *Chatterton*, with score by Leoncavallo, if you please. Also three or four music-hall sketches, mostly called "historic episodes," and played by sundry variety stars. The best of these was one in which the boy-poet was very beautifully acted by the usually comic male impersonator, Vesta Tilley, now Lady de Frece.

Alas ! even this true and touching tragedy of the youthful, starving, and eventually poisoned poet, did not escape the attention of the burlesque merchants. I am sorry to say that one of the most uncalled-for of these travesties, and a very poor one at that, was written by my late beloved old friend, Albert Chevalier, and was produced at the Vaudeville Theatre with great failure.

It was bad enough surely to " skit " such awful crime plays as *The Bells*. One of the travesty purveyors went so far as to call his skit *The Bells Bellesqued, and the Polish Jew Polished Off; or, Mathias the Muffin, the Mystery, the Maiden and the Masher.*

Even a worse title was that used by Chivvy for

his tasteless Chatterton travesty, namely, *Shattered-Un.*

As to infanticide plays and baby-farming dramas, many examples could be given ; but perhaps it is enough to quote the most popular of the first-named class, namely, the almost numberless dramas founded upon Sir Walter Scott's great romance, *The Heart of Midlothian.* This shows the killing of her infant babe by Effie Deans, and the self-sacrificing, ceaseless struggles of her great-hearted sister Jeanie to save that poor girl from the scaffold. It was based by Sir Walter upon a real infanticide case.

The most striking and most enduring drama concerning this crime was that concocted by the hereinbefore-mentioned Colin Hazelwood of the " Brit " and the City of London theatres, for that great actress, the late Miss Marriott. That splendid tragedienne toured this drama for many years. My theatrical uncle whom I have mentioned several times, namely, W. W. Lacy, toured with her almost all the time in order that he might enact one of the minor villains who strive to bar Jeanie's progress and is pushed by her over a wooden bridge over a terrible chasm. In this episode my very acrobatic, pantomimic uncle did a back fall from far up in the flies, down . . . down below the depths of the stage, where he was caught by a convenient mattress. A marvellous feat !

Hazelwood, hack writer though he was, made a very fine job of this play. It was not even beaten by the great Dion Boucicault's dramatization which he called *Effie Deans ; or, the Lily of St. Leonards.* In spite of that version being played by several important stars, it failed to attract.

Dion did this infanticide drama, with its big trial scene, at Astley's Theatre, which he took for the nonce, renaming it, I remember, the Theatre Royal, Westminster. Other versions of this baby-slaying story were written or nailed up (mostly the latter) by such melodramatists as Fitzball, Dibdin Pitt (the Sweeney Todd dramatizer), the prolific Moncrieff and others too numerous to mention.

There were two or three operas upon the subject, the most important being *Jeanie Deans*, with libretto by Joseph Bennett (then musical critic of the *Daily Telegraph*), and the score by the famous Caledonian composer, Hamish McCunn. This opera was first produced at the Edinburgh Lyceum, and I caught it when it was brought to Daly's just over thirty years ago.

Concerning baby farming, the notorious Mrs. Dyer and several such awful criminals of the sort were treated under various names all over the country. The most important drama of the sort, however, based upon these real murder crimes, was one produced by the late Sir Augustus Harris, at Drury Lane Theatre, under the name of *Human Nature*. It was written by Harris in collaboration with that splendid play constructor Henry Pettitt, and its baby-farming scenes aroused very strong emotions among the audience.

An earlier play on this baby-farming business was of course the one which I have mentioned earlier in this volume, a play which also dealt with the starving and slaying of poor, illegitimate little girl slavies. That play was written around that unspeakable miscreant, Mrs. Brownrigg.

CHAPTER XLIX

Some Gallows Dramas

I may mention, by way of winding up, that there are many plays which deal with executions, and in most cases they are carried out with extreme realism.

Three of these plays have already been mentioned in detail, namely, *George Barnwell, Maria Martin; or, The Murder at the Red Barn*, and dramas dealing with the doom of the *Flowery Land* Pirates.

The other principal execution dramas (I speak only of those concerned with real crimes or treason) include, of course, most of the three- or four-score plays written around Mary Queen of Scots.

These Mary plays, beginning in Elizabethan times and continued by way of Schiller, the Poet Banks, and later W. G. Wills, Tom Taylor, etc., culminated in a peculiar version written for, and played by, that lovely but not particularly great American actress, Mrs. Brown Potter, now a Queen among Theosophists. This play was chiefly remarkable for the fact that whenever that lady had to mention Mary Stuart she described her as " Murry, Queen o' Scarts."

Other Queens executed in dramas have, of course, included poor Lady Jane Grey, and often have I seen her execution take place upon the stage.

One of the latest of the Lady Jane Grey plays, which date from the early seventeenth century onwards, was by the hereinbefore-mentioned Robert

Buchanan, and was played at the Old Gaiety under the title of *The Nine Days' Queen*.

Two other hapless Queens whom I have seen beheaded upon the boards are Anne Boleyn, and especially (and more often) Catharine Howard. In the case of this Queen most of the players concerned showed the husband to whom she had been faithless in marrying Henry the Eighth turning up at the block as Executioner! Often have I seen him raise the Fatal Axe to chop off his guilty wife's head! Usually, however, suppressed love burst forth and he dropped the woeful weapon and died at the foot of the scaffold, while poor Catharine waited for another executioner, as the curtain fell.

One popular tragedian who was very fond of playing this would-be headsman was William Creswick, and I often saw him act this part with three different Catharines. One was the great favourite, Miss Pauncefort, at the Surrey Theatre. The second was Miss Page, an enormously popular leading lady at the Standard, Shoreditch. The other, Miss Sarah Thorne. The popular Sarah was not only the eldest of the far-flung acting Thorne family, but was also for so many years manageress of the Theatre Royal, Margate. She was likewise the tutor of several of our present-day leading stage favourites. These include Irene and Violet Vanbrugh and the late Arthur Bourchier, to name no others.

I forgot to mention that the Catharine Howard Headsman-Husband play, written by Frederick Phillips for the Surrey, had the alluring title of *Ambition; or, The Throne, the Scaffold, and the Tomb*.

Also that this very story in another form, but leading up to the husband's yearning to use the Fatal Axe upon his faithless wife, was called *Hinko*. I saw this at the old Queen's Theatre, Long Acre, many years ago, with Hermann Vezin as the would-be wife executioner.

It needs but to add that these execution plays include various versions written around Charlotte Corday, the murderer of Bolshevist Marat. Also the *Dead Heart* and *The Only Way*. Also several thrilling " scaffold" real crime melodramas, entitled *Eliza Fenning, the Female Poisoner*.

The other gory specimens of the sort comprise Douglas Jerrold's fine naval drama, *Mutiny at The Nore*, in which poor Richard Parker is swung up to the yard-arm. Likewise *Her Wedding Day*, a crime drama with the heroine (falsely accused, of course) about to be hanged by the neck, when it is suddenly found that the necessary Jack Ketch is too ill to officiate !

An understudy appears at once with ropes, etc., all ready, and proves to be the villain, whom the heroine is charged with murdering ! He, finding her still obdurate in yielding to his " passion," places the rope about her neck !

At that moment a muffled reporter in a corner fires a revolver. The shot pierces the Fatal Rope, and the shooter dashes forth and proves himself to be the heroine's long-lost bridegroom ! With the arrest and pending "gallowsing" of the would-be executioner-villain, the poor bride now looks forward to realizing the play's title, and peacefully spending *Her Wedding Day*.

THREE TIMES HANGED

The last real crime execution drama calling for our attention is one of several which arose at the time when John Lee was accused of murdering his lady employer at Babbacombe, Devonshire, some years ago.

It is a strange case, well within the memory of my readers. John Lee was sentenced (wrongfully as it would appear) and was led to the gallows. He was led thereto on three separate occasions, but each time, as though by some special interposition of Providence, the rope broke, or the drop failed, and John Lee stood unscathed.

Naturally after this third failure at Capital Punishment Lee was reprieved. Whereupon sundry plays soon arose.

The best and most successful of these John Lee execution-failure plays is a still current specimen. It was written by Ben Landeck and the late Arthur Shirley, and was entitled, *Saved from the Sea*.

The would-be execution scene in this drama was really a wonderful piece of realism. It caused shrieks of horror " in front "—especially from the feminine part of the anguished audience !

Still more such horrifying shrieks are (as I write) being emitted nightly at the Elephant and Castle Theatre in the tremendously successful revival of *Maria Martin; or, The Murder in the Red Barn*. The hanging of the wretched murderer therein is performed in full view of the audience and in the most appallingly realistic fashion !

For more of these executions, see *The Hangman's Record*.

EPILOGUE

And now it is perhaps time that I spoke my Tag (as we say on the stage).

Did space and time permit I could describe many other real crime dramas and melodramas, but doubtless the foregoing batch will serve as special samples.

In thanking my Kind Friends in Front, I would add this. Although it can be said, as regards most of these blood-and-thunder and similar dramas, that they are often bombastic in dialogue, and mostly morbid in subject, I would ask this question.

Are these dramas any worse, indeed are they not mostly better, and certainly cleaner and more wholesome, than many plays and so-called " comedies " of the eternally triangular and wretchedly " Sexual " type which now disfigure and degrade the British Drama ?

It has been my privilege—as a dramatic critic, and I shall always feel it my duty—to denounce every specimen of unwholesome play. And when I depart from this Stage of Life, I hope it may be said of me—now so many of my confrères have joined my crusade—that like the Irish gossoon who " fell full soon on the first of June," I " bade the rest keep fighting."

CURTAIN

INDEX OF PLAYS

INDEX